W9-BJS-120

About Island Press

Since 1984, the nonprofit organization Island Press has been stimulating, shaping, and communicating ideas that are essential for solving environmental problems worldwide. With more than 1,000 titles in print and some 30 new releases each year, we are the nation's leading publisher on environmental issues. We identify innovative thinkers and emerging trends in the environmental field. We work with world-renowned experts and authors to develop cross-disciplinary solutions to environmental challenges.

Island Press designs and executes educational campaigns, in conjunction with our authors, to communicate their critical messages in print, in person, and online using the latest technologies, innovative programs, and the media. Our goal is to reach targeted audiences—scientists, policy makers, environmental advocates, urban planners, the media, and concerned citizens—with information that can be used to create the framework for long-term ecological health and human well-being.

Island Press gratefully acknowledges major support from The Bobolink Foundation, Caldera Foundation, The Curtis and Edith Munson Foundation, The Forrest C. and Frances H. Lattner Foundation, The JPB Foundation, The Kresge Foundation, The Summit Charitable Foundation, Inc., and many other generous organizations and individuals.

The opinions expressed in this book are those of the author(s) and do not necessarily reflect the views of our supporters.

AMERICAN URBANIST

American Urbanist

How William H. Whyte's Unconventional Wisdom Reshaped Public Life

Richard K. Rein

⬤ ISLANDPRESS | Washington | Covelo

Library of Congress Control Number: 2021939623

All Island Press books are printed on environmentally responsible materials.

Manufactured in the United States of America
10 9 8 7 6 5 4 3 2 1

Keywords: Bryant Park, *City: Rediscovering the Center,* cluster zoning, conformity,
conservation, creativity, *Fortune* magazine, group dynamics, Jane Jacobs,
The Last Landscape, Laurance Rockefeller, New York City, open space
preservation, *The Organization Man,* pedestrian safety, Princeton University,
Project for Public Spaces, public parks, *The Social Life of Small Urban Spaces,*
sociology, St. Andrew's School, Street Life Project, Time Inc.,
urban planning, walkability

To my partner, Nell Whiting, who offered warm encouragement along with cool, critical analysis.

And to my sons, Rick and Frank, who provided a brass band of support.

And to my parents: Marian, who believed that books enabled a high school graduate to stand toe to toe with a guy from a fancy college; and Dick, an organization man who knew when to resist, a trait that on one occasion took him from Endicott, New York, to Tom Watson's office at IBM headquarters in Manhattan.

Contents

Preface

Spend a few hours with William H. Whyte and you may begin looking in a new way at the neighborhood where you live and the company where you work. My first exposure to Whyte came in the fall of
1965, when some eight hundred freshmen gathered in the Princeton
University Chapel to listen to a welcoming address from the college
president. In addition to the usual platitudes, he offered a word of cau-
tion to these postwar baby boomers: things might not always be the
same. Then he quoted an alumnus who had probably sat through a
very similar opening exercise in the very same place thirty years before:

> Every great advance has come about, and always will, because some-
> one was frustrated by the status quo; because someone exercised the
> skepticism, the questioning, and the kind of curiosity which, to bor-
> row a phrase, blows the lid off everything.[1]

The quotation was from William H. Whyte, author of the 1956
best seller *The Organization Man*, the book that defined a generation
of men and women who committed themselves to the big corporations and other institutions where they expected to be employed for a
lifetime.

As a college freshman I couldn't imagine how frustrating the status
quo would soon become: The fact that there were no women in that
freshman class and only about a dozen Black students. The fact that if
you were a Princeton undergraduate, you would be expected to subject
yourself to a superficial selection process to become a member of an
"eating club" and have a place to socialize during your junior and senior
years. The fact that the biggest corporations waiting to employ you
upon graduation were likely to evaluate you in much the same way as
those eating clubs did in their selection process. The fact that a war in

Southeast Asia was escalating. The fact that civil rights advocates were beginning to march in what would soon become an explosive movement. A lot of lids were about to be blown off.

William Hollingsworth "Holly" Whyte was quite familiar with the status quo. After studying at St. Andrew's School in Delaware and at Princeton, Whyte served in the United States Marine Corps on Guadalcanal and eventually became a top editor at *Fortune* magazine, the influential business magazine in the flourishing Time Inc. publishing empire. Whyte was no long-haired hippie or flag-burning radical. Many years later an associate wrote that he could not recall ever seeing Whyte dressed in anything other than a coat and tie. But Whyte appreciated the fact that not everyone was cut from the same cloth as he. One of the greatest failings of The Organization, as Whyte referred to it in his book, was that it often missed the input of the unorthodox thinker. The companies often wanted execution, not exploration. "All the great ideas," some company people believed, "have already been discovered. . . . So the man you need—for every kind of job—is a practical, team-player fellow who will do a good shirt-sleeves job."[2]

By the late 1960s college students, even at staid Ivy League institutions, were challenging the status quo. When some students in Princeton's School of Architecture were assigned to create a public housing design, they turned their obligatory balsa-wood model into a political statement by adding an ironic touch of urban reality: a live cockroach. The same group of activist-architects, including a future cofounder of the Congress for the New Urbanism, formed a People's Workshop in nearby New Brunswick to bring architectural services to the city.

While my memory of that freshman welcome speech has faded with the years, some of the message may have been absorbed. I became one of a small group in my class who did not participate in the upper-class eating club system. As the editor of the student newspaper, I oversaw a news board that supported coeducation and cast a favorable light on the rabble-rousers who protested in Chicago in the summer of 1968.

As a young reporter at *Time* magazine, I reported for a new section founded less than a year before the first Earth Day was celebrated in 1970. It was called The Environment. Shortly after that, I took a job as a writer for an environmental planning firm in Pittsburgh. As part of my work, I read *The Last Landscape* by William H. Whyte. I soon moved back to Princeton, became a freelance writer, and decided to stay long enough to buy a house. The real estate agent showed me 1950s-era split-levels on the outskirts of town—the sprawl described in *The Last Landscape*. Then she showed me one side of a duplex, with a teeny backyard, in the heart of town. I recalled Whyte's advice about how a small space can be made to seem bigger by enclosing it. I bought it.

In 1984 I had an aha moment. Several miles from the heart of Princeton, a new corporate community was blooming in office parks on the four-lane highway officially designated as US 1 but informally called Route 1. Newspapers carried alarming telephoto shots of traffic at rush hour, with grim-faced commuters in cars stacked in long lines. But I was skeptical. What would possess those people, I wondered, to enter that rush hour traffic, morning and evening, day in and day out? The answer was that some exciting work was going on in those offices. It was a community of its own, I realized, and it deserved its own community newspaper. I called the paper *U.S. 1*. It continues to this day.

The Princeton–Route 1 corridor attracted national attention. The *New York Times* profiled the corridor and its eponymous newspaper in 1987.[3] In his 1988 book, *City: Rediscovering the Center*, Whyte described a consulting job he had taken in the Princeton–Route 1 corridor. Whyte criticized the new corporate corridor for its inefficient use of land and its inability to support a healthy mix of uses. He quoted the corridor's own "sprightly newspaper," my newspaper (!), which had proclaimed that the Route 1 corridor's trouble was "not too many people, but too few."[4]

Over the years *U.S. 1* covered many of the issues addressed by Whyte: suburban sprawl; an unsuccessful battle to convert acres of parking lots at the busy Princeton Junction train station into a mixed-use transit village; New Brunswick's successes and Trenton's failures in efforts to revitalize their downtowns; and a squabble between the university and townspeople over moving the Princeton train station 460 feet farther away from the center of town, among others.

Meanwhile, in my own neighborhood a group of artists and designers had volunteered to transform a vacant alley into an outdoor sculpture garden, art gallery, and performance space. It was an under-utilized space ten feet wide and eighty feet long in the heart of down-town. As I walked past the alley one day, I met one of the designers, Kevin Wilkes, an architect and general contractor. I remarked that taking an unused space—as small as it was—and putting it to good use was exactly the kind of action that William H. Whyte had en-couraged. I referred to Whyte fully expecting that I would then have to explain who he was. No need. "Holly Whyte!" exclaimed Wilkes. "Holly Whyte's my hero!"

Another aha moment. Time to learn more about William H. Whyte.

Introduction

A Man of Many Missions

This book is about William H. Whyte. Today the name will ring a bell with many people in the field of urban planning, who remember his analyses of cities and suburbs and his observations that showed what made public spaces work, or not work. Whyte stands among the leading American urbanists of the twentieth century, one whose work has become even more relevant in the twenty-first century. But in December 1956, when sociologist C. Wright Mills reviewed a new book called *The Organization Man* for the *New York Times* Sunday Book Review, Whyte's name was virtually unknown except to the readers of *Fortune* magazine.

Mills, a professor at Columbia University, was a reviewer with impressive credentials. As a PhD sociologist and author of *The Power Elite*, which declared that American society was controlled by an unelected upper echelon from the leading business, political, and military institutions, Mills dismissed Whyte as "an energetic reporter" tackling "a very old theme." While Whyte "adroitly reports various facts and trends," Mills noted, "he manages to keep the tone of his book that of an earnest, optimistic Boy Scout. The trouble is he really isn't prepared."[1] Mills, the academician, may not have been impressed with

Whyte's unconventional and deliberately simple opening sentence: "This book is about the organization man."

Within six weeks *The Organization Man* was on the *Times* bestseller list, where it stayed for most of 1957. Eventually its worldwide sales would be measured in the millions. Not bad for an unprepared Boy Scout.

Soon Whyte could not be categorized so glibly. In 1957 the American Library Association awarded Whyte $5,000 for the best book in the field of contemporary affairs and problems. In 1958, at an alumni program sponsored by Whyte's alma mater, Princeton University, three academic departments—politics, economics, and sociology—based their discussions on *The Organization Man*. In 1959, after he had left *Fortune*, a foundation president trying to interest Whyte in a project asked directly, "What are you now, anyway? Private eye? Pundit? Consultant?"[2] As Whyte's focus shifted from organizations to the sprawling suburbs in which many organization people lived and then to the cities where many of them ultimately would hope to live, his public stature became even more difficult to describe. He was called a conservationist, an environmentalist, an urbanologist, a sociologist, an urban planner, an urban anthropologist, or—a most convenient catchall—a public intellectual.

In fact Whyte was a bit of all of these things, but he was also an organization man in the best sense of the term. Rather than dismissing large institutions, Whyte knew how to function within them without being blindly acquiescent to them. His "optimistic premise," as he wrote in the opening pages of *The Organization Man*, was "that individualism is as possible in our times as in others." The fault was not in any of the accoutrements of the organization, from station wagons to gray flannel suits, or in the organization itself. The fault was "in our worship of it."[3]

Whyte could appreciate organizations of all sorts, especially "deep organizations," institutions that maintain a sense of public purpose beyond their bottom-line, short-term objectives.[4] Whyte was educated at St. Andrew's School, which he entered shortly after it was founded by the Du Pont family and which immediately began storing archives—a sign of a deep organization. He studied at Princeton University, founded in 1746. And he enlisted in the United States Marine Corps, where he honed his analytical skills writing for its professional military journal, which began publication in 1916. He worked with other "deep organizations" to effect changes in land use and urban design. These included, among others, Time Inc.'s *Fortune* magazine, which allowed reporters months to produce a finished article; the Rockefeller Brothers Fund, continuing a philanthropic purpose that began in the nineteenth century; and the New York City Planning Commission, a rare government agency that, in the late 1960s, at least, openly criticized its own work.

Whyte noted in the *New York Times* in 1986: "Some years ago I wrote a book about the people who work for large organizations. I called them organization men. Some people got mad at me for this. They said I was calling them dirty conformists. But I wasn't. I was an organization man myself . . . and I meant no slight."[5]

This biography rediscovers Whyte's work as a journalist, an author, an advocate of sustainable land use and engaging public spaces, and, yes, an organization man. It explores his critical thinking, his skepticism, and his curiosity—attributes that would serve anyone well today. This book hopes to encourage readers, and the organizations with which they are affiliated, to tackle the continuing issues—and occasional crises—of our urban and suburban realms.

William Hollingsworth Whyte, known to family and friends as Holly, lived from 1917 to 1999. Born and raised in a small town about twenty-five miles west of Philadelphia, Whyte spent his high school years at a brand-new—and then very small—private boys' school. A prescient headmaster attributed Whyte's lackluster grades to poor time management and declared that he could not be "classified in the ordinary way." On the strength of that recommendation, Whyte was accepted at Princeton, where he majored in English and wrote for the literary magazine. After graduating in 1939 and spending a brief time selling Vicks VapoRub, Whyte eagerly enlisted in the Marine Corps a few months before the attack on Pearl Harbor. His combat service may well have included the classic story line of the small-town boy growing into a man of the world. But during Whyte's tour as a Marine Corps intelligence officer he also witnessed the tension that exists between an individual and the group around him. And he learned how to distill information into intelligence. For Whyte "military intelligence" was a serious endeavor, not an oxymoron or a comedian's punch line.

Looking back at the 1950s, when the "silent generation" was just beginning to enter the workforce and the corporate world appeared to favor conformists and company loyalists, the innovation going on in the background is easy to miss. Whyte and his colleagues on the staff at *Fortune* magazine in the 1950s challenged the corporate establishment in ways that few business magazines today would dare. In 1952, as a thirty-four-year-old reporter, Whyte cast a wary eye on the emerging discipline of business communications and the accompanying loss of "intuition, inspiration, perception, and the like."[6] Whyte introduced the term "groupthink," which remains in common use.[7]

In *The Organization Man* Whyte declared that the Protestant ethic and its survival-of-the-fittest code had quietly been supplanted by a social ethic, in which an individual, "by sublimating himself in the group," could help "produce a whole that is greater than the sum of its parts."[8] Survival of the fittest had become survival of those who fit in best. "Group" had become the more important word in "groupthink." Despite the common perception, however, Whyte did not condemn conformity or organizations. Whyte advised his readers how to work with The Organization and how to—when necessary—resist it. He noted that the lure of The Organization was not limited to business enterprises. It could be experienced just as much in the halls of academe and on the hallowed grounds of religious institutions.

The Organization Man may appear to be only an early accomplishment before Whyte turned to his true calling as an urban critic. But the book set the stage for much of his later work by studying in depth the "packaged villages," as he referred to the suburbs housing the organization men and their families. These new developments might have met the immediate needs of the postwar baby boom, but they would fail to be a sustainable alternative to vibrant cities and downtowns. "Urban sprawl," a term used (but not coined) by Whyte in a 1958 *Fortune* article, became his next area of interest.

In the 1960s, as protests on the streets captured the public's attention, Whyte and other insiders quietly transformed the conservation movement into the environmental movement and expanded its focus to include the urban landscape as well as the fields and streams of rural America. Whyte and his allies developed their own unconventional tactics to work with, and sometimes against, developers and bureaucrats.

In *The Last Landscape*, published in 1968, Whyte continued to develop antidotes to the seemingly inexorable spread of urban and suburban sprawl. The book also brought into focus the enduring joys of city life, the potential of the smallest plots of land when put into use rather than left abandoned, and the perils of poor planning. Whyte discovered one egregious example as he edited New York City's unorthodox master plan of 1969. Privately owned public spaces that were intended to provide public benefits in exchange for increased building sizes turned out to be a bad deal for the public. Identifying what made spaces work for the public and then specifying how zoning laws could be changed to accomplish that consumed Whyte in the 1970s and 1980s. That work became the basis for his film and accompanying book in 1980, *The Social Life of Small Urban Spaces*.

Published in 1988, *City: Rediscovering the Center* was Whyte's last major work. In that book Whyte described the potential downside of corporate moves to the suburbs, and the reasons why small up-and-coming businesses would continue to seek out and thrive in urban locations. In the city, Whyte wrote, "truly critical negotiations" can be done "informally, on common meeting grounds equally accessible to both parties." These places, such as restaurants, coffee shops, even street corners, "are the heart of the city's intelligence networks, and a company that cuts itself off from them loses something that no electronic system can ever provide."[9] Not even Zoom, as noted in chapter 18.

* * *

William H. Whyte died at the age of eighty-one in 1999. His death was the moment for history to form its first impression of the man. In Whyte's case it was favorable. But like most first impressions, it would eventually need to be revised and supplanted by a broader view—one that comes into focus in this book.

Shortly after Whyte's death, Harvard sociologist Nathan Glazer wrote that Whyte "seems fated to be known as *The Organization Man* man." Glazer viewed him as "one of America's most influential observers of the city and the space around it."[10] On January 2, 2000, the *New York Times Magazine* called Whyte "The Observation Man" and alluded to both his social criticism and urban planning: "After writing 'The Organization Man,' his groundbreaking study of corporate culture, he applied his analytical skills to the urban center."[11]

Whyte nurtured and encouraged many people who would make their own significant contributions in open space preservation, urban planning, and public space management. At a time when women were seldom heard of in the fields of architecture and urban planning, Whyte jump-started the career of a relatively unknown writer, Jane Jacobs. On the strength of Whyte's recommendation, the Rockefeller Brothers Fund provided money to enable Jacobs to write *The Death and Life of Great American Cities*. Urban economist and author Richard Florida, a professor at the University of Toronto, visited with Jacobs on several occasions in Toronto, where she lived during the last thirty-three years of her life. Florida asked Jacobs about her life in Manhattan. She answered that she had only a few friends there, her editor, Jason Epstein, and Holly Whyte. "Without Holly Whyte," Florida says, "there might not have been a Jane Jacobs."[12]

When Whyte turned his attention to urban design, he quickly generated a legion of disciples, many of whom are still active today (as we will see in chapter 18), marching under the various banners of new urbanism, ecological cities, and urban sustainability. Some see themselves as part of another divide in American society—walkable urbanism versus car-dependent suburbanism. Some of the leading advocates for walkable, vibrant, sustainable downtowns—in big cities as well as small towns—employ tactics described by Whyte in *The Last Landscape*. Proponents of privately owned public spaces—created by negotiations between developers and municipalities and championed by Whyte—make sure that the public is aware of its right to use these spaces. Many of these same public space advocates also share the concern raised by Whyte in 1958: "More and more, it would seem, the city is becoming a place of extremes—a place for the very poor, or the very rich, or the slightly odd."[13]

We are now thinking about cities—large and small—more critically than ever. It may take years to assess the full impact of the COVID-19 pandemic on a particular city's economic footing, social support system, transportation infrastructure, and racial and economic diversity. But the pandemic immediately made clear that cities and towns needed to rethink the way they use their streets, parking lots, and public spaces. Whyte suggested these changes decades ago; the pandemic accelerated their implementation in many places.

With so much changing so quickly, we need benchmarks by which we can judge the civic realm. We may like, or not like, the downtown section in our community, but why? What works, what doesn't, for pedestrians, bicyclists, residents, workers, motorists, and commuters? In part because of Whyte, professional planners now routinely include public input in their process. But that process draws on increasingly specialized disciplines. Laypeople, the committed members of a community or organization whose role Whyte valued highly, still need to consider the ultimate questions: Will that "walkable urban" lifestyle become as stultifying as the suburban sprawl of a few decades ago? Will the Starbucks logo replace the McDonald's arches as a symbol of our uniformity? Will the organization men—and now women, of course—who constitute this new urban aristocracy supplant the middle- and lower-income people who have made the cities so diverse and dynamic over the years? If Whyte's legacy endures, it will be largely because people have realized they do not need to be a practitioner (or even a student) of urban planning to help shape the future of their community.

*　*　*

William H. Whyte's considerable curiosity and observational skills took him down many different paths. If he were operating in today's hyperactive media environment, he might have been caught up in a single intellectual silo along the way, with a social media platform needing to be constantly fed. Luckily for us, however, Whyte did not feel constrained by any one area of expertise. And he usually explored most of one path before starting down another, allowing us generally to follow his life decade by decade, from one focal point to the next.

But Whyte often remained active in one subject even as he was turning his attention to something new. The narratives overlap at several points. Whyte's years at *Fortune*, discussed in chapter 4, occurred during the golden age of print journalism, dramatically different from today. At *Fortune* Whyte also received a significant dose of management training. His dose ended with a slightly bitter pill, but the experience served him well as he moved into the world of wealthy philanthropists, high-powered developers, and sometimes wily conservationists and public officials. But within this same time period, Whyte produced three remarkable books that remain relevant to this day. Those books are addressed in chapters 5, 6, and 7—the last of which marks Whyte's pivot into open space preservation and urban planning issues in the 1960s and beyond.

Whyte's reputation as an analyst of organizations and their management persisted through the 1950s and into the first half of the 1960s, overlapping his work in open space preservation. In the late 1960s Whyte was wrapping up his work in open space and turning his eye to poorly designed public spaces in Manhattan. Then he heard about the challenges faced by landmark preservationists and realized that the conservation easements he had developed for rural and suburban America could be employed to save historic buildings in the city—the subject of chapter 12.

Over the course of his life, Whyte developed a framework for the study of people, their organizations, and their physical surroundings. We could call it Whyte's Way. His analytical approach helped fuel the discipline of urban studies and placemaking. It empowers laypeople, as Whyte was himself, to stand their ground among the most highly trained professionals. The lesson of *The Organization Man*, which is not to condemn the organization but rather to understand its strengths, weaknesses, and inherent biases, gains a new currency in the complex world of urban and suburban planning. And sometimes, as Whyte has instructed us, a great advance still requires someone "frustrated by the status quo" who "blows the lid off everything."

Whyte's Way of critical thinking can be illustrated by an image he describes in *City: Rediscovering the Center*. He asks readers to envision a telescopic view of Fifth Avenue in Manhattan, "eight blocks of people, tense and unsmiling, squeezed into one." If the image were being used in a film to represent the popular and unflattering view of city life at that time, the soundtrack would feature "jackhammers, sirens, and a snatch of discordant Gershwin." Beware of compressed, telescopic views, Whyte argued. His observation point was on the sidewalk itself, looking laterally as the people moved before him. Why were those people in that river of humanity? For all sorts of good reasons, it turned out, and the long stream of pedestrians was not an unending, anonymous flow of humanity. People ran into friends and stopped to talk. Others lingered at newsstands. People chatted with strangers. The "ultimate reality," Whyte concluded, "was people in everyday situations."[14]

Whyte never lost his enthusiasm for empirical evidence. In doing research for a 1982 reprint of the 1939 *WPA Guide to New York City*, for example, Whyte used the home addresses of the people on the Social Register to determine how much Manhattan's Upper East Side had changed between 1939 and 1982. Very little, he discovered. The geographic center of those socialites had moved only a few blocks.[15] On another occasion, Whyte measured the sound level of the water wall at Paley Park in Midtown Manhattan and discovered it was higher than that of the street outside—despite the claim by visitors that they went to the park for peace and quiet.[16]

In making his arguments, Whyte often sought out the most powerful argument against his position and then turned it into a positive. Was his beloved prep school, St. Andrew's, "out of step" with mainstream academies? Certainly, Whyte conceded. But "the key question," he added, "is whether it is out of step enough."[17] Some observers believed that big companies fleeing to the suburbs meant that cities were dying. But, Whyte argued, the smaller start-up companies replacing them sometimes generated more jobs than were lost when the big companies left.

Architects, Whyte believed, did their best work when faced with seemingly impossible conditions, as opposed to a blank site leveled by a bulldozer. Space wasted on car parking in the urban landscape, he noted in *The Last Landscape* in 1968, could be put to a higher use.[18] Whyte even had a positive view of the slightly off-kilter individuals hanging out in downtown areas. "In many ways, the odd people do a service for the rest of us," he said in his narration of *The Social Life of Small Urban Spaces* film. "They reassure us of our own normality."[19]

Don't overthink things, Whyte counseled. In *The Organization Man*, he wrote about an anthropologist's study of a strike by factory workers in Massachusetts. The anthropologist traced the discontent to the fact that mechanization had destroyed the "hierarchy of skills" that used to be a source of satisfaction and status in the workplace. Whyte thought the workers' demands should be taken at face value: they were on strike because they really wanted what they said they wanted: more money. Whyte proposed that someone could "create a stir" by creating "a radical new tool" for the human relations field: the face-value technique.[20]

Similarly, in studying the social life of public plazas and streets, Whyte and his researchers searched for common denominators among the most widely used places. People simply sat where there were places to sit. Nothing more complicated than the addition of chairs could transform a plaza. What Whyte discovered, he cheerfully admitted, "may not strike you as an intellectual bombshell."[21]

Whyte conveyed his direct empirical evidence in straightforward, declarative sentences. As an author he began all but one of his books with the elemental assertion that "this book is about" whatever the subject at hand might be. While some academicians today still look askance at Whyte in favor of other urbanists who present their findings in a theoretical framework, Whyte's work was a precursor—and almost certainly a contributor—to the emergence of public space design as a discrete field in the architecture and planning professions.

People today with a cursory knowledge of Whyte often assume he was some form of PhD-level academician, often an anthropologist or a sociologist. But if he had been part of the academic establishment, he would have been an outlier with an unconventional approach. As he reflected in his 1992 preface to *The Exploding Metropolis*, "I found in my work on urban spaces that many of the most rudimentary questions were neither posed nor answered. . . . The customary research plan didn't help much because the research was vicarious, that is, once or twice removed from the reality being studied. There is no substitute for a confrontation with the physical. You see things that theory misses."[22]

Of course, to talk the talk about confronting the physical you ought to walk the walk. Whyte literally did just that on many occasions. As recounted in chapter 16, Whyte attended a meeting of developers at the Carnegie Center on Route 1 just outside Princeton, New Jersey, by walking from the center of town to the office complex. "They thought I was some kind of nut," he wrote.

Walking the walk, Whyte realized, exposed not just the breadth and length of a place but also the ups and downs, the topology. Elevation matters. Whyte observed that if people have to descend or ascend more than about three feet into a public plaza, they will visit that space less often than a similar one at street level. The two-dimensional bird's-eye view might be great for city planners sitting at their desks, and better yet for presentations at zoning boards, but it does not expose the literal ups and downs of reality.

At the end of his career and his life, Whyte worked on a memoir of his time with the United States Marines fighting the Japanese on Guadalcanal. Whyte and his battalion relied on maps based on information from civilian visitors to that South Pacific island before the war. The maps were crude and lacked one critical detail: the location of the ravines and cliffs that pockmarked the terrain. Exploratory patrols provided ground-level reconnaissance that spared a significant force of men from almost certain disaster.[23] Later in life the leatherneck would not forget the lesson.

For William H. Whyte, mapmaking and observational skills were nurtured not in the big city or in the Ivy League classroom but rather in his small hometown in southeastern Pennsylvania and at a brand-new prep school brimming with high hopes in a rural corner of Delaware.

Chapter 1

The Cast of Characters, from White to Whyte

W illiam H. Whyte, observer, critic, and ultimately great defender and promoter of the city, wherever it might be located, always had a quick answer when asked to list his three favorite cities: "New York, New York, and New York." *New Yorker* writer Brendan Gill likened Whyte's scrutiny of Manhattan to Henry David Thoreau's observation of Walden Pond.[1] The Whyte equivalent to Thoreau's cabin was a brownstone on a narrow lot on East 94th Street in Manhattan. But the big-city urbanist had small-town roots, in West Chester, Pennsylvania, with a population of just under twelve thousand.

Its size notwithstanding, West Chester was laid out in the classic grid system of a big city by Thomas Holme, a surveyor associated with William Penn. The downtown "skyline" is punctuated by the 1848 Greek Revival Chester County Courthouse with its declarative clock steeple, designed by Thomas U. Walter, the architect of the Capitol Dome in Washington, DC, and by the six-story 1908 Farmers and Mechanics Building. In 1930 the town added a touch of modern architecture, the Art Deco Warner Theatre, open every day but Sunday in accord with the town's Quaker influence.

West Chester was and still is walkable. The town measures a little more than a mile on any side. An energetic kid like Whyte could easily pedal his bicycle out into the lush countryside of the Brandywine Valley, where George Washington's troops were defeated by the British in 1777. As a kid in the 1920s, Whyte found the countryside enthralling. He described the scene in a fictional account in his college literary magazine.

> Five miles north of West Chester, in the heart of the rolling hills that have been a fox-hunter's paradise for years, the Brandywine Creek is flanked on one side by a cornfield and several flat meadows, on the other by a thickly wooded hill. It was on the top of this hill that old Tom Marshallton had built his house eighty years ago, and had stoutly claimed that he had chosen the most beautiful spot in all the world. . . . It is still as charming today.[2]

Whyte's physical surroundings influenced him throughout his life. His immediate family and forebears also played a role, though how much of Whyte's independent, contrary thinking was inherited rather than nurtured by circumstances cannot be determined. But tracing Whyte's family back several generations on both sides suggests that several of his forebears challenged the status quo and resisted institutional constraints—traits that somehow became imbued in Whyte.

John Campbell White (the family name was not yet Whyte) came to America from Ireland in 1798 and began to practice medicine in Baltimore. One of his sons married a daughter of William Pinkney, who had served as attorney general of the United States and as US senator from Maryland in the early 1800s. Their son, William Pinkney White, born in 1824 in Baltimore, became a pivotal figure in the family lineage.[3]

Tutored by Napoléon Bonaparte's former private secretary, White had to interrupt his studies at the age of eighteen because of family financial difficulties and went to work for a Baltimore-based counting house. In 1843, at age nineteen, he took a new job with a law firm and then entered Harvard Law School. At some point early in his career, as a result of a bitter dispute with an uncle over the management of a

family-owned distillery business, William Pinkney White took a dras-
tic step. He changed the spelling of his last name to Whyte.[4]

This first Whyte not only changed his name but also brought it into
the national spotlight. Whyte, whose death in 1908 was reported on
the front page of the *New York Times*, served as US senator, Maryland
governor, mayor of Baltimore, and state attorney general. He was also a
family man, in 1847 marrying Louise B. Hollingsworth, the seventeen-
year-old daughter of a Baltimore merchant. The eldest of their three
sons was William Hollingsworth Whyte, born in Baltimore in 1849
and destined to be the first of three William Hollingsworth Whytes
(the last being the subject of this biography).

William H. Whyte I's first marriage did not last long, but he had
one daughter, Mary Whyte, probably born in the early 1880s. On June
15, 1887, he married his second wife, Caroline Hartshorne, daughter
of Joshua Hartshorne, a Civil War iron merchant who in 1867 had
built a handsome estate in West Chester, Pennsylvania, on a large lot
bordered by North Church Street, Virginia Avenue, and High Street.
The wedding took place on a Wednesday afternoon in the parlors of
the Hartshorne mansion with Senator Whyte, father of the groom, in
attendance. It was described by a reporter as "a *recherche* affair in every
particular. . . . Within the open hallways and parlors and over the piaz-
zas of the palatial home there was a profusion of flowers everywhere,
combined with which was the elegant attire of the ladies, the whole
making a scene of exquisite beauty and loveliness."[5]

That glowing review marked the arrival of the Whyte family in West
Chester. The reverie was short-lived, however. William H. Whyte I
died in February 1888, six months before the birth of his namesake,
William Hollingsworth Whyte Jr.

The family's subsequent press was not always so positive. In 1901 the
Daily Local News, West Chester's newspaper since 1872, printed a story
that was scandalous at the time.

Assistant Fire Chief Michael Mearra . . . is missing from his home
in this place, where his absence is mourned by a wife and four children, the youngest being about ten months old. Absent from town
is also Miss Mary Whyte, daughter of the late W. Hollingsworth

Whyte, of Baltimore, and granddaughter of Judge Pinkney Whyte,
the eminent Maryland jurist.... It is alleged by Mrs. Mearra that
Michael and the girl left this place on Thursday evening and are now
together at some point unknown.... Detectives are now searching
for Mearra and Miss Whyte. If found the latter will have to stand
a suit for alienating the affections of the husband of Mrs. Mearra.[6]

A search of *Daily Local News* editions published over the next several weeks revealed no further airing of the affair. Aunt Mary Whyte,
nevertheless, was certainly another notable character in the Whyte
family lore.

Raised by his mother, who never remarried after his father's death,
Whyte Jr. attended the Delancey School in Philadelphia and then was
part of Harvard University's Class of 1911. He married Louise Troth
Price of Whitford, Pennsylvania, on September 9, 1913. Their first son,
William Hollingsworth Whyte III, was born October 1, 1917. Another
son, Robert, was born in 1923. In the tenth reunion yearbook of his
Harvard class, Whyte Jr. listed his occupation as "railroader," with an
office in Philadelphia and memberships in the West Chester Golf and
Country Club and the West Chester Club.

Louise Troth Whyte's family had its own remarkable characters.
She was one of four girls and three boys born to Dr. Joseph Price and
Louisa Troth of Philadelphia. Dr. Price earned his medical degree from
the University of Pennsylvania in 1877 and founded the gynecological
and obstetrical departments at the old Philadelphia Dispensary. The
setting was described as a slum, with inhabitants "in daily contact with
disease, especially those incident to vice and poverty." Despite the circumstances, Dr. Price attained "an unequalled record of 100 sections
for pelvic suppuration with but one death."[7]

In 1891 he opened a private hospital at 241 North 18th Street in
Philadelphia, considered one of the largest hospitals in the country
for abdominal surgery. According to a tribute presented shortly after
his death, Dr. Price and his hospital exceeded the standards of the day.
"Cleanliness was his slogan, two general baths per day and an ever-
lasting scrubbing of face, hands, and head, between times, with soap,
alcohol, and bichlorid." The tribute, written by a former colleague, Dr.

A. P. Butt of Elkins, West Virginia, suggested that Dr. Price thrived because he practiced outside the comfort zone of a large organization: "Price was destined to be a free lance; fetters would not have set well and perhaps this slum stage was better suited to his talents than the more pretentious one of some large endowed hospital. One wonders what effect such a hospital appointment would have had; would it have developed or starved him? I think the latter."[8]

By the time Whyte III was born, in 1917, his parents were living in one side of a modest duplex at 407 West Barnard Street in West Chester. Soon they would move to more spacious quarters and closer to the extended Hartshorne family. The Whytes' new home, at 539 North Church Street, was built in 1869 on a lot that was carved out of a corner of the much larger Hartshorne estate. The main house, a two-and-a-half-story Italianate brick mansion built in 1867, is now on the National Register of Historic Places and divided into office suites. The three-bedroom, two-story brick house occupied by young Holly Whyte and his family was not a mansion, but it was solidly middle-class.

In West Chester, Holly enjoyed the kind of boyhood that only a small town—or a close-knit neighborhood in a big city—could provide. "We had gangs in West Chester," he wrote in his memoirs, obviously employing some of the hyperbole that would color many of his personal recollections throughout his life. "My cousin, Alec Hemphill, led the dreaded East End gang. They had twenty Daisy and Benjamin air rifles and even a single-shot .22 to our gang's miserable collection of six Daisys and Benjamins. We called ourselves, without much imagination, 'The Club,' and we thought we were safe in our own tunnel system, essentially a trench covered over with several sheets of galvanized iron."[9] Whyte would write sixty years later in *City: Rediscovering the Center*, "It is often assumed that children play in the street for lack of playgrounds. But many children play in the streets because they like to."[10]

Another favorite play space for young Holly was a summer home near a pond in Wellfleet on Cape Cod owned by his grandmother Price. On Cape Cod, he learned a skill that would serve him well in World War II combat on Guadalcanal as well as in the study of public spaces and pedestrians in Manhattan—the creation and reading of maps. On his visits to Wellfleet, young Whyte discovered the location of the best blueberry bushes. He drew his own maps so that he could find them again on his next visit.

In that same favorite summer place he observed another memorable family character, his uncle Joe Price, son of the eminent physician. In 1931 or 1932, with the Great Depression dampening personal finances, Holly observed Uncle Joe, who had never had a real job, suddenly arrive on the Cape with a new sailboat and car. The puzzle was solved when Holly and a buddy camped out one night on the shore. They were awakened by the sound of an approaching boat. Many years later, Whyte reported in his partial memoir: "Bootleggers! Now we were really scared. A truck pulled up on the beach, and we saw three men unloading what appeared to be cases of whiskey from the boat and putting them in the back of the truck." One of the bootleggers was Uncle Joe.[11]

When Holly reached his high school years, the family was wealthy enough to consider a boarding school but likely not so wealthy as to send him off to Exeter or Andover or any of the other very elite destinations. His grandfather, the first William H. Whyte, certainly had improved the family fortunes by marrying into the Hartshorne family. And Holly's father inherited the portion of the Hartshorne estate that passed through his mother, Caroline Hartshorne Whyte. Her will bequeathed virtually all of her assets either directly or through a trust to Holly's father and then to his children. Her daughter-in-law, and Holly's mother, Louise Price Whyte, was to be given only "the sum of one hundred dollars, clear of collateral and inheritance taxes." In a codicil dated December 5, 1927, Caroline stipulated that nothing was to be kept in trust and that all assets should be transferred to Holly's father "absolutely, to be his sole property and to be disposed of by him as he may see fit."[12] Some of the Hartshorne inheritance flowed eventually to Holly, though it was not enough for anyone to live the life of the idle rich, as we will see in chapter 17.

On February 24, 1929, Caroline Hartshorne Whyte died in the St. James Hotel in Philadelphia, where she was spending the winter. The will provides no clue as to how much money was in her estate, nor does it explain who took ownership of the Hartshorne mansion, the setting for her recherché wedding to Whyte Sr. But the mansion did not stay in the family for long. By 1936, it and the large lot surrounding the Whyte house had been sold to two benefactors of the Society of Friends, the Quakers. They in turn gave it to the church, which converted it into a nursing home with about thirty rooms.[13]

There may have been another cloud looming over the family: the impending divorce of Whyte Jr. and Louise. By the end of the decade the marriage was over, with Louise remaining in the West Chester house and Whyte Jr. living in the Chestnut Hill section of Philadelphia with a new wife, Margaret Perry. In 1969, when the nursing home proposed to add several structures to the property, Louise Whyte protested in a letter to the *Daily Local News*: "Years ago I thought I had that part sold to a man of great taste for a proper sum. I was away one month and before my return the Provident Trust Co. sold the house to two Quakers who told the would-be buyer and Provident the house was 'falling to pieces.' As a matter of fact, the house was always in beautiful order. So the two Quakers got it for next to nothing."[14]

Whatever the impetus, the family hoped to place William H. Whyte III in a new boarding school that offered "need-blind" admissions, St. Andrew's School in Middletown, Delaware. St. Andrew's was the creation of the Du Ponts of Delaware. Young Holly's uncle John Hemphill (the husband of Louise Price Whyte's sister) was a close friend of A. Felix du Pont, who believed there should be a private school in Delaware that was accessible to all boys regardless of wealth. Its quintessential collegiate Gothic buildings would later provide the setting for the 1989 movie *Dead Poets Society*.

St. Andrew's opened on September 19, 1930, and was formally dedicated on October 14. On November 4 of that year, Louise Whyte requested the school's catalog and noted that she was "anxious to get my 13-year-old boy in either this spring or next fall if it is possible."[15]

When W. Hollingsworth Whyte III, as he then called himself, showed up for eighth grade in the spring semester of 1931, he got off to a rocky start. "As a latecomer, the smallest and newest boy, it was only natural that they should beat me. And beat me," Whyte recounted in *A History of Saint Andrew's School at Middletown, Delaware: The First Thirty Years, 1928/1958*. "For someone who had just left a small-town

Figure 1.1 St. Andrew's School, founded by A. Felix du Pont, opened its doors to students in the fall of 1930. Holly Whyte, fourth from right in the first row of standees, would eventually become a school trustee. (St. Andrew's School.)

home, it was a devastating experience. It wasn't just the beating. It was entry into a society which seemed run by the boys themselves."[16]

But within months, Whyte made his presence known. The official school newspaper, *The Cardinal*, had already begun publication. "The younger boys were frozen out of its direction by the older ones," Whyte recalled. Out of the blue, an alternative paper appeared. Printed on the school's mimeograph machine, it was called *The Textbook*. Under its hand-drawn logo, showing a handful of books on a shelf, was the first editorial, signed by the editor-in-chief, "W.H. Whyte."

> This paper was created, not with the intention to interfere in any way with the doings of the Cardinal, but to record the minor doings and seemingly trivial affairs of the school, which of course, the Cardinal has no room for. It is independent and depends enturely

[sic] upon its advertisers. Any contributions will be gladly accepted and the author will get due credit for his work. . . . Absolutely any article that is sensible will find its way to the Mimeograph Machine.

The editor-in-chief, thirteen years old, cranked out another ten issues. *The Textbook* was, as promised, filled with trivial affairs. A question:

> X—Which would you rather have—a million dollars or twelve daughters?
>
> Z—Twelve daughters—because if I had a million I would want more but twelve daughters would be enough.

Then came volume 1, issue 11. The lead editorial began with a simple declarative sentence: "This is the last issue of the Textbook. The Textbook and the Cardinal have merged to make weekly, the Cardinal." In the 1928/1958 St. Andrew's *History*, Whyte provided the backstory. "Since the older boys who ran the Cardinal were always persecuting us and rifling our files, we left a checkbook in our drawer which showed a handsome but entirely spurious balance of $40. A few days later we were approached by the management of the Cardinal. How about a merger? We agreed."[17]

While the combined papers may have taken the name of *The Cardinal*, Whyte made clear from the beginning who was in charge. In the combined publication, produced with a typewriter, two boys were listed as editors-in-chief. One of the names was crossed out and re-typed in the list of coeditors. Whyte's name remained as editor-in-chief. He was still only an eighth grader.

By the fall term of his senior year at St. Andrew's, Whyte was cocky enough to spoil for a fight. In a November 20, 1934, editorial he wrote that he was looking for something, anything, "to write a humdinger of an editorial about." Alas, he continued, "the school still continues in its peaceful routine. . . . We have often secretly wished that Mr. Pell [the headmaster] would pass some other tyrannical bill of legislation or that a master would horsewhip a boy. Then we could put something more in the editorials than a plea for subscriptions."

Decades later, in 1980, Whyte would be the keynote speaker at the

Figure 1.2 Whyte, in foreground with pen poised, did not always excel academically. But as his headmaster said, he could "scarcely be classified in the ordinary way." (St. Andrew's School.)

school's fiftieth anniversary. "The school has always been congenial to self-expression, and the tradition started with Walden Pell. He was strong for us doing things of our own devising. He was also quite tolerant," Whyte said at the anniversary event. Whyte recalled one St. Andrew's faculty member in particular, an English teacher named William H. "Bull" Cameron, who came to St. Andrew's in 1931 at the age of twenty-three. Whyte remembered Cameron as "a rigorous taskmaster."

[He was] someone who won't let you talk it out, but forces you to re-write, and re-write again. And with little sympathy for your feelings. I have a collection of harsh marginal comments with the initials WHC at the end of them. Here are some: "This is a pile of cliches. Write it over, and just one metaphor per paragraph please." "What are you trying to say here? I can understand none of it." "Where are your topic sentences? Where is your topic?" But we did learn. We did master the English declarative sentence. And we should be grateful.[18]

Declarative sentences became a hallmark of Whyte's writing. His first book, *Is Anybody Listening?*, began, "This is a book for laymen by a layman." As noted in the introduction to this biography, *The Organization Man* started in a similar vein. Whyte introduced *The Exploding Metropolis* in 1958 with the sentence "This is a book by people who like cities." His memoir, *A Time of War*, written at the end of his life, began, "You can draw an outline of my life with maps."

Whyte began his handwritten letter to the admission office at Princeton University with a declarative sentence. "I have selected Princeton for several reasons. As a college preparatory to taking a law course it has been recommended highly to me; a good many of my friends are or will be at Princeton; my father, although a Harvard man himself, favors Princeton mainly because of the associations I would make there; its undergraduate activities cover a wider ground than do most colleges; and materially its location is convenient to me."[19]

The Princeton application form included this question: "Are you an applicant for any scholarship, or loan, or self-help earnings at Princeton?" Whyte's answer was "Yes," another indication of his upper-middle-class—but not wealthy—status.

But would Princeton choose Whyte? While the prep school senior may have mastered the declarative sentence, he was not always on top of his academic game. Headmaster Pell filled out the "General Estimate" for the Princeton admission office, which requested "as full and accurate an estimate as possible of this applicant as regards his industry, initiative, perseverance, sense of honor, reliability, force of character, and influence on his fellow students."

In today's world it is hard to imagine a principal or a headmaster taking the significant amount of time needed to distill and to reconcile the objective and subjective components that make up the "general estimate" of any student's life. Yet that is exactly what happened in 1935 at St. Andrew's. In a lengthy handwritten statement, excerpted here, the headmaster chose his words carefully.

Hollingsworth Whyte has taken the initiative in many fields of ex-tra-curricular activities—publishing, dramatics, photography, even medicine and architecture! His time has been so divided among a multitude of interests, including football and a passion for rowing, that he has never given himself a fair showing scholastically. His marks must be discounted, therefore. He is a brilliant & versatile boy who has made a special contribution to the School from the funds of his particular genius.

Whyte is usually too pre-occupied to bother much with the details of "surface order," though his promptness, attention to his "jobs" and neatness in caring for his room have improved as he has grown older.

He is a connoisseur of entertainment, and this interest in-volved him in the taking of a few small drinks during our Sixth Form Dance. In common with the others involved, Whyte con-fessed his part voluntarily. . . . The suspensions given are not to be interpreted as the School's severe censure on the characters of those involved. We trust Whyte and prize his presence in the School, though we deplore the softness & thoughtlessness that led him into this trouble, and that seems often to be the converse of the artistic & creative intellect.[20]

Along with the "General Estimate," Pell provided the Princeton admission office with the "principal's final report on applicant." The marks for the final term were not pretty.

Sacred Studies	B
English	D+
Latin	D
American History	D
Chemistry	D

The good news: Whyte graduated tenth in his class. The bad news: There were only twelve in the class.

On the back of the grade report, Pell answered some additional questions. Is he an unusually good student, or an average student, or

Figure 1.3 Whyte, in the back row on the right, posed with his senior year classmates in 1935. Eleven years later he was the school's graduation speaker. (St. Andrew's School.)

slow and persistent, or generally poor? Pell's comment: "Unusually good, but he has so many other irons in the fire that his studies do not get the benefit of all his time & energy."

Has he exhibited special mental qualifications or unusual ability in one or more subjects which would qualify him for high-stand sections in certain college courses? Pell: "Certainly in English."

Within ten years William H. Whyte would be a United States Marine Corps combat veteran, writing in the *Marine Corps Gazette* about the difference between information and intelligence. Within twenty years Whyte would be writing his best-selling book, *The Organization Man*, and would rail against the psychological tests that companies were using in hopes of divining who would—and who would not—fit into the culture that the company believed was critical to its collective success. At the other end of the testing industry, standardized aptitude tests were coming into vogue—objective measures believed to be predictors of success in higher education. The subjective middle ground between these two extremes was the quaint process by which Princeton University and St. Andrew's School were sizing up Whyte. The headmaster's "General Estimate" was prescient: "Hollingsworth Whyte is an unusually brilliant boy whose temperament is such that he can scarcely be classified in the ordinary way."

The Princeton admission office was convinced and made an offer to Whyte. The grateful seventeen-year-old sent a handwritten response to Princeton's director of admission, Radcliffe Heermance.[21]

Dear Sir.
I have recieved [sic] your notice of my admission, and I hereby wish to accept it so that a place will be reserved for me.
Very truly yours,
W. Hollingsworth Whyte III

The mnemonic device of "i before e, except after c" may have been another form of "surface order" for which Holly—another character in the White-Whyte lineage—did not have strict regard. But spelling errors would not hold him back.

Chapter 2

Princeton—from Rower to Writer

In the fall of 1935, William H. Whyte gathered with his fellow freshmen in the Princeton University Chapel to hear the president, Harold W. Dodds, welcome the new class to the university. "At no time since the Great War," the president began, speaking at a time when numerals were not yet needed to identify world wars, has peace "been in such uncertain balance." In 1935, at the height of the Great Depression, Dodds also had a warning: "Light-hearted, haphazard acceptance of new things, a care-free willingness to try anything once, in private life or in politics, is not experimentation in any scientific sense. It is gambling."[1]

Living in a single room in North Edwards Hall, Holly Whyte took a while to make his mark at Princeton. A faculty adviser offered an early estimate of Whyte's academic progress in a report dated October 9 of his freshman year. "Probably an erratic student," the adviser wrote. On November 22 the adviser added some good news: "Spanish very much better." Whyte rowed on the freshman crew and was captain of the boat that won the freshman title. But the text of a story in the student newspaper referred to "Bill Whyte's yearling eight," suggesting that the reporter had never bothered to talk to the young man who referred to himself as Holly, never as Bill.[2]

In his sophomore year Whyte again lived alone, at 211 Foulke, a dormitory reminiscent of the buildings at St. Andrew's School, and successfully gained admission into an undergraduate eating club, Quadrangle. Whyte's club was not one of the elite clubs such as Ivy or Cottage that caught the fancy of F. Scott Fitzgerald and attracted the upper crust of undergraduate society, but it was socially acceptable nonetheless. (A year later Quadrangle accepted Robert F. Goheen of the Class of 1940, one year behind Whyte and destined to follow Dodds as the next university president.)

As a junior, Whyte became an English major. He saw his position on the crew move laterally, from the heavyweight to the lightweight (150-pound) crew, but not upward toward the first string. Whyte nevertheless found rowing on Lake Carnegie, a ten-minute walk from the heart of campus, to be a welcome diversion. In the Class of 1939's fiftieth reunion yearbook, Whyte described one of his favorite college memories: "In a shell on Lake Carnegie, late afternoon, the boat is going nice and easy. Just the sound of the slides and the church bells, and then the long walk back up, dead tired but sharing an experience that one must recall with deep pleasure."

By the end of his junior year Whyte had a new calling as a writer of fiction for the student-run *Nassau Literary Review*, informally known as the *Nassau Lit*. In the June 1938 issue, the first among four featured short stories and critical essays was a submission by William H. Whyte III '39, as his byline read in the publication. Whyte, a first-time contributor, drew from something that he knew well—the Pennsylvania farm country. From the opening paragraph of his 5,250-word narrative, Whyte made obvious that the title character, with a name based on a slight misspelling of a derogatory term for a German soldier in World War I, would not be a conventional hero.

> Hienie Schmidt climbed up the last step to the front porch of the brown frame house and flopped himself wearily onto the swing suspended from the porch roof. . . . For only seventeen Hienie was a big boy; large with that loose-jointed, big-boned, yet heavy frame that characterizes the Pennsylvania Dutch strain. His head, in contrast to the rest of his body, was even larger. . . . His face, while not flabby,

Figure 2.1 A Princeton faculty adviser guessed that the freshman Whyte was "probably an erratic student." (Seeley G. Mudd Manuscript Library, Princeton University.)

was soft and pudgy, his eyes an innocuous blue, and his mouth broad and loose, hanging open as if in a constant state of surprise.[3]

Overweight and unappreciated, Hienie is taunted by his own family as well as the more sophisticated kids in town. But he finds his moment when he falls into cahoots with two ne'er-do-wells in town. Even the ne'er-do-wells sense an easy mark in Hienie, who is set up to take the fall in their plot to steal a week's worth of cash from the neighborhood grocery store. Whyte's carefully scripted chase scene has a surprise ending—Hienie finally gets away with something and joins his fellow conspirators at a bar to savor the moment. The reader knows the moment will not last long.

By his senior year Whyte had become a regular contributor to the *Nassau Lit* and was listed as story editor on the masthead. His short stories included "The Country Gentleman," a reverie set in the Brandywine Valley, quoted in the previous chapter, which celebrates the beauty of the unspoiled countryside and also picks up the idiosyncrasies of a real-life character in Whyte's life, the unforgettable uncle Joe Price.

> "Where was I—oh yes—your grandfather. He was a real man; could cuss and drink with the best of them. I betcha Lou never told you that!" He chuckled heartily and then became grave. . . . "Dammit—Joe was a good man; would have made the best farmer in Chester County if the family had left him Valley Farms. Your mother said he didn't even know how to milk a cow right, but I'm tellin' you he would have amounted to something if he'd stuck around here." "Well, Mr. Marshallton," I interjected, "as a matter of fact he's making pretty good money now up at Cape Cod. He's got control of several businesses in Wellfleet." "Businesses!" my host snorted. "He doesn't belong in business any more than I do. Joe Price running a store!" "Well, what's wrong with that, Mr. Marshallton?" "Nothing wrong, I suppose . . . if you're cut out for that sort of thing. But anybody born and raised in the country running a store—huh!"[4]

Another *Nassau Lit* story, "We Meet the East End Gang," is a fictionalized account of Whyte's childhood exploits back in West Chester, also described in the previous chapter. The East End Gang story won some praise from a faculty reviewer who critiqued the *Nassau Lit* in the *Daily Princetonian*: "Mr. Whyte's slice of adolescent experience . . . rings true. Lacking in economy, it is nonetheless well told, and the author manages a large group of characters skillfully; he wisely limits himself to types, individualizing only Buddy, on whom the story pivots. The climax is both effective and satisfying."[5]

In at least one instance, Whyte seemed determined to break loose from his small-town roots. The December 1938 issue of the *Nassau Lit* featured a story called "Driftwood," with a byline that may have been intended to strike a more sophisticated tone: W. Hollingsworth Whyte '39. The setting was far from West Chester: a Parisian haunt that Whyte called Harry's American Bar, no doubt inspired by Harry's New York Bar, already famous as a Parisian hangout for Ernest Hemingway, Fitzgerald, and other literary lights. The young Whyte may have been channeling some prominent writer of the day.

> I was in Harry's American Bar one night. . . . For eleven o'clock it was doing pretty well. In one of the corners there were several Yale men, who, laboring under the delusion that they were at Maury's, had turned up their pant cuffs one more notch and undone their ties, a sure sign of their inclusion in that exclusive circle of the Big Three [along with Princeton and Harvard]. They were flipping a coin to determine which of them was to approach a group of Smith girls who were ostentatiously ignoring them. . . .
>
> It was at this juncture that there was a furious scuffling outside the swinging doors. They parted with a bang to reveal a small man of about thirty-five who looked like Robert Benchley. The bartender muttered "Mon Dieu!" and absently reached for the bottle of "Nectar of Old Kentucky" that was sitting on the top shelf.[6]

Just two months past his twenty-first birthday, our "W. Hollingsworth Whyte" presented a piece of fiction narrated by a sophisticated man of the world. The narrator resembled Whyte most likely only in the latter's imagination. During his college years, Whyte's mother on several occasions had alerted the society pages to her son's activities. A holiday trip from West Chester to New York in December 1936, for example, earned a mention in the *Philadelphia Inquirer*. There was no evidence of any trip abroad, but Whyte could have absorbed details from a classmate or club mate who had made the pilgrimage to the real Harry's New York Bar in Paris.

The most telling detail in the piece may have been the young Princeton writer's characterization of the vain Yale men at the bar (continuing a long tradition of Princetonians having fun at the expense of "Yalies" and vice versa). A little more than a decade later, the managing editor at *Fortune* magazine told the young reporter, Whyte, that the Class of 1949 at Yale was considered "the best crop in years—wonderful for business." He wanted Whyte to do a major feature on the graduating classes at Yale and other prestigious schools. But, like the fictional character at Harry's in Paris, Whyte was less than impressed with the Yale men and others in the Class of 1949 on campuses across the country. He found them fearful of another depression, looking to business as a "storm cellar" to protect them. The resulting article in *Fortune* was the germ of *The Organization Man*.

By the spring term of his senior year, Whyte, who otherwise might have been working solely on his senior thesis for the English department, due in early April, was also overseeing the production of his first play. It would be staged at Princeton's small Theatre Intime, founded in 1920 and a venue where Jimmy Stewart, Joshua Logan, and other aspiring college actors had performed. Whyte's play, *We Rileys*, was another creative effort drawing on Whyte's small-town roots. Set in a neighborhood drugstore, the plot revolved around the soda jerk, his political ambitions, and what he called his "splendiferous" concoction, the Passion Fruit Varsity Ice Cream Split. Two women characters, played by town residents, added to the intrigue.

Whyte, no doubt practicing some reverse snobbery, dedicated the play to "those maligned beings of our great American public who use chewing gum, read the Sunday magazine supplements, suffer with Joan Crawford and Tyrone Power, dance the shag, and who do not subscribe to the *New Yorker*." The dedication was the first of several lighthearted digs at the *New Yorker* that Whyte would take in his career. The review in the *Daily Princetonian* was written by the president of the Princeton Triangle Club, Sanders Maxwell, who would become a prominent Madison Avenue ad man.

"We Rileys," unveiled last night by the Theatre Intime, offers plenty of laughs and a melodramatic climax that is effective enough to keep the audience on its toes. W. H. Whyte III '39 has built his story around the latest thing in eternal triangles, boy-girl-soda fountain, and a mythical Nazi spy ring.... The keynote of the production is the small-town atmosphere presented via the drugstore set, and the total scorn of any sophisticated pretensions turns out all to the good.[7]

We Rileys was named best student play of the year, an award that carried with it a cash prize of $50, equivalent to almost $900 today. Whyte listed the award on his page in the senior year photo book, the *Nassau Herald*. From Whyte's point of view, another satisfying notice may have been the presence in the audience of Edith Pell, wife of the headmaster at St. Andrew's, who traveled up from Middletown, Delaware, and who later added her ticket stub to her collection of St. Andrew's memorabilia.[8]

With the play done, Whyte needed to turn his attention to the senior thesis, a rite of passage to this day for most Princeton students. An English major, as well as a produced playwright, Whyte titled his thesis "The Renaissance of the English Drama and George Bernard Shaw." What was most surprising about Whyte's thesis may have been that he was even allowed to write it. His subject was a living literary figure: in 1939 Shaw was eighty-two years old, and he would live until 1950, writing several more plays after Whyte left college. The Princeton English department in Whyte's day, and for years later, looked askance at seniors who chose as their thesis subject a contemporary writer whose literary reputation was not yet firmly established.[9]

Moreover, Whyte relied not just on his subject's literary works but also on Shaw's writings in nonacademic journals, noting the cause-and-effect power of Shaw's literary criticism. The thesis also took Whyte outside the musty confines of academic arguments over dead poets. And it may have emboldened him decades later when he worked without credentials alongside professionals in two other disciplines: architecture and urban planning.

The thesis was submitted on April 10, 1939. Whyte by then had achieved honors status, not in the elite "first group" of seniors but in the more populous "second group." On June 20, 1939, Whyte was one of 509 seniors graduating at Princeton's 192nd commencement. Other classmates included Temple Fielding, the travel writer, and Walter

Lord, the narrative historian whose account of the sinking of the *Titanic*, *A Night to Remember*, became a best seller a year before Whyte's *Organization Man*.

In Whyte's four years at Princeton, changes were unfolding abroad and in Princeton University's own backyard. The senior class poll, published in the 1939 *Nassau Herald*, asked the usual questions about social customs. Drinkers far outnumbered abstainers; smokers outnumbered nonsmokers; and conservatives slightly outnumbered liberals. The poll also included some questions not asked of prior classes.

> Would you fight for your country? At home: Yes, 431, No, 20. Abroad: Yes, 141, No, 247.
>
> Do you believe there will be a world war within A. One year, 27; B. Three years, 157; C. Five years, 123. Another 133 predicted there would be no world war.
>
> Who, in your opinion, was the outstanding personality for 1938? Hitler, 293; Chamberlain, 57; Roosevelt, 21.

In the spring of 1939, when that poll was published, the appeasement policy of British prime minister Neville Chamberlain was still in effect. The United States was still operating under the 1935–1937 Neutrality Acts. It was not until September 1, 1939, when Germany invaded Poland, that the world finally saw the wisdom of Winston Churchill's warning about appeasing Adolf Hitler: "The belief that security can be obtained by throwing a small state to the wolves is a fatal delusion."

Two contemporary events unrelated to the impending war also occurred during Whyte's college years. Both would prove relevant to issues in Whyte's professional life. In April of Whyte's senior year, the 1939 New York World's Fair opened in Flushing Meadows, New York. Its theme: "The World of Tomorrow." The most popular exhibit was General Motors' Futurama, a ride designed by architect Norman Bel Geddes that imagined a world twenty years in the future. It was a working miniature model of a superhighway to whisk motorists from their job in the dreary city to their single-family house with a manicured lawn and welcoming garage in the suburbs. The ride was filled to capacity almost every day. By the time Whyte wrote *The Organization*

Man, the families of those men were living in just those sorts of houses. They would soon commute to work on the first stretches of the new Interstate Highway System.

Meanwhile, in Princeton, a massive physical transformation was taking place on the other side of Nassau Street, within a few hundred yards of the university. A zinc baron named Edgar Palmer, a 1903 graduate of the university, had a dream about a downtown center scaled to mimic the footprint of the new Rockefeller Center in New York. Palmer retained architect Thomas Stapleton to design a mixed-use center of retail shops on the ground floor with apartments above, anchored by a reconstructed Nassau Inn and a large movie house. It would be built in the Colonial Revival style to complement Princeton University's collegiate Gothic.

Preparation for the new Palmer Square began in 1929, when houses in the heart of the town's Black neighborhood were either torn down or moved to the far end of the neighborhood. The original plan called for the new development to continue several more blocks to the north, which most likely would have resulted in the razing of the house at 110 Witherspoon Street, birthplace of the singer, lawyer, athlete, and civil rights activist Paul Robeson. But work was halted as even the wealthy struggled under the weight of the Great Depression. The scaled-back project was revived in 1936 and the first phase completed in 1939 as Whyte and his class were preparing to graduate. More houses in the old neighborhood, occupied by many people on the service staffs of the university and the eating clubs, were razed. The mostly low-income residents had to relocate.

The new square presented some of the best elements of a mixed-use center that Whyte would later advocate in his writing. It also had some of the worst, especially the vast parking lot behind the new movie theater that separated Palmer Square from the new boundary of the primarily Black neighborhood. Even worse, the theater and its parking lot had been constructed at the expense of those neighbors, many of them families with deep roots in the Princeton community.

Undergraduates at any school are often oblivious to their surroundings beyond the campus boundaries. During Whyte's time in Princeton the college was all White, the town still segregated. Robeson wrote that "Princeton was spiritually located in Dixie."[10] Black students could attend the "colored school" but had to travel to Trenton or Somerville for high school. In 1937 a community organization, which provided Black children with arts programs not available in their segregated elementary school, invited the diva Marian Anderson to perform at McCarter Theater. There was one problem: the hotels in town did not accommodate Blacks. Albert Einstein solved that problem by inviting Anderson to stay at his house.[11]

A few students did investigate life across the street from the campus. The October 1938 issue of the *Nassau Lit* carried a striking piece of nonfiction, appearing just four pages after the end of Whyte's short story "The Country Gentleman." The piece, titled "Bad Housing Bad Business," documented the overcrowded circumstances in the Black neighborhood, including three and four families sharing not only a house but also an outhouse; buildings with no running water (relying instead on wells); and sometimes buildings with no electricity. For every house torn down during the Palmer Square construction, there was almost no place left to build a replacement house.

According to the *Nassau Lit* article, the town attempted to address the substandard, overcrowded housing issue by establishing a nonprofit housing authority, which would create ten new units adjoining the overcrowded neighborhood. The undergraduate journalist had a matter-of-fact tone in describing what today would be a blatantly racist policy. The new subsidized housing would be "open to white families only. . . . Therefore, the only way in which the new project can help the colored people of the lowest income-group is by loosening up the occupancy of dwellings now in use."[12]

As Whyte and his classmates completed their senior year of college, urban renewal and affordable housing in the town of Princeton were not pressing issues. In 1939 jobs were still a major concern. On February 9 of that year the *Daily Princetonian* listed ten organizations scheduling visits with seniors to discuss possible employment: B. F. Goodrich Company, W. R. Grace & Company, Insurance Company of North America, McCreery & Company (retailing), Provident Mutual Life Insurance, Shaeffer Pen Company, Texas Company Petroleum

Figure 2.2 As a Princeton senior in 1939, Whyte was hired as a sales trainee by the maker of Vicks Vapo-Rub. (Seeley G. Mudd Manuscript Library, Princeton University.)

Products (stenography recommended), Aetna Group and Pension Department, International Business Machines Corporation, and the maker of a most mundane household product, Vick Chemical Company, which was seeking applicants to a sales training position. Applications, the announcement from Vick stated, "must be accompanied by a photograph" and were due on February 15, less than a week away.

One week later, on February 16, the *Daily Princetonian* published another set of notices for senior interviews. The list included another notice from the maker of Vicks VapoRub, which may not have had enough response to its ad the week before. The February

16 announcement took a different approach: "Vick Chemical Company has a few scholarships available in their training school for selling. Proficiency in writing is a requisite. Application should be made immediately."

In June 1939, war clouds were gathering. But Whyte and his classmates—many of whom did not believe there would be a war—had other concerns. "We worried about our careers," he wrote. "We talked about individualism a lot, but we didn't practice it much. My friends were joining big corporations, early examples of *The Organization Man* at work. I moved into the management-training program of the Vick Chemical Company."[13]

Chapter 3

Vicks and the Marines— Information to Intelligence

Four years at an Ivy League college would have been a life-changing experience for any young man in the waning days of the Great Depression. But William H. Whyte apparently did not perceive that time as a great transformation. In fact, in his subsequent body of public writing, Whyte reflected on his Princeton University career in less than a paragraph. Two subsequent endeavors proved more noteworthy. The first, selling Vicks VapoRub, was eye-opening but not life changing. The second, service in the US Marine Corps, was eye-opening, life changing, and a building block for his subsequent career, but not in the way one might expect.

The manufacturer of Vicks VapoRub recruited Whyte to sell a product that could be traced back to the 1890s, when a Greensboro, North Carolina, pharmacist named Lunsford Richardson cooked up a line of twenty-one home remedies. The best seller was Vicks Croup and Pneumonia Salve, possibly named after Richardson's brother-in-law, Dr. Joshua Vick. The salve was made with menthol, a recently discovered balm derived from peppermint plants. When the salve was rubbed onto the skin, body heat would vaporize the menthol and release medicated vapors, or so the company claimed. In 1911 the company discontinued all of its other products and renamed the salve Vicks VapoRub.

In 1918 and 1919, when the so-called Spanish flu hit the United States, sales of Vicks VapoRub soared from $900,000 to $2.9 million.

Three months after his college graduation, the future author of *The Organization Man* signed on with the Vick School of Applied Merchandising, the company's sales training program. Vick Chemical Company paid the room, board, and travel expenses of the young trainees plus a monthly salary of $75 (the equivalent of about $1,300 today). The company also held a bonus of $25 per month in escrow until the end of the course. That was an incentive for the young men to stick with the program. It was, Whyte wrote in *The Organization Man*, "the essence of the Protestant Ethic."[1]

In Vick's case, that ethic meant every man for himself in a competition in which not everyone might continue to the next level—full-time employment. Whyte was assigned to a sales territory in the hill country of eastern Kentucky. Whyte later wrote in his partial memoir, "On a typical day I would get up at 6 or 6:30 a.m. in some bleak boarding-house or run-down hotel and after a greasy breakfast set off to staple Vicks signs on barns and telephone poles. At about 8:00 I would make my first visit to one of the local general stores." Whyte described the owners of the country stores, his sales prospects, in contemporaneous letters he wrote to his father. "Most of them are friendly, but some of them are mean as the devil. They're really scared to death of salesmen, afraid we'll 'put something over' on them."[2]

Putting something over on them was exactly what the Vick sales corps was hoping to do. Whyte described attempting to sell a single store a year's worth of supply, or even more, so that the store proprietor wouldn't have any room for a competitor's product (principally Penetro, made by Plough Inc.). When making a sales call to a store, Whyte would make sure he was not spotted by the owner of a nearby pharmacy—no need for him to know that a nearby competitor would also be stocked with a ton of VapoRub.

At one point in the training Whyte admitted feeling sorry for some of his potential customers, storekeepers who were buying the product on "a precarious credit relationship" with the wholesalers. The parent company sent a supervisor out to the Kentucky backwoods to review Whyte's work. "Fella," the supervisor told Whyte, "you will never sell anybody anything until you learn one simple thing. The man on the other side of the counter is the enemy." Whyte's sales picked up immediately, from 48 percent of sales to calls made to 74 percent.

As Whyte recalled the experience many years later, the initial field of thirty-eight men, including Whyte, dwindled to about two dozen after six months. By the end of the year, only about six or seven would be hired full-time. Another Vick sales training "alumnus," Tom Shepard, who would later become publisher of *Look* magazine, had a similar memory. Vick "was about the toughest thing I'd ever done in my life," said Shepard, who enrolled in the program after graduating from Amherst College in 1940 and before enlisting in the US Navy.[3]

While Whyte portrayed his experience as brutally competitive, he conceded that "as a cram course in reality it was extraordinarily efficient." Although Whyte referred to the Vick School in both *The Organization Man* and *A Time of War*, he did not answer the question, Did he make the grade or not? Vick company records show that Whyte was one of those hired for full-time employment, but the records also reveal that the program was not quite as cutthroat as Whyte portrayed it. In fact, of the twenty-five "cadets" in Whyte's group who made it to the end, fourteen were offered jobs by Vick, seven were placed with other companies, and only four received no offer.[4] It was another instance of Whyte embellishing the facts in favor of a good story.

Meanwhile, another organization, with a tradition that dates back to 1775, was waiting. By 1941 both Whyte and his father were interventionists, believing that the United States could no longer ignore the war raging in Europe. In October 1941, Whyte enlisted in the Marine Corps, the second-smallest branch of the United States armed forces (only the Coast Guard is smaller), but one with an outsize reputation as the only branch of the services made up exclusively of volunteers. (The Marine Corps did not rely on draftees to fill its ranks until the height of World War II and the Vietnam War.) "Ego was involved, I suppose," Whyte wrote in his memoir. "If you're going to go, why not go with the one truly elite outfit in the U.S. armed services?"[5]

The Marine Corps changed Whyte's life in two ways. The first was what you would expect to happen when a young man such as Whyte and his comrades in arms are exposed to the rigors of military life and to the horrors of war. Whyte, a kid from a small town, a very small prep school, and an Ivy League school in a small-town setting, was introduced to a raft of characters, including eccentrics who rivaled his uncle Joe from childhood, the types of characters for whom he would have a special admiration throughout his life.

The second life changer was not what you would expect. The Marine Corps exposed Whyte to an analytical side of military operations. As a contributor to the *Marine Corps Gazette*, which functioned as a professional military journal, Whyte wrote perceptively about organizations, the role of individuals within them, and the gathering and interpretation of information and intelligence. In the Marine Corps, Whyte also encountered one memorable soldier who would become a model of the best kind of organization man—one who could draw on the strengths of the institution to which he belonged and also function at a heroic level as an individual when necessary.

Whyte's Marine Corps transformation began on October 28, 1941, the day he was sworn in at the Officer Candidates School in Quantico, Virginia. The first roll call announcement of "Whyte, William Hollingsworth Third" drew an exasperated comment from the drill instructor: "Jesus, what a moniker." The new enlistee quickly became Whyte, William H. Jr., and, after graduation from the officer training school, a second lieutenant. As he was when he peddled Vicks Vapo-Rub, Whyte was a letter writer in the US Marines. He wrote numerous letters to his father and stepmother, then living in the Chestnut Hill section of Philadelphia.

Dear Dad and Margaret: This is a very belated thanks for the swell weekend in Washington. . . . Would have written sooner but we've been having night problems lately and I haven't hardly even seen a newspaper.

The night problems are something—tramping and scrambling around brush and wood and mud soaked to the skin. Get in about 10:30 p.m., clean equipment, bed at 11:00 p.m. Up at 5:40 a.m. As a result when we all had our physical exams a lot of us had heart flutters never noticed before. I'm scared stiff my former 'Y' exam

Top: (l to r) Holly with Ches Baum and Walden Pell at the Headmaster's
House. Above: The Intelligence Section, Third Battalion, First Marines after
four months on Guadalcanal. Holly is front row, center, with mustache.

Figure 3.1 Whyte, at left in top photo, and fellow alumnus Ches Baum reminisce with former St. Andrew's Headmaster Walden Pell. Two months before Pearl Harbor, Whyte enlisted in the US Marines. He is in front row, center, in photo at Guadalcanal. (St. Andrew's School.)

may not pass. If it does I get my commission on the 31st. Find out tomorrow or Thursday about the exam. . . .

P.S. I MADE IT! Just got the news. Physical exam okay.[6]

Whyte and his fellow officers who made the grade would soon be assigned platoons. What kind of men would they be commanding? Whyte recognized them as colorful characters who could match his uncle Joe "eccentricity for eccentricity, any day." With the war clouds thickening, the Marine Corps was rapidly expanding. The new second lieutenants would find their platoons populated with new enlistees who had just completed boot camp as well as much older men, including a few who had seen combat duty in World War I. They were the "Old Breed" marines, unlikely to be impressed by anyone's college degree or, for that matter, successful completion of the Officer Candidates School.

To take over command of these men was the ultimate organizational challenge for Whyte and his fellow officers in training. On December 7, 1941, less than two months into their three-month officer training school, Whyte and his fellow "ninety-day wonders," as the new second lieutenants were known, knew who their ultimate enemy would be. But first they headed to the training camp of the First Marine Division at New River, North Carolina (now known as Camp Lejeune), and faced another formidable force, the Old Breed marines who would be assigned to the platoons that the ninety-day wonders were expected to command. "We were all scared to death," Whyte wrote.[7]

Whyte's reckoning with the Old Breed brought with it a conflict between two schools of thought. One school, endorsed by all but one of Whyte's fellow second lieutenants, was to try to be one of the guys, essentially a commander who not only commanded but also tried to get along with the Old Breed. The other school of thought was advanced by just one of the young officers in training. Harold Kirby Taylor had stood out from the beginning of the officer training school. He had an outstanding academic record. But, as Whyte would write later, "the period of his life of which he was proudest was his days as a Boy Scout. This naturally provoked derision from us, and I can't begin to tell you all the nicknames we coined on the strength of his idealization of the Boy Scouts of America. Worse than this, he lectured us incessantly on our somewhat lackadaisical attitude towards the military profession. While we played bridge he studied, and often as we were going to sleep we could hear the click of his rifle as he practiced the manual of arms in the shower room."[8]

Taylor earned the nickname "Ramrod." Whyte compared Taylor's approach with that of the other new second lieutenants.

That first day we took over our new platoons, we suffered. The old gunnery sergeants didn't conceal their amusement; the men smiled knowingly as we marched them into ditches. We forgot all the commands we'd been taught, and generally made fools of ourselves. After those terrible first days we grew more confident, more able, but we still hesitated to exert our authority. We wanted to be liked, and so we pretended not to notice when the men didn't salute us; we dismissed them as early as we could in the afternoon. We couldn't have been more ingratiating.

But not Taylor. His men marched and trained from dawn to dusk and frequently half the night; anyone who failed to salute him got extra duty.... We were sure that this spit and polish, this strict discipline, were obsolete. Our policy was to talk things over with the men and not worry if their close order drill was a little sloppy. We were going to have one great, big, happy family! ... With smug self-satisfaction, we agreed that Taylor's men would turn against him at the first opportunity, that their hatred of him would take active form if we ever got to battle.[9]

That prediction would be put to a test within months as Whyte, Taylor, and the other marines were shipped off toward the Pacific theater. By July 1942, Whyte's letters were arriving from overseas, first from New Zealand, where the marines were assembling for their attack on Guadalcanal.

The marines were headed toward what would be a decisive encounter. The Japanese, after their stunning attack on Pearl Harbor on December 7, 1941, had captured Wake Island, Guam, Singapore, the Philippines, and the Dutch East Indies. They captured the island of Tulagi, just north of Guadalcanal and boasting a natural harbor, on May 3, 1942. The US Navy managed to slow the advance with a victory in the Battle of Midway on June 4 and 5, 1942. But on July 1, the Japanese landed combat troops and construction crews on Guadalcanal, an island about ninety miles long and thirty miles wide, roughly the size of Long Island. The goal was to build an air base there, from which the Japanese could launch attacks on New Guinea and push onward to New Zealand and Australia.

In New Zealand Whyte and his fellow marines anticipated that they would undergo six months of intensive training before seeing any combat action. Whyte wrote home to report that "morale and spirit are very high. We've only got picked men here—all the gold bricks and bums (among officers and men alike) were left behind in the U.S."[10] The morale was tested quickly when training was abruptly curtailed. The order was received to prepare for an amphibious attack on Guadalcanal and to retake Tulagi. A dress rehearsal landing on Fiji did not go well. Worse yet, aerial maps of Guadalcanal were lost in a bureaucratic snafu and never delivered to the troops.[11] Nineteen thousand marines, including Whyte, nevertheless landed on Guadalcanal on August 7, 1942.

Guadalcanal soon became a celebrated World War II battle arena, in large part because several widely read war correspondents covered the early weeks of the campaign there. Richard Tregaskis, writing for the International News Service (which later became United Press International), quickly produced a combat memoir, *Guadalcanal Diary*. Published on January 1, 1943, by Random House, it was turned into a movie starring William Bendix and released on November 5, 1943. But, as Whyte would point out in a letter home, many of the newspaper correspondents stayed only a few days and would leave immediately at the first instance of heavy naval shelling. Even Tregaskis's reporting was conducted before the "really hot" fighting began.

Some of the hottest fighting began on October 23, 1942, when Japanese tanks attacked at the Mantanikau River. Whyte's description in his memoir, *A Time of War*, draws on his letters home as well as on captured Japanese diaries. Whyte's analysis criticizes both Japanese and American operations and also acknowledges his own foibles. He describes an American patrol of about thirty men who "stumbled out into the field at noon" and "became so engrossed in eating their rations and watching the dogfights overhead, they failed to notice more than nine hundred rifles aimed their way." But, as Whyte learned much later from a diary captured from the Japanese, the major commanding the Japanese forces declined to fire upon the marines because he did not want to give away his position. Whyte said he blanched when he read the diary—"I was the leader of that happy-go-lucky patrol."[12]

In his letters home, Whyte began to display the even-keeled tone of a detached journalist. One of the longest letters Whyte wrote reflected the period of greatest action, and greatest danger, for Whyte and his comrades.

November 1942.

As events have developed it now has become plain the Japs are throwing everything into their drive to get the islands back. As you've read in the papers, they haven't given us a moment's rest—almost daily bombings (plus night bombers), naval bombardment and land fighting. They have lost frightfully but they keep coming. However, they can't keep it up forever. . . .

When the battles die down there is ceaseless patrol activity in the jungle—a sort of no man's land. . . . We ran into a bunch of Japs some time ago. I had a patrol of six and myself. Our mission was to locate the Jap positions as our offensive began at dawn the next morning. We spotted one area in front of a 75 mm gun a friend of mine had taken the breech block out of the day before (while the Japs slept). His patrol was pumping tommy guns at them, so we swung north and went through the jungle to the beach and went along the ridges to his north, finding two Jap 35 mm guns emplaced and camouflaged at a bend in the road. As the gun crew was obligingly sleeping or eating somewhere we tinkered with the guns with the aid of a screwdriver until it would take a mechanical genius to put it back together again (still have a part of the breech block as a souvenir). We then skirted the coral formations (caves, etc.) along the shore until I spotted a Marine standing up behind a sort of coral "igloo" with a gun port in it about 20 yards away. Then I heard the Jap bird call signal and the Marine turned around and saw me. For a Marine he looked very very Japanese. I shot at him with my .45 missing him quite completely. I ducked for cover (as my Niponese was likewise doing) and the rest of the patrol flopped down into firing positions behind logs, trees, etc. We had evidentially surprised the gun crews of the 37 mm for they started rushing around for cover by the little coral "igloos." Fortunately all the men on our left had Thompsons and three Japs who tore across for cover were literally torn to shreds. The rest of the Japs started shooting (at what I don't know as their shots came nowhere near us) and jabbering quite excitedly. A couple stuck their heads up to see what was going on. The man on my right got one, and I got the other.

That simple statement was the only reference Whyte ever made in his collected letters to his killing an enemy soldier. The matter-of-fact tone continued through another paragraph, a brief description of the death of Ramrod Taylor, about whom Whyte would write much more later in the war: "Incidentally the friend of mine who had the other patrol operating to our south was killed that day. After his men withdrew from their contact with the Japs he went back to 'find out something.' If you read about an officer who dismantled two Jap 75 mm guns while the crews were sleeping that's him. I certainly miss him."

Whyte clearly appreciated the courage of his comrades. One letter home included a photograph of himself and his section. "The most insignificant ones were the ones who did best in the hand to hand fighting," Whyte wrote. "The one second from the right at top with the simple grin killed four in two minutes!" Stories like that were already the stuff of movies such as *Guadalcanal Diary* and part of a long legacy of Marine Corps valor. At Guadalcanal, according to documents later captured by the Americans and eventually read by Whyte, the Japanese soldiers were told the Americans they were fighting had been "chosen from the scum of the prisons and insane asylums of America for love of killing. They were so dreaded in the U.S.A. that they were invariably kept under guard there lest they lash out in uncontrollable massacre." They were "fierce brutal murderers known as Marines."[13]

To maintain some semblance of normalcy on Guadalcanal, Whyte slept on muslin sheets he had sneaked ashore on landing day and enjoyed "cocktail hour." His concoction was made with a base of canned grapefruit juice, "several squeezes of toothpaste [Pepsodent]," and medicinal alcohol. The sheets, he admitted, "were the subject of some derision," but the cocktail, according to the budding epicure, was "quite tolerable."

Whyte would call his time at Guadalcanal "the most exciting four months of my life." But he still had two more years to serve, a time that

Figure 3.2 First Lieutenant Whyte, standing on right, posed with his fellow marines during a lull in the fighting at Guadalcanal. (Official photo United States Marine Corps / Seeley G. Mudd Manuscript Library, Princeton University.)

would prove less exciting but equally transformative. On December 17, 1942, he shipped out to Tasmania, where he ended up in a hospital for treatment of malaria, the first of several bouts he would endure. Whyte was then reassigned as a regimental intelligence officer in Australia, training snipers and teaching map reading. But he suffered another malaria bout and was sent back to West Chester, Pennsylvania, for more recuperation.

There wasn't much action at home. In July 1943 Whyte spoke at a launching ceremony for a destroyer escort built at the Dravo Corporation's shipyard in Wilmington, Delaware.[14] He also wrote to Brigadier General Clifton B. Cates, commander of the Marine Corps Schools at Quantico, who had been Whyte's regimental commander on Guadalcanal, requesting a chance to teach combat intelligence at the staff command school. It was a natural extension of his combat duties as an intelligence officer. On September 23, 1943, Whyte was back at Quantico. The assignment began with three months of coursework for Whyte to prepare him to train other marines. Classes began at 8:00 a.m. and ended at 4:30 p.m., every day but Sunday. "The course sounds fascinating and is quite tough," he wrote to his father and stepmother.

At Quantico brains counted as much as brawn. In teaching his own course, Whyte, now promoted to captain, employed various exercises to sharpen his students' observational skills. Whyte described a "hearing test" administered to the trainees. They were told that a recording had been made at a Japanese prisoner of war camp in Hawaii, where several hundred prisoners were ordered to stage a mock banzai attack, yelling out American slang phrases that they had been taught to use to intimidate the marines, such as "Marine, you die," and "Stupid fool." The recording was played and the students were asked to write down every English phrase they could discern. Their notes included the foregoing examples as well as "Yankee pig" and "Marine, you yellow." Then the students were told the truth: the recording was not from a prisoner of war camp but came from the soundtrack of a prewar Japanese film that did not contain one word of English. "The average man is a very poor reporter," Whyte concluded.[15]

Whyte's analyses soon appeared as in-depth articles for the *Marine Corps Gazette*, a publication founded in 1916 that was and still is dedicated to advancing the "knowledge, interest, and esprit in the Marine Corps" and to "the dissemination of military art and science."

At the time of the *Gazette*'s first issue, military strategists from all service branches were still processing the lessons of the Allied forces' failed amphibious landing in 1915 on the Gallipoli Peninsula in the Dardanelles.[16] British and French troops made their land invasion against Turkish troops on April 25. By the middle of October, they had made little headway, and by December they were evacuating—after incurring nearly two hundred thousand deaths. Among many military strategists, particularly the British (with the exception of Winston Churchill), the defeat created the "Gallipoli syndrome"—the belief that any amphibious military invasion was fraught with danger and probably inadvisable. It soon became clear that the Marine Corps had a different view. In the first issue of the *Marine Corps Gazette*, in March

1916, a future marine commandant, then Colonel John A. Lejeune, addressed strategies of landing troops on beaches and how to defend against such landings. By 1921, the Marine Corps had created a school at its headquarters in Quantico "devoted to the science of amphibious warfare." The causes of the failure at Gallipoli were part of the classroom discussion.

Also in 1921 Earl H. "Pete" Ellis, then a Marine Corps lieutenant colonel, wrote a thirty-thousand-word paper that predicted the Japanese would eventually attack the United States in the Pacific Islands and that fighting them on heavily fortified islands would require amphibious landings. Ellis wrote that such landings required "careful training and preparation, to say the least; and this along Marine lines. It is not enough that the troops be skilled infantry men or artillery men of high morale; they must be skilled water men and jungle men who know it can be done—Marines with Marine training."[17] In 1934 the Marines revised the Ellis paper as a more explicit guide to amphibious landings. It was adopted virtually word for word by the navy in 1937 and named Fleet Training Publication No. 167. "It flew in the face of conventional wisdom," Whyte wrote in his memoir.[18] It was the guide for amphibious landings in the Pacific, and it was used to prepare for Normandy as well. As some Marine Corps enthusiasts say, when reminded that the marines did not fight at Normandy, yes, the army and the navy provided the muscle, but the marines provided the brains.

When Whyte arrived at Quantico in late 1943 to begin his training as an instructor, the *Gazette* had just transitioned from its original quarterly publication to a bimonthly schedule. In 1944 the *Gazette* became a monthly. Any concerns about having enough content to fill this expanded editorial calendar may have been allayed somewhat by Whyte, who provided articles for both the March and April issues in 1944 and wrote six more that would be printed between July 1945 and May 1946. The *Gazette* articles created another set of contemporaneous notes—unvarnished by the passage of time—about the war and Whyte's experiences in it.

Whyte's first piece in the *Gazette* reexamined the story of Ramrod Taylor. In his letter home dated November 1942, Whyte had made only a cursory reference to Taylor's death. In Quantico a year and a half later Whyte painted a more detailed picture, one that foreshadowed his postmilitary examination of the tensions between organizations and individuals within them. In late October 1942, Taylor requested permission to lead a patrol behind the enemy lines to disarm two Japanese 75-millimeter artillery emplacements that had been harassing American troops. The mission was risky: the enemy guns were on high ridges and protected by infantry and forward observers. Given that the guns were lobbing fourteen-pound shells into the American positions from several miles away and had withstood all attempts to take them out from the air, Taylor was given the go-ahead.

On that raid Taylor and six volunteers came upon one gun while the Japanese soldiers manning it were sleeping. The marines disabled the breech block, the part of the gun that holds the shell in place for firing, and rendered the weapon useless. Then Taylor moved alone to the next suspected location. This gun was also unattended. But as Taylor approached the emplacement, he saw four Japanese soldiers observing him from a distance. He calmly waved to them, and they waved back. Then Taylor disabled the weapon, gave another wave, and nonchalantly walked away.

At the time, according to Whyte, some men in the unit thought Taylor's success was an example of an individual soldier ignoring procedures and singlehandedly—and heroically—achieving his objective. Whyte took a different view of the raid.[19] Taylor based his foray on a set of essential elements of information (EEI), creating what Whyte called "a sound estimate" rather than "slipshod thinking." After receiving permission to execute the raid, Taylor requested a full twenty-four hours in which to plan it. He and Whyte determined five likely places where the Japanese guns could be located. After analyzing the next round of shelling, two of those locations were eliminated. Taylor and Whyte plotted the locations of known enemy soldiers to determine the best possible route to the first suspected location. They also mapped out a primary route for withdrawal along with a secondary route. Taylor was "well known in the regiment as an extreme stickler for 'correct' procedure," Whyte wrote. "Not because he could recite the book, but because he understood its basic principles so well, could Taylor so unhesitatingly follow sound staff procedure in an operation involving but seven men." The organization played its role. So did an individual operating intelligently within it.

Whyte's article for the *Gazette* described only the successful mission. Two days later an unsuccessful and tragic one took place. On October 31 both Taylor and Whyte were ordered to take small patrols out to destroy additional Japanese gun positions. Whyte, wary of taking the same route twice, directed his men on another path and surprised a dozen Japanese soldiers. After exchanging fire, with both sides missing their targets, Whyte's platoon retreated. Taylor's platoon took the same route he had followed two days before. This time the Japanese were waiting and attacked first. Taylor held them off, buying time for his men to retreat, but lost his life doing so. In his memoir Whyte called the order to send Taylor out on the same patrol on the same route two days later "an incredibly stupid mistake."[20]

Whyte's second article for the *Gazette*, "Observation vs. the Jap," published in April 1944, analyzed techniques for training observation personnel in battle conditions. "A critical element was to bring all incoming reports together in a centralized location so that an up to date, digested, and cross-checked picture of the situation is available to the unit. It is amazing after an action to find out how much information of the enemy had been available but never acted [upon], because many of the small items were independently acted upon or 'lost in the shuffle' and hence never found their way to the situation map, where together they would have been quite significant." The takeaway, as marine captain Whyte described it, was simple: "As in every intelligence function it is not the individual report which counts, but the mass. See that you control that mass."[21]

After Whyte's death some historians questioned how Whyte would have reconciled that advice with his criticism of groupthink (chapter 5). Whyte would emphasize the second sentence in the foregoing quotation. Controlling the mass, he wrote in the *Gazette*, required that the people gathering the information "restrict themselves to reporting what they see and hear" and refrain from offering interpretations. Otherwise, "the wish being father to the thought, they unconsciously start describing more than they actually saw."

Moreover, the material collected by the group was information, not intelligence. "There is a world of difference between the two." Whyte addressed "the heart of modern intelligence theory—the process by which raw information is turned into intelligence"—in a two-part series, more than six thousand words in total.[22] Considering the history and future possibilities of his subject, Whyte praised George Washington for his systematic intelligence gathering. "His instructions to his agents concerning the data he desired on British activities in New York reads almost like a 'school solution' intelligence plan." The Civil War offered a "fertile ground for espionage," with many prisoners taken and communication facilitated by the telegraph. But there was "no real intelligence for a simple reason. In no unit was there one authority responsible for collecting all the scraps of information from various sources—patrols, civilians, prisoners—and lumping them together in an information 'pool' where in the mass they might make some sense." Whyte even speculated about intelligence gathering far into the future—the 1960s. He imagined a remote-controlled television observation post with marines in space suits defending a radar station on the moon. All those changes notwithstanding, Whyte contended, "the basic principles are as valid now and will be as valid in the future as they were centuries ago."

The dust jacket of *The Organization Man* said that Whyte "was educated at Princeton and in the United States Marine Corps at Guadalcanal."[23] What were the lessons of Guadalcanal? The first was to judge people by their capabilities rather than by their intentions. The Japanese, in fact, had based their attack on Pearl Harbor on a misguided sense of what Americans would choose to do rather than on what they were capable of doing. "Because we realize that in the fog of war we rarely know enough about the enemy to justify making sweeping generalities and premises that will hold true in all cases, we prefer the method of inductive reasoning, the method by which we let the facts point to the conclusions rather than taking a conclusion and finding facts to support it," Whyte wrote.[24]

Thirty years later, Whyte recalled that lesson when he began to observe the use of public space in Manhattan. He realized then that the assumptions made by city planners at their desks did not always match the realities of the streets below. The fact that a space was labeled public open space did not mean that the public could or would use it.

The second lesson was about terrain. Maps are important not just to show the relationship of one object to another in two dimensions. There is also a third dimension—elevation—to consider. On Guadalcanal both Japanese and American forces literally walked into life-threatening situations because they had no knowledge of the vertical terrain they would encounter between points A and B on a two-dimensional map. This was another lesson that Whyte applied thirty years later in Manhattan. Public plazas that were up or down a flight of stairs were used less frequently than those at street level.

The third lesson was that information had to be gathered systematically. In the *Marine Corps Gazette*, Whyte described the virtues of a set routine for gathering information and then the importance of sorting that information into subject areas. Ignore the growls about paperwork, Whyte advised in the *Gazette*, and make the soldiers on the observation posts fill in every line of their journals. "This drives home to the men the necessity for accurate designation of the object seen, time, direction, etc."[25]

Even during his wartime experience with the US Marines, Whyte envisioned an information age approach to data management. As he wrote in the *Gazette*, "Corps and division headquarters may be equipped with automatic machines for recording and classifying incoming data, much like the machines that sort and file fingerprints, but the principle will remain the same. Get the data recorded, then classify it."[26]

By the time these articles were published in the *Gazette*, Whyte was a civilian. "As far as I could tell," he wrote in his memoir, "I had no marketable skills."[27] But, at the age of twenty-eight, he already had an appreciation for the tension that could exist between a powerful organization and a strong individual operating within it—a foreshadowing of the best seller he would write a decade later. Whyte articulated his views in a commencement address he delivered on June 1, 1946, at his alma mater, St. Andrew's School. Just eleven years out of high school himself but obviously seasoned by his time in the Marine Corps, Whyte warned against both "fear of censure" from the group and, "at the other extreme," people "who make a fetish of unortho-doxy." But within this range, Whyte contended, there was room for an intelligent, well-prepared individual willing to "stick his neck out" in order to effect change. To make his case, Whyte related the heroic but ultimately tragic story of Ramrod Taylor, from the group's initial derision of his Boy Scout–like training regimen to the group's ultimate admiration and willingness to be led into battle by him: "Taylor had the complete courage of his convictions; he had known that group disapproval was more apparent than real; that where men collectively scoffed, they might as individuals be filled with unexpressed respect."[28]

The civilian Whyte also had "a taste for writing," as well as clippings of the eight articles he had written for the *Marine Corps Gazette*. Those pieces represented an impressive body of work for a young journalist. More important, they were not the ordinary inverted-triangle formu-laic news stories such as those that a daily newspaper reporter might use in a job hunt. Whyte's pieces were substantial and insightful. He was hired at *Fortune* at a salary of $75 per week—his monthly pay when he started out as a Vicks VapoRub salesman. If the Marine Corps had been no ordinary branch of the military, then the same could be said about *Fortune*'s place in the world of journalism. It was another well-established organization with its own set of eccentric individuals and another one in which Whyte would soon make his own mark.

Chapter 4

Fortune Magazine—the Foundation for a Career

A fter William H. Whyte was discharged from his post at the Marine Corps training school at Quantico, Virginia, in October 1945, he returned to his mother's home on North Church Street in West Chester, Pennsylvania. By June 1 of the next year, he was looking ahead. When he gave his commencement address at St. Andrew's School about maintaining personal convictions in the face of a group's disapproval, Whyte prefaced his remarks with a sober (but not totally accurate) self-assessment.

> Traditionally commencement speakers are men who have achieved success in some field, rich in experience, of mature judgement, eminently fitted to counsel young men about to leave school. You can see, then, that it poses somewhat of a problem when a person in my circumstances is called upon to make such an address. There are many like us, who, though they have graduated some time ago, are still struggling, still groping, and not too sure of just what the future holds.[1]

The speech's introduction may have built some rapport with Whyte's youthful audience, but there was also considerable literary license in his self-assessment. Whyte already had a connection at Time Inc. A Marine Corps buddy, George Hunt, a 1939 Amherst College alumnus, had run a scout and sniper school with Whyte in Australia. Hunt had started working at Time Inc. as an office boy in 1940. After the war Hunt returned to join Time Inc.'s *Fortune* magazine (he would later become managing editor of *Life* magazine). Whyte, armed with that connection and his clippings from the *Marine Corps Gazette*, was able to end his "struggle" with the future three days after his address to the St. Andrew's senior class. On Tuesday, June 4, 1946, he began his career at *Fortune* magazine in New York.[2]

Soon Whyte had another self-deprecating story to tell. As he claimed later in various forums, upon his arrival at *Fortune* Whyte considered himself "the worst writer." He theorized he had been kept on board only as "a kind of exhibit" to show others how not to write. Whyte pleaded guilty to a "weakness for clichés" and a delight for "ornamentation" and "elaborate metaphors and analogies." He repeated this claim in a statement he made to his college class on the occasion of its fiftieth reunion: "Most of my life has been UP—Princeton, the Marines, *Fortune*. I've had the good luck to be affiliated with some very good organizations. On the DOWN side was the apprentice part of writing. I was tremendously unhappy at my plodding ways and the low opinion my colleagues had of my efforts."[3]

Could it be? Could Whyte, just twenty-eight years old, have already forgotten the tutelage of his St. Andrew's English teacher, Bull Cameron? Not likely. More likely, Whyte was indulging in his penchant for telling—and retelling—a good story and not letting the facts get in the way. *Fortune* editors who looked at Whyte's body of work from the *Marine Corps Gazette* would have recognized that the young writer represented exactly the kind of talent that Time Inc. sought. Whyte's lack of business experience might have been an advantage. As Time Inc. founder Henry R. Luce had claimed, it was easier to turn a poet into a business journalist than to turn a bookkeeper into a writer.[4]

But there certainly was an apprenticeship.[5] In May 1947 Whyte continued to list North Church Street in West Chester as his permanent address. And his name did not appear in the staff box of *Fortune*—as an associate editor—until October 1948. Such a delay between being hired and appearing in the staff box was not uncommon at Time Inc. publications. But Whyte quickly moved into *Fortune*'s fast lane. By 1951 he was promoted to assistant managing editor, one rung below the top. Whyte became both a participant in and a witness to the growth of Time Inc., one of the country's largest media companies.

Whyte's time at the magazine was the foundation for his life's work. In a six-year period at *Fortune*, Whyte's editorial projects led to the publication of three books (discussed separately in the next three chapters). Whyte and other enterprising *Fortune* writers seized opportunities to engage in long-term reporting and writing projects, sometimes challenging the magazine's own editorial positions, often set by Luce himself. In his early years at the magazine, Whyte would occasionally hobnob after work with fellow "alumni" of the Vick School of Applied Merchandising. By the end of his career at *Fortune* he was socializing at the Century Association, a private men's club in Manhattan (which excluded women until 1988). Whyte the writer even turned himself into a bit of bookkeeper as he bumped heads on one occasion with the Time Inc. business department. At *Fortune* Whyte became an organization man, honing his skill at working with and within a large and powerful institution without being seduced by it. He would benefit greatly from that skill for the rest of his life.

Luce announced the imminent birth of *Fortune* in its parent magazine, *Time*, three days before Black Thursday, October 24, 1929, when the stock market began the plunge that preceded the Great Depression. But that crash did not deter Luce from forging ahead with the first edition of *Fortune* in February 1930. With nearly two hundred pages in its first issue, printed on wild wove antique paper (a special stock that eliminated glare), the magazine measured a grand 11.25 by 14 inches, much larger than most periodicals. The cover price was one dollar (compared with *Time*'s fifteen cents). It was a beacon of optimism in an otherwise bleak environment for business. The *New York Times* called *Fortune* "sumptuous to the point of rivaling the pearly gates."[6] In the first issue the editors already were bragging about the second issue, March 1930, which would include a piece with an intriguing title, "Hemingway on Bullfights."

Fortune's circulation in its first year reached thirty thousand. Ad space for the first year—at $500 per page—was sold before the first issue was published. Intended by Luce to be America's "most beautiful magazine," *Fortune* featured art by the likes of Ben Shahn and Saul Steinberg and photographs by Margaret Bourke-White and Walker Evans. *Fortune*'s circulation grew fivefold by 1937. The cover of its tenth anniversary issue in 1940 was printed in gold—the ink had metallic gold embedded in it.[7]

Much of the magazine's success has been attributed to the writers brought on board without the usual journalistic credentials. The staff included Archibald MacLeish, who won the Pulitzer Prize in 1932 for a poem written while he was at *Fortune*. James Agee spent eight weeks reporting and then more weeks handwriting his impressions of sharecroppers in the rural South. When he was about fifty thousand words into the process and indicated he had no end in sight, Agee was granted a leave of absence. In 1941 the work, with photos by *Fortune*'s Walker Evans, was published as the literary classic *Let Us Now Praise Famous Men*.[8]

Fortune in the 1940s and 1950s revolutionized business journalism. "The early *Fortune*, more than any other journal anywhere in the industrial world, saw the large modern corporation as a primary economic and social force," wrote the economist John Kenneth Galbraith, a staff writer from 1943 to 1948.[9] Business journalist Joe Nocera has described the "enormous intellectual ferment" among *Fortune* writers, who sensed "they were creating a new kind of business journalism. They began viewing business the way a sociologist might, reporting not just on which company was doing what, but on what companies had in common, on how corporate strategy was devised, and on what life was like inside a big company."[10]

As a new hire, Whyte started out doing short pieces of a thousand words or so for "an ill-begotten department called Shorts and Faces." The editors also turned to Whyte to produce what he called "cats and dogs, rejects, stories 'for the bank' (i.e., never to run)."[11] One Shorts and Faces item, appearing in the January 1948 issue, profiled Herman Frederick Willkie, elder brother of the 1940 presidential candidate Wendell Willkie. The headline of the piece was "Outside the Groove." The article marveled at the unorthodox Willkie, vice president in charge of production for Joseph E. Seagram & Sons, at the time the largest distiller in the United States. "What is to be made of a businessman who looks upon present-day free enterprise as 'the prototype for bureaucracy' and charges that industry systematically 'keeps new and useful things off the market because it loves monopoly'? How should his corporate superiors view a man who encourages his key executives to leave the company whenever they wish . . . ?" The *Fortune* archives do not reveal the writer of this unbylined article, but the themes raised are similar to those that would soon be explored by Whyte in *The Organization Man.*

Within his own family, Whyte quickly became a celebrity—the small-town boy making it in the media capital of the world. During the Christmas holidays, recalled Whyte's stepbrother, Jim Perry, Whyte would up show up at the Chestnut Hill home of his father and stepmother with "not one but two bottles of Chateau d'Yquem. Greater love hath no stepbrother."[12] Whyte, now a well-paid journalist, was a decade removed from the days of his homemade Marine Corps libations. (Inspired by Holly, Perry would go into journalism himself with the *National Observer* and *Wall Street Journal.*)

Like many of those before him, Whyte also found time to flex his literary muscle outside the pages of *Fortune.* He dabbled in the dream of his college days—to be a playwright or dramatist of some sort. The Rockefeller archives in Tarrytown, New York, contain a half dozen handwritten and partial scripts for plays and radio shows. One was a proposed episode for *The Aldrich Family*, a radio (and later television) sitcom that ran from 1939 to 1953. Another was a synopsis of a proposed three-act play called *The Silver Box.* In this work in progress, Whyte set the play at a boys' school, where a conflict unfolds between the hero and the group of which he is a part. People prefer "a certain tyranny" to "an uncertain freedom," Whyte noted in a list of possible themes for the play.[13] More seeds were being planted for *The Organization Man.*

No evidence suggests that the Whyte scripts were ever produced. But he had better luck with a tongue-in-cheek nonfiction piece regarding the New York literary scene, pitched by Whyte in 1951 to the managing editor of *Harper's* magazine, Russell Lynes. Whyte got some editing advice from Eric Hodgins, a *Fortune* managing editor and publisher whose novel *Mr. Blandings Builds His Dream House* was turned into a 1948 movie.[14] Whyte's piece, published in *Harper's* in October 1953 and titled "You, Too, Can Write the Casual Style," was another salvo in an ongoing war of words between Time Inc. and the *New Yorker* magazine. *Fortune* had drawn first blood with an August 1934 article detailing the *New Yorker's* commercial success rather than its literary accomplishments. The *New Yorker* fired back in 1936. In a long profile of Luce and his business empire, Wolcott Gibbs, the *New Yorker's* theater critic, lampooned *Time's* peculiar literary style. Gibbs mimicked "Timespeak" to make his point: "Backward ran sentences until reeled the mind. . . . Where it all will end, knows God!"[15]

Whyte jumped gamely into this literary mosh pit. "A revolution is taking place in American prose," he began. "No longer the short huffs and puffs, the unqualified word, the declarative sentence. We have come to the age of The Casual Style." Whyte attributed this new form to writers for the *New Yorker*, who employed various editorial sleights of hand, including the omitted word ("Man we know told us . . ."), the Hedge ("British upper classes have always seemed reasonably droll to me, at least in moderation"), and what Whyte termed "the Cancellation." To illustrate an elegant execution of the cancellation clause, Whyte cited a theater review in the April 30, 1949, *New Yorker*. After a long and complicated recapitulation of the play's plot, Whyte noted, the reviewer needed to get back to his main point. So he used this cancellation clause: "It was all exactly as foolish as it sounds and I wouldn't give it another thought."[16] The writer of that review: Wolcott Gibbs, who had mocked *Time* in 1936. Whyte, an organization man, was also a team player.

All great fun (to employ the casual style).

But Whyte and his *Fortune* colleagues were also tackling more serious subjects. As they did, they exhibited an openly irreverent tone compared with the pro-business approach of the magazine's editorial positions. Luce announced "the American Century" in 1941. In 1948 Luce redefined *Fortune's* mission as "not just the reporting of private enterprise but its active defense and articulation." In May 1949, a *Fortune* article advised the business community that "only good Public Relations—i.e. good performance that's understood and appreciated"—would guarantee the long-term success of a business.[17]

The magazine's stated values seemed to mesh easily with the public relations imperative of the National Association of Manufacturers (NAM), which promoted the virtues of the American enterprise system through print advertising and outdoor billboards in the 1930s and 1940s. NAM's "Industry on Parade" was a staple of 1950s television. In the late 1940s NAM created a $100 million campaign (equivalent to about $1 billion today) to promote American business, discourage unionization, and counter what it considered misinformation promulgated by the left-leaning policies of Harry Truman and others. It was called the Free Enterprise campaign.

The creators of that campaign must have been pleased to hear that *Fortune*, Luce's influential business magazine, was beginning a series of articles on business communication. *Fortune* tackled the project in its robust, spare-no-cost way. Whyte spent more than four months preparing the series. He consulted more than sixty books along the way. He was assisted by sixteen *Fortune* stringers, who conducted interviews with one hundred business leaders. The magazine sent another hundred questionnaires to public relations men (like most professions in the 1950s, public relations was a man's world). The series began in September 1950. The sponsors of the Free Enterprise campaign must have felt their jaws drop when they read the core paragraphs of Whyte's first article, "Is Anybody Listening?"

> All in all, the Free Enterprise campaign is shaping up as one of the most intensive "sales" jobs in the history of industry—in fact, it is fast becoming very much of an industry in itself. At the current rate, it is accounting for at least $100,000,000 of industry's annual advertising, public relations and employee-relations expenditures. More to the point, it is absorbing more and more of the energies expended by the top men in U.S. management.
>
> And it is not worth a damn.[18]

The expensive ad campaign, Whyte charged, antagonized labor unions and insulted the intelligence of average Americans. Without explicitly stating it, the campaign was pro-business and pro-Republican. Yet the sponsors insisted they could be "politically persuasive and nonpartisan in the same breath." The problem was simple. The Free Enterprise campaign lacked authenticity. Whyte noted that absence, just as he would later in assessing new towns and public plazas.

Fortune's 1950 article bit the hand that fed it. What appeared to be a full-page ad accompanying the article showed two men talking outside a corner drugstore, with a newspaper boy peddling papers in the foreground. The headline said "Bull Session—Sometimes it doesn't take much to get a guy to wondering." The copy underneath avowed that taxes on big business and pleas for government handouts were hurting the American Way, represented by that enterprising newspaper boy. Careful readers could see a disclaimer at the top saying "Not an Advertisement." But some people believed it, and one company even requested permission to reprint it. The writer of the faux ad copy was the same person who wrote the article: Whyte.

As the Time Inc. in-house newsletter reported, the magazine was braced for brickbats, but it got more bouquets. One unnamed Time Inc. executive reported that reaction to the article was greater than anything he had seen in fifteen years. It was mostly appreciative, and much of it came via phone calls. "A lot of people don't want to have their names signed to anything so controversial," said the executive.[19]

Whyte's stock rose commensurately outside the company as well. Jack Goodman, executive editor of Simon and Schuster, wrote to him in October 1950. "I understand you are responsible for the brilliant article, 'Is Anybody Listening?' . . . I wonder if we mightn't have a talk about the possibility of a book stemming out of this? If you are not already committed to it, of course." It was a heady time for a writer who had just turned thirty-three. Even sweeter: the letter was directed to Whyte as he was on assignment at Time-Life International offices at 4 Place de la Concorde, Paris.[20]

In two subsequent articles the next year, Whyte tackled a subject that was lurking in the shadows of corporate personnel offices but never fully addressed: the wives of management. The articles were based on 230 personal interviews with corporate executives as well as additional interviews with many of the executives' wives. *Fortune*'s research showed that half of the executives interviewed for the story reported that they screened wives before a final hiring decision was made about their husbands. Describing the company country clubs that IBM built for its employees and their families, Thomas J. Watson explained that the goal was the creation of "a fairly cohesive social system in which home and business life are brought into increasing harmony." Revlon, Whyte reported, tutored the wives of managers in the fine points of entertaining. In these pre-feminist days, the goal was men's liberation, not women's. "We have an obligation to deliberately plan and create a favorable, constructive attitude on the part of the wife that will liberate her husband's total energies for the job," explained one executive.[21]

In March 1952, in the final article in the communication series, titled "Groupthink," Whyte took up several of the themes that he would develop four years later in *The Organization Man*. One was the view that individualism had been subsumed by the group to which the individual belonged. "We have had to learn how to get along in groups. With the evolution of today's giant organizations—in business, in government, in labor, in education, in big cities—we have created a whole new social structure for ourselves, and one so complex that we're still trying to figure out just what happened."[22] Another theme was that social engineering, in the form of "human relations," could help individuals fit into a group. Whyte was highly skeptical of both assertions.

The book that grew out of the series, *Is Anybody Listening? How and Why U.S. Business Fumbles When It Talks with Human Beings*, ended with a sentence that differed in one word from the concluding line of the magazine article on which it was based. The change was one that reflected a recurring theme in Whyte's thinking during his *Fortune* years. Here is the ending that appeared in the article:

> We need, certainly, to find ways of making this bewildering society of ours run more smoothly and we need all the illumination science can give us to do it. But we need something more. . . . A new respect for the individual must be kindled. A revival of the humanities, perhaps, a conscious, deliberate effort by the corporation not only to accommodate dissent but to encourage it—possible approaches to a problem so fundamental cannot easily be spelled out.
>
> Only individuals can do it.

Figure 4.1 In 1952 Whyte published his first book, *Is Anybody Listening?* (*Princeton Alumni Weekly* / Seeley G. Mudd Manuscript Library, Princeton University.)

In the book, there was a telling change in the last sentence: "Only the layman can do it."

Why the change? Whyte aimed his message not at solo entrepreneurs or lone adventurers but rather at people within a group or organization. Whyte clearly saw a struggle that was particular to a conscientious individual who was part of an organization, in other words, a layman. By its first definition, certainly in the 1950s, a layman was a committed member of the congregation rather than of the clergy who led it. But Whyte also used the term when referring to the business owners and managers in urban business districts—stakeholders, as they might be called today. Whyte amplified his view as he was participating literally as a layman at his church, the Episcopal Church of the Epiphany on Manhattan's Upper East Side. On Sunday, October 18, 1953, Whyte preached on a "laymen's Sunday." His remarks were reported in the next day's *New York Times*, which quoted at length from Whyte's address.

> The key problem of an age of huge organizations is not better human relations; the great problem of our bureaucratic society, if it is to continue vigorously, is ideas and new thoughts and conflicts.
>
> Today, as many interpret it, human relations means that the worker, whether he is in the shop or in the carpeted office, fulfills himself by making peace with the system.[23]

The laymen's sermon ended with Whyte's call to arms against the status quo and his assertion that every great advance had been the result of someone ready to "blow the lid off everything" if necessary. This premise of *The Organization Man* had been on Whyte's mind since at least the time of his graduation speech at St. Andrew's School in 1946. Whyte seized on an opportunity to further develop his thinking a few years later. The president of Yale University, Charles Seymour, had boasted that his seniors in the Class of 1949—the first postwar class to enjoy four uninterrupted years of college—were the most talented Yale students ever, destined to be the leading lights of capitalism in the second half of the twentieth century. Seymour passed the idea on to *Fortune*'s managing editor, R. D. "Del" Paine Jr., who thought it could be the starting point for an in-depth piece on the graduating classes of elite colleges throughout the nation.

The assignment went to Whyte, who drove 2,200 miles to visit colleges in the East and Midwest. Another dozen *Fortune* correspondents made campus visits in other parts of the country. Whyte sent out questionnaires to placement directors and deans at around sixty colleges. A researcher interviewed personnel directors at corporations in Chicago, Cleveland, Boston, and New York. Mindful of his Marine Corps intelligence work, Whyte didn't look for information that would confirm his conclusion. Instead he found one refrain that "was not at all what we had expected. Get ready, the seniors were saying, for catastrophe.

They were headed for business alright, but not because they liked the idea. They wanted a storm cellar for the great depression ahead. And so, on the verge of the greatest peacetime boom in history, the class of 1949 girded for the future, looking to big business for security."[24]

As was the case with the articles leading up to *Is Anybody Listening?*, Whyte's reporting flew in the face of *Fortune's* stated editorial direction. In July 1950, for example, *Fortune* had surveyed the new possibilities presented by the use of psychological tests. Could tests determine executives' ability to use scientifically determined strategies, rather than seat-of-the-pants decisions, in their business planning? Whyte's reporting took a dim view of all such personality tests.

A year later the *Fortune* editors had extolled the increased professionalism of the new managers overseeing much of the corporate landscape. "Today's businessman brings a new professional responsibility to his day-to-day problems. And because he measures himself more in what he does than what he owns, industry, itself, has achieved a greater stature in life and progress of the country." The headline above this statement read "The Tycoon Is Dead."[25] But Whyte's reporting, fleshed out in *The Organization Man*, showed that the greater stature did not necessarily result in increased performance. Reading Whyte's reporting would make you mourn for the lost tycoons, who often single-handedly transformed the business landscape. Creative leadership, Whyte would conclude, was often being removed from the leader's hands and transferred to lower-level staff.

In October 1952, the Carnegie Institute of Technology in Pittsburgh dedicated its new Graduate School of Industrial Administration. One event was an informal closed roundtable session with sixteen leading administrators, educators, and researchers. The attendees included the heads of Standard Oil of New Jersey; Goodrich Rubber; Westinghouse; Gulf Oil; the graduate business schools at Harvard University, the Massachusetts Institute of Technology, and the University of California, Los Angeles; and Whyte, by then assistant managing editor of *Fortune*. The agenda called for a discussion of fundamental research for management. In his remarks, Whyte cried out for those rare unmanageable people in the corporate ranks.

There is really a fantastic amount of work, of various degrees of usefulness, in progress on how people get along in groups. Are we not in danger of overlooking a critical new problem—how do we provide a favorable environment and proper incentives for the independent spirit? How do we nurture that type of individual? He may not fit at all well into groups. He may be almost destructive in his interpersonal relationships. But he may be that rare individual who has the genius and the drive that can spark a sleeping organization, who can really make the difference between life and death for a firm.[26]

Fortune then offered Whyte an opportunity that any magazine writer would jump at—the time to stitch this reporting into a book. By then, however, Whyte was already a published author with a well-received first book. *Is Anybody Listening?* was reviewed favorably in both the *New York Times* Sunday Book Review and the daily *New York Times* in April 1952. Within a month Arthur Godfrey saluted Whyte's book on his morning radio show, a favorite of housewives across the country. "If your husband is in business—if you gentlemen who are listening are businessmen—let me recommend a book. . . . I read about half of it last night and I think it is the most intriguing book I have yet read—or one of the most intriguing. . . . Get hold of it and read it. I wish everybody would."[27]

Meanwhile Whyte also proved to be the rare writer who had "turned himself into a bookkeeper," to borrow from Luce's hiring maxim. In negotiating the contract for *Is Anybody Listening?* with Simon and Schuster, the Time Inc. business office convinced Whyte that it would be to his advantage to have Time Inc., rather than Whyte, sign the contract for him. But in doing so, Whyte soon discovered, Time Inc. also made itself an equal partner with the writer and shared fifty-fifty in all royalties after sales exceeded a certain level. Whyte wasn't happy. He drafted by hand a spreadsheet charting the negative effects as sales increased, with an accompanying pie chart. In a two-page memo to his boss, Del Paine, Whyte warned that the company's claim to half of the royalties would discourage personal incentive. "A ceiling, in effect, is put on the dream."The policy, Whyte wrote, "is not only against my interests, but those of the organization as well."[28]

Time Inc. archives do not reveal the terms of Whyte's deal with Simon and Schuster for his new book, *The Organization Man*. But a November 1953 memo from *Fortune*'s managing editor, Hedley Donovan, to his two top associates suggested that this time Whyte had total royalty rights in the forthcoming book. Donovan spelled out how Time Inc.'s largesse would be leveraged for the magazine journalist turned author.

> Holly Whyte and I have agreed that he should have six months to work on his book, starting January 1st. Two months of this would represent his 1953 and 1954 vacations; two months would be charged to the Publisher (during which Holly would do some part-time work on promotion material); the other two months would be carried by Editorial on the presumption that Holly's work on the book would also lead to more *Fortune* articles. During the same period Holly will also be called upon for criticism of manuscripts in his general territory, and perhaps for production of an editorial short or two.
>
> Holly's contract with the publisher of his book will give *Fortune* the exclusive magazine rights.[29]

No mention was made of *Fortune* or Time Inc. having any rights in the book itself. The memo stated only that "perhaps" Whyte would produce an editorial short or two during the course of this paid leave. But Whyte probably was aware that the boss's wife, Clare Booth Luce, once had staff writers' outside work bound in leather with a pointed legend embossed on the cover: "Created on Harry Luce's time."[30] Whyte came through with several substantial pieces during his leave of absence.

In the April 1954 issue Whyte took a satirical view of the increasing use of personal identification systems, symbolized by the new punch cards that were read by data processing machines. The article, "The Case for the Universal Card," carried a byline of Otis Binet-Stanford, a nom de plume borrowed from the names of the creators of the most prominent IQ tests of the time. With the article was a photograph of a "Universal Card" for an individual named George B. Follansbee. The card provided everything that a data-driven personnel manager would seek in considering a job applicant: date of birth and eye color, academic credentials, and fingerprint. The *St. Louis Post-Dispatch* denounced the totalitarian implications of the card and its inventor. *Punch*, the British humor magazine, took the *Fortune* article very seriously and responded with a sarcasm-laden attack.

It was a frightening view of a brave new world. But it was also totally fictional, fabricated by Holly Whyte.

In October and November 1955, Whyte reported and wrote a two-part series on the major private foundations (which he also wove into *The Organization Man*). The series posed a question: "Those uniquely American institutions, the big foundations, have recently come under attack for being too bold. Are they?" The series asserted that the three biggest foundations—Ford, Carnegie, and Rockefeller—were not bold enough. "One measure is their support of the scholar who is not a member of the 'team'—the independent researcher. Their record is un-impressive." Whyte also criticized the large foundations for preferring to make large grants to large institutions rather than smaller grants to smaller, but possibly equally worthy, nonprofits.

The Rockefellers must have taken notice of Whyte's coverage. In September he had an interview scheduled with John D. Rockefeller III at 30 Rockefeller Plaza for an article described only as "Foundations of the U.S." It would be followed by many more visits by Whyte to the Rockefellers' aerie (chapter 8).[31]

In December 1956, *The Organization Man* was published, with its cut-to-the-chase opening line: "This book is about the organization man." Within four months the book had sold thirty thousand copies, at $5 apiece. The gross of $150,000 would be equivalent to almost $1.4 million today. The successful launch of *The Organization Man* was immediately noticed at Time Inc. In an interview for the company's internal newsletter, *F.Y.I.*, Whyte said, "I knew there were some people who would be interested in what I had to say, but I never dreamed there were that many."[32]

Though the timing could have been coincidental, one week after a favorable *New York Times* review Luce received a note from Eric Hodgins, the former *Fortune* editor and author. Hodgins told Luce that he and Russell Lynes, editor of the "Casual Style" essay in *Harper's*, had proposed Whyte for "resident membership in The Century." The Century Association, as it is formally known, was then (and still is) one of the top private social clubs in the city, with a membership roster that included many artists and literary figures. Hodgins asked Luce to write a letter in Whyte's support. Seven days later Luce wrote to the Committee on Admissions. "Holly Whyte has been a valued colleague of mine for ten years, and it gives me pleasure heartily to endorse this nomination. He is presently Assistant Managing Editor of *Fortune* and has achieved, both within and without the company, a respected position as an editor and writer."[33]

The following year Whyte fielded invitations from various conferences and offers of honorary degrees. His sudden status as a celebrity notwithstanding, Whyte continued to pursue more stories for *Fortune*. An article that appeared in January 1958 was the first in another series that would culminate in a book. The subject was urban sprawl. Whyte centered his story on development that was consuming prime acreage in the Brandywine Valley of Chester County, Pennsylvania, near his childhood home, the setting for some of the short stories he had written as a college student.

The series continued with a relatively short article for *Fortune*, "The Businessman's City." Whyte made a plea to the *Fortune* audience—including the concerned laymen—to look at themselves as the beginning point for the solution to problems of cities. It was a simple thought but necessary at the time, according to Whyte. The federal government, through its Federal Housing Administration, was favoring suburbs over cities. City planners (many of whom lived in the suburbs, Whyte noted) were dreaming of starting over again in the exurbs. Many were still caught up in the Radiant City dream formulated by the famed French-Swiss architect Le Corbusier. Whyte and the city planners with whom he consulted had another approach in mind: revitalizing the cities. To address that issue, Whyte recruited Jane Jacobs, then a staff writer for *Architectural Forum*, another Time Inc. publication. Jacobs's piece in *Fortune*, "Downtown Is for People," published in

April 1958, generated "one of the best responses" Whyte could recall (chapter 7).[34]

These *Fortune* articles became the building blocks for the third book published under Whyte's name (this time as editor). *The Exploding Metropolis* would foreshadow the breadth and depth of the urbanism movement that came into its fore in the second half of the twentieth century.

As Whyte was creating all this content for *Fortune*, he was also taking seriously his responsibilities as an organization man, as would be expected of an editor at a Time Inc. publication. On November 12, 1952, shortly after being promoted to assistant managing editor, Whyte issued a memorandum to Del Paine, his immediate boss, and to Hedley Donovan, the magazine's top editor. It began, in the Whyte style, with a simple declarative sentence: "This memo is about *Fortune*: where it is, and where it is going."

Before even suggesting there were any changes needed, Whyte reminded his audience that *Fortune*'s star was rising quickly and that "this is not due to some mystique, but to something that can be analyzed, and therefore improved upon and strengthened. . . . That something is this: that in an era of bewildering social and economic changes, *Fortune* is the organization most aware of the changes and most vigorous in discovering them and their implications for management."

Whyte attributed the magazine's healthy status to following "our own natural curiosities and inclinations" rather than by the "conscious retailoring" of the organization. "It's no great exaggeration to proclaim that the *Fortune* men's room provides the most advanced forum in the country" on the topic of organizational management. In the male-dominated world of the 1950s, the men's room reference needed no apology.[35]

In a memo a year later Whyte played the role of organization man and cheerleader, sharing reactions to an article titled "The Crown Princes of Business." Whyte enumerated thirteen responses to the article by the business community, including reprints being distributed to fifty executives at Western Electric and the listing of the piece as reading material for Harvard Business School's advanced management course.[36] In July 1956 Whyte wrote a three-page memo aimed at a job applicant who sought advice about how to write short pieces for the "b.o.b.," or back-of-the-book section, similar to the Shorts and Faces section that existed when Whyte first joined the magazine. Donovan circulated the memo to four of his top lieutenants. "Holly puts the b.o.b. problem so well that I thought his memo deserved wider circulation."[37]

Within a week of the publication date of *The Organization Man*, Whyte found himself defending Time Inc. against a potential hostile reporter from "our favorite newspaper," as Whyte described the *New York Post* in a memorandum to Donovan. The *Post* had drawn parallels between *The Organization Man* and the inner workings of Time Inc. Whyte had tried to disavow the *Post* reporter of his contention that *Time* was using personality tests in its hiring process. "I explained we did not give the things. It was highly unlikely that we ever would."[38]

Whyte's status at *Fortune* and Time Inc. was about to change. Donovan clearly valued Whyte as a writer and editor. But was he equally confident about Whyte's ability as a manager? The test came in 1958, when Luce picked Donovan to be his successor as editorial director of all magazines at Time Inc. At that time Whyte and Duncan Norton-Taylor were both assistant managing editors under Donovan. They would take turns as "acting managing editor" when Donovan was on vacation or on assignment. But Donovan, looking ahead to his eventual promotion, decided he had to have a "clear number 2" and an heir apparent. He chose Norton-Taylor. In what he would describe as a "painful conversation," Donovan explained to Whyte that he would have more fun and be more valuable to the magazine as a writer and editor rather than as a managing editor, whose time creating content would be limited. Whyte was "deeply disappointed."[39]

In looking for an outcome that would feel less like a demotion, Luce held a few discussions with Whyte about starting a new magazine that would be under his direction. Donovan gave "Mr. Luce" a progress report in a memo on June 30, 1958, marked "Confidential."

I've had two or three more rounds with Holly Whyte. He's still considering your "proposition." Also a variant that I proposed to him: work here until mid-1959, at which time you would owe him another reading on the future; then (to take advantage of the tax-and-royalty situation he will be in during 1959–60) he could take a leave of absence which might perhaps run 12–18 months without impairing his *Fortune* prospects. Or if his absence *was* beginning to hurt his prospects, we would tell him so.

I think he wants to see you once more on this, and then will be making up his mind by the end of the week.[40]

The next meeting with Luce did not go Whyte's way. When Luce subsequently appointed Norton-Taylor as Donovan's successor, Whyte, at age forty and still single, had every reason to reconsider his future. His father had died on August 8, 1958, at the age of seventy—a rite of passage for any son. Whyte also had no other choice but to reconsider. A curriculum vitae of Whyte in the Time Inc. archives has a handwritten note across the top: "Resigned Oct. 1958 to freelance." Above that note another handwritten comment, dated October 24, 1990, disputes the first comment. "False, according to [a name that is undecipherable]. She says he was fired in 1959." Both comments were no doubt from Time Inc. researchers who, as Whyte would later write, were "nicely assertive, but assertive."[41]

Whyte did not burn any bridges. By October he was off on a working holiday to Finland and Sweden. In a letter to Del Paine, the former *Fortune* managing editor, Whyte sounded more like an enterprising freelancer than a disgruntled former employee. He suggested that he might have some "gleanings" from his trip that could be of use to either *Fortune* or *Architectural Forum*. Still a good organization man, Whyte reported that *Fortune*'s "Exploding Metropolis" series had been favorably viewed in Sweden. He felt that one project in particular in the center of Stockholm would make a good story for *Architectural Forum*. He revealed no bitterness about being passed over at *Fortune*.[42]

Whyte, the organization man, was leaving the most generous and most accommodating organization he had known until then. But the seeds of his next endeavors had been sown: He had connected with the Rockefellers, especially the middle brother, Laurance, who would become his benefactor and accomplice though the 1960s, 1970s, and 1980s. The *Fortune* series on urban issues had become a book, *The*

Exploding Metropolis, and had put one of its contributors, Jane Jacobs, in the national spotlight. And Whyte's *The Organization Man* had been through multiple printings and had already been reissued in paperback.

On top of that he had been admitted to the Century Association, where he strengthened a friendship with Peter Cook, who had preceded him at Princeton University by two years. By then Cook was an accomplished landscape and portrait artist. His wife, Joan, was the daughter of prominent Bucks County painter John Follinsbee. The Cooks, who lived just outside Princeton, also had a young friend, Jenny Bell Bechtel, a former model turned fashion designer. Jenny Bell and Holly would soon meet.

By the end of his time at *Fortune*, Holly Whyte was well known as a journalist and author. But he was moving quickly to a larger role. Cornell historian Robert Vanderlan sized up the literary lions of Time Inc., including Whyte, in a 2010 book, *Intellectuals Incorporated: Politics, Art, and Ideas inside Henry Luce's Media Empire.* To Vanderlan these writers, including, among others, James Agee, Daniel Bell, John Hersey, Dwight Macdonald, Archibald MacLeish, T. S. Matthews, Theodore White, and John Kenneth Galbraith, as well as Whyte, were more than journalists and authors. They were "connected critics."[43] Vanderlan borrowed the phrase from philosopher and political theorist Michael Walzer, who defined the "connected critic" as one who operates in "the everyday world" and is able "to study its internal rules, maxims, conventions, and ideals, rather than to detach . . . from it in search of a universal and transcendent standpoint."[44]

The everyday world—especially its rules, maxims, conventions, and ideals—had become William H. Whyte's oyster.

Chapter 5

Is Anybody Listening?—the High Cost of Harmony and Groupthink

The 1950s and 1960s, the dawn of consumer electronics, were also the days of do-it-yourself electronics. If you wanted a television or a stereo system you could have paid a high price at a store, or if you were handy you might have built one yourself from a kit. Some tinkerers and even more accomplished inventors subscribed to *Science and Mechanics* magazine or its sister publication, *Radio-TV Experimenter*. The spring 1961 issue of *Radio-TV Experimenter* reviewed one gadget with an unusual name. The magazine described it as follows:

> Called the Group-Thinkometer by its inventors, this electronic device registers your opinion. You can vote against the boss, and nobody will be the wiser. Let's say that around a conference table are gathered engineers, scientists, test pilots and designers. The project leader points to a chart and says, "All those in favor of this nozzle design vote Yes by pressing the button." Instantly, the total vote in favor is indicated on a dial.
>
> This idea was developed and experimentally marketed by the Harwald Company of Evanston, Ill., and it was found that the "Thinkometer" does more than just speed up a voting procedure.

The chairman can instantly determine the group opinion at any moment during a discussion. And of course, the vote is completely secret, as long as each person conceals the button in his hand. The "personality factor" in voting is eliminated, and each person is free to express his opinion, in favor or against, without fear of offending a friend, a co-worker, or a boss.[1]

The handy Group-Thinkometer would enable anyone in the room to express an opinion—free from the opprobrium of the group. The record does not indicate exactly when the Harwald Company first produced the Group-Thinkometer, but the gadget was certainly in existence in 1956 when William H. Whyte referred to it in *The Organization Man*. "Most group-relations people would probably disown it as too stringent a tool, yet it seems a perfectly logical development," he wrote.[2]

Whyte coined the term "groupthink" in a 1952 article for *Fortune*, a fact that several subsequent writers have overlooked. In 2004 a Senate Intelligence Committee reported on the blunders surrounding the Iraq War: "The committee concluded that the intelligence community was suffering from what we call a collective groupthink." In a footnote the committee attributed the word "groupthink" to a professor of psychology at Yale University, Irving Janis. William Safire, the *New York Times* language columnist, noted the error. "If the committee's other conclusions are as outdated as its etymology, we're all in trouble," Safire wrote.[3] That correction notwithstanding, the *Yale Alumni Magazine* in 2008 referred to Janis as the originator of the term. In a recent essay a Yale alumnus noted Whyte's first use of the term but insisted that "Janis was the progenitor of the word in its current sense."[4]

The fact remains that, after coining the term in the magazine article, Whyte elaborated on the groupthink concept in a chapter by that name in his subsequent book *Is Anybody Listening? How and Why U.S. Business Fumbles When It Talks with Human Beings*. Published within weeks of the final article in *Fortune*'s series, *Is Anybody Listening?* was reviewed in the *New York Times* Sunday Book Review and then in the newspaper's Books of the Times column on consecutive days in April 1952.[5] The second review called the book "lively but scrappy and disorganized." It was a fair complaint. As entertaining as it was, the chapter on corporate wives was more of an internal personnel issue for managers than a corporate communication challenge. But the free-flowing book turned up plenty of fascinating insights that would be further explored in Whyte's next, and much bigger, book, *The Organization Man*.

Whyte's newly coined word, "groupthink," was no doubt inspired by George Orwell's *1984*, published in 1949 and cited by Whyte in his 1952 *Fortune* article. No one needed to work hard to figure out what this portmanteau meant, and it was a broad term that could be used to cast any number of aspersions. The following was Whyte's definition:

> Groupthink being a coinage—and, admittedly, a loaded one—a working definition is in order. We are not talking about mere instinctive conformity—it is, after all, a perennial failing of mankind. What we are talking about is a rationalized conformity—an open, articulate philosophy which holds that group values are not only expedient but right and good as well. Three mutually supporting ideas form the underpinning: (1) that moral values and ethics are relative; (2) that what is important is the kind of behavior and attitudes that makes for the harmonious functioning of the group; (3) that the best way to achieve this is through the application of "scientific" techniques.[6]

At least two historians later raised their eyebrows at the apparent contradiction of Whyte's denunciation of groupthink in *Fortune* and his earlier description in the *Marine Corps Gazette* of wartime intelligence gathering: "As in every intelligence function it is not the individual report which counts, but the mass. See that you control that mass."[7]

James C. Bradford, a professor of military history at Texas A&M University, wrote in the introduction to Whyte's war memoir that his "call for adherence to standard operating procedures and group norms at the end of World War II stands in sharp contrast to the views expressed in *The Organization Man* a decade later. . . . It would have been interesting to ask him if he believed that the criticisms he leveled in *The Organization Man* applied to military as well as civilian institutions, and in time of war as well as in time of peace."[8] Robert Vanderlan, who featured Whyte and other prominent Time Inc. writers in his 2010 book *Intellectuals Incorporated*, also referred to Whyte's *Marine Corps Gazette* articles. "Curiously for the future author of *The Organization Man*, his prescriptions emphasized a strict adherence to correct 'procedure' and the necessity of subordinating the individual to the organization."[9]

But Whyte's thinking was more nuanced than that. Bradford quoted only the first sentence of Whyte's summary statement quoted here. He left out the second sentence: "See that you control that mass." Vanderlan, in turn, based his conclusion on Bradford's analysis. And though he never referred directly to his *Gazette* article, Whyte did elaborate on groupthink in *The Organization Man*: "People very rarely *think* in groups; they talk together, they exchange information, they adjudicate, they make compromises. But they do not think; they do not create."[10]

The greatest peril of groupthink may have been that its adherents confused "the harmonious functioning of the group" with the quality of the thought that was produced. Groupthink was thought to be "not only expedient but right and good as well."[11] Groupthink was no doubt as alluring in the 1950s as it is today. It is not "instinctive conformity"—anyone, after all, can just meekly go along with the crowd. It is a "rationalized conformity," often arrived at after great deliberation. The rationalizing is important. To this day sincere institutional administrators will say that they reached a consensus but only after a vigorous debate. An opinion forged from a group will most likely be perceived as better and more righteous than one held by a lonely individual on the edge of, or outside of, the group. A good creative idea, like a rope, would be stronger by virtue of the number of individual strands woven into it. Those sincere administrators, Whyte would say, are indulging in groupthink.

In the mid-twentieth century, Whyte believed, harmonious decision making had become a goal of academe, corporate America, and most other organizations. To achieve that goal, personality tests purportedly could identify the people who would best fit into a harmonious group. Once the group was in place, other "scientific techniques," the third point of Whyte's definition, could be utilized to help create a harmonious march toward consensus.[12]

After the *Fortune* article on groupthink was published in 1952, Whyte spoke at a management conference. About halfway through the session the program chairman called an intermission and rearranged all the chairs into circles of four each. What's this? Whyte asked. It was a "buzz session," he was told, intended to stimulate ideas through interactions within the small groups. The proceedings were restarted, but there was no "buzz" that Whyte could detect. Groups of four were probably too small, the chairman conceded. At the next such meeting, he would try the buzz session again but with groups of six to eight. Whyte remained skeptical.[13]

The chairman of that event, Whyte discovered, was a graduate of a summer program at the National Training Laboratories for Group Development in Bethel, Maine (now known as NTL and based in Baltimore, Maryland). One of its innovations was the T-group, a training session in which participants used role-playing, feedback, and problem solving to gain better understanding of groups and of themselves. The Bethel laboratory had also experimented with "leaderless groups" that would experience a period of chaos as individuals let their opinions fly. That in turn would lead to a valuable catharsis and, ultimately, some creative thoughts. That was the theory. One noted sociologist, William Foote Whyte (no relation to Holly), participated in a leaderless group and concluded that without a leader, "such a high premium is placed upon fitting into the group and being sensitive to the group's wishes that the individual who shows some initiative . . . becomes suspect and is likely to be discouraged."[14]

Long after William H. Whyte's identification and analysis of groupthink, concerns about avoiding it and fostering creative thinking in the workplace rippled through the business and academic worlds. In 1956 *Life* magazine published a cover story titled "The Course Where Students Lose Earthly Shackles." The subject, John E. Arnold, founder of the Creative Engineering Laboratory at the Massachusetts Institute of Technology (MIT), was "one of the many intellectuals taken by Whyte's thinking."[15] Arnold took his innovative approach to Stanford

University's engineering school in 1957. From there Arnold's vision of creative thinking—an antidote to groupthink—was passed via various disciples to David Kelley, who had formed a design firm, IDEO, that was credited with creating the first Apple computer mouse. In 2003 Kelley had an epiphany, which was to call the company's creative process "design thinking." The process, which emphasizes rapid prototyping and repeated iterations, has become a blockbuster product. IDEO has since grown to more than seven hundred employees. Harvard, Cornell, and Stanford Universities, among others, offer certificate programs in design thinking.

Possibly because of the opprobrium associated with groupthink, IBM's chief executive officer Thomas J. Watson Jr. in 1957 took note of the firm's longtime motto, "Think," and elaborated on it. "Thinking things through is hard work and it sometimes seems safer to follow the crowd. That blind adherence to such group thinking is, in the long run, far more dangerous than independently thinking things through."

In 1961 an MBA candidate at the MIT Sloan School of Management, James A. F. Stoner, pondered the accepted wisdom that groupthink was the cause of overly cautious decisions, militating against innovative decisions that might be viewed as risky. But, Stoner wondered, was it really true, and if so, what caused groups to think more conservatively than individuals? Stoner conducted some studies of his own for his master's thesis. The result was the opposite of conventional wisdom. Groups could come to risky conclusions, just as IBM's Watson had suggested. Mike Clayton, a project management consultant and author, described Stoner's research.

> Groupthink can get out of hand. Not only do group members seek to conform with one another, but as some members shift their point of view, the center of gravity of the group's thinking will move. In seeking to conform with this, other group members shift their perspective, and the result of this cascade of small changes is a polarization of the group, and a result that is known as "risky shift."
>
> Therefore, groups can endorse higher risk decisions than any of the individuals would—perhaps due to the degree of confidence re-

sulting in group members agreeing to decisions that they would not make as individuals.[16]

After writing *Is Anybody Listening?* and establishing his expertise in corporate communications, Whyte could have carved out a lucrative career as a business school professor or management consultant, counseling institutions of all types and sizes on how to discourage groupthink, encourage creative thinking, and better manage a thoughtful workforce. He could have used a memorable line from his own *Fortune* article as his company motto: "The great enemy of communication . . . is the illusion of it."[17]

But Whyte had bigger topics to tackle at *Fortune*. And he was not yet thirty-five years old.

Chapter 6

The Organization Man—More than an Epithet

On Friday, October 4, 1957, William H. Whyte played the role of "outside troublemaker" at a weekend retreat for an executive training program. The topic was how to foster creativity within an organization. As the author of *The Organization Man*, by then a reigning best seller, Whyte did not disappoint the executives—he made trouble. His message was that major institutions, with their belief in a group approach to work, were losing the independent thought, curiosity, and skepticism often provided by individuals who failed to fit into the group. The cost of such an approach was high, Whyte told the executives. It was "nowhere more evident than in the conduct of industrial research laboratories." Some of the most venerated research laboratories in the United States were recruiting people not because of their brilliance but because of their ability to fit in with the group. In his book Whyte had quoted a young trainee at a national research lab. When asked whether the organization should hire a true genius if the genius also turned out to be antisocial, the trainee replied, "I would sacrifice brilliance for human understanding every time."[1]

The thirty senior executives at the retreat didn't buy Whyte's argument. They gave him "a very hard time indeed," Whyte would recall. One corporate vice president scoffed at Whyte's pessimism—top people always break through the group setting. Why wouldn't that continue to be the case? Another executive boasted that his corporation sponsored creativity sessions to stimulate new ideas. Several offered a single piece of evidence in rebuttal to Whyte: the Manhattan Project. That group effort during World War II, after all, had produced the atomic bomb that made the world safe for democracy. Take that, Holly Whyte.

Then, "something dreadful happened," as Whyte recalled. "Someone came in with a note. A strange object had just been hurtled up into the skies and it hadn't been put there by American know-how."[2]

That strange object was *Sputnik*. The launch of the Soviet Union's orbiting satellite, what some would later call the Pearl Harbor of the Cold War, helped make *The Organization Man* a definitive story of life in the corporate world in mid-twentieth-century America. Whyte had been critical of the commercial approach to research that favored projects with well-defined objectives and a high chance of success. Projects that were deemed science for science's sake were less likely to be funded. In fact, Whyte reported, only about 4 percent of research and development money was allocated to "creative research."

Even primary education was being affected by concern for the group over the individual. While the smartest kids in the Soviet Union were being fast-tracked into advanced math and science, American kids were being taught social skills. In Park Forest, Illinois, the suburb where Whyte conducted much of his research on organization men and their families, the prevailing view of parents, when asked what they most wanted from the high school curriculum, was that it should "teach students how to be citizens and how to get along with other people."[3]

The Soviet advances in the space race brought the American approach into question. Maybe the group approach was not the answer. On the morning after the *Sputnik* news, at the next session of the executive training session, "an almost unpatriotic note crept into the proceedings," Whyte reported. "If we could be beaten like this, the feeling seemed to be, maybe, just maybe some comforting assumptions needed to be re-examined."[4]

Whyte presented his recollection of the *Sputnik* news just three weeks after the launch, in a speech at Grinnell College in Iowa. At that point the United States still had more setbacks to endure in the space race. The main American effort had been assigned to a team from the US Naval Research Laboratory. Its first satellite launch, attempted in December, after yet another successful Soviet Union launch, exploded a few feet above the launchpad. "Kaputnik" was a popular newspaper headline.

Meanwhile, however, another satellite effort was underway in the United States. The director, Wernher von Braun, had been viewed warily by the mainstream effort because of his prior affiliation with the Nazi V-2 missile program. But after the *Sputnik* launch, Pentagon officials were more receptive. Von Braun told them he had been in "silent cooperation" with several other agencies and could have a satellite in space within sixty days. A successful launch was made in January 1958. Von Braun was the kind of organization man Whyte would have admired—one ready to work outside as well as inside the system.

Less than a year after its publication, *The Organization Man* had become something Whyte never intended it to be—synonymous for an obsequious conformist, a company cheerleader. "I am rather sorry that the term 'organization man' is used as an epithet," Whyte told his audience at Grinnell. Whyte said he used the term "simply for a person, good, bad, or indifferent, who works in large-scale organizations. I would hardly dream of demeaning him for he is to be found, not only in General Motors, but in the University of Chicago, in the Cowles Publications, the Columbia Broadcasting System, the Oak Ridge Laboratories, *Fortune* magazine, and Grinnell College."[5] Whyte the *Fortune* editor and the Grinnell students in his audience were in the same boat. Their "blood brothers," as Whyte had written in the book's introduction, included individuals at organizations of all sizes, not just the large-scale ones: "the seminary student, doctor, physics Ph.D., intellectual on a foundation-sponsored team project, engineering graduate at Lockheed, and young apprentice at a Wall Street law factory."[6]

The social ethic and the organizations that followed it had their positive attributes, as Whyte made clear. "The energies Americans have devoted to the co-operative, to the social, are not to be demeaned," Whyte wrote in *The Organization Man*. Nor was he condemning conformity. "Nonconformity is an empty goal, and rebellion against prevailing opinion merely because it is prevailing should no more be praised than acquiescence to it. . . . There will be no strictures in this book against . . . ranch wagons, or television sets, or gray flannel suits"[7]—the latter an obvious reference to the best-selling novel and Hollywood movie of the 1950s, Sloan Wilson's *The Man in the Gray Flannel Suit*.

Whyte illuminated what he saw as a sea change in American society—the replacement of the Protestant ethic by the social ethic. Many people, especially businesspeople, still gave lip service to the Protestant ethic. Defined by the German philosopher Max Weber in the early 1900s, the ethic was based on the belief that a hardworking, competitive individual could single-handedly achieve success. It was a great fit for the American dream. The social ethic, however, cast the individual in a larger context. An individual could be more productive, possibly even more worthy, by working side by side, harmoniously, with others. The perceived benefits of the group setting were similar to the belief that decisions made in group settings were likely to be better than those clung to by one lonely individual. But the individual, Whyte argued, did not have to conform to the social ethic. The individual could resist the blandishments of the organization when circumstances warranted.[8]

Whyte saw real costs associated with the social ethic. In *The Organization Man* he worried that straitjacketed personnel managers would screen out the "brilliant but erratic scientists" who were responsible for breakthroughs in fundamental knowledge. Whyte challenged readers to examine the list of commercial inventions over the previous thirty years. Most did not originate in a corporate laboratory—Kodachrome film, for example, was invented by two musicians in a bathroom, Whyte wrote (perhaps with some dramatic license). A recruiting film for Monsanto Chemical Company, in contrast, showed three young men in lab coats chatting amiably with each other. "No geniuses here," the narrator intoned. "Just a bunch of average Americans working together." Whyte quoted a policy manual from the Socony-Vacuum Oil Company: "Few specialists in a large company ever work alone. There is little room for virtuoso performances."[9]

Whyte praised one lab as an exception to the rule: Bell Labs, which did make room for virtuosos. Mervin Kelly, president of Bell Labs from 1951 to 1959, has been compared to an "able concert hall conductor" who "sought a harmony, and sometimes a tension, between scientific disciplines; between researchers and developers; and between soloists and groups." Kelly, as described by Jon Gertner in *The Idea Factory*, had not allowed the quest for harmony to supplant the lab's real goals: the development of the transistor, solar cell, and laser. Bell Labs, Whyte noted, accommodated the brilliant theoretical physicist Claude Shannon, who roamed the halls on a unicycle while simultaneously juggling tennis balls.[10]

Whyte had witnessed the transformation from the Protestant ethic to the social ethic in his own life. He trained to be a Vick salesman in the late 1930s, when the Protestant ethic was firmly in place at the company. The men in the program toiled individually, fighting against competitors for business and then competing against each other for what they believed to be a limited number of full-time positions. "Business was survival of the fittest," they were told. After the war, when he and other Vick alumni gathered for drinks in New York, they would marvel at the company's new training program. It reflected the social ethic—"all but a handful" got hired for full-time jobs. Security was "reasonably guaranteed."[11]

For people of the 1950s with vivid memories of the Great Depression, the advent of the large corporation was practically a salvation. Adolf Berle, a prodigy who had a law degree from Harvard University by age twenty-one, provided a blueprint for New Deal economists in the 1932 book he coauthored, *The Modern Corporation and Private Property*. Berle contended that large corporations had replaced the tycoons of the late nineteenth and early twentieth centuries as the driving economic force in America. A managerial class ran the corporations with little need to answer to stockholders. Government therefore needed to harness these corporations for the public good. By 1954 Berle estimated that nearly half of the nation's industrial assets were owned by just 135 corporations. The rise of the corporation, he wrote, "shows no sign of slackening."[12]

These large corporations and their legions of managers became

Whyte's Walden Pond in *The Organization Man*—the first of several figurative ponds that Whyte would focus on in his career. The corporations, nearing their apogee in the 1950s and 1960s, offered employees alluring job security and sometimes even lifelong benefits. In 1955 *Fortune* magazine, by then the nation's most widely read business publication, initiated its annual Fortune 500 survey of the nation's leading companies. The top ten on the inaugural list: General Motors, Jersey Standard (Esso), U.S. Steel, General Electric, Esmark, Chrysler, Armour, Gulf Oil, Mobil, and DuPont. The corporations offered on-the-job training and subsidized attendance at night school. IBM, number 61 on that first Fortune 500 list, offered employees $1 memberships in country clubs with golf, tennis, swimming, and bowling. Many companies offered employees discounted stock purchase plans. Some lifelong employees invested their entire retirement plan in their own company's stock.

The benefits of corporate life were magnified in the 1950s by two other important social institutions, each of which came under Whyte's critical eye: (1) nuclear families, with their stay-at-home mothers, which provided the workforce for the organizations; and (2) the suburbs, which provided the comfortable setting for those men and their families. Each one came into full bloom in the post–World War II era.

The nuclear family had risen while the number of multigenerational families living under one roof had declined. As depicted by television shows such as *Leave It to Beaver* and *Father Knows Best*, nuclear families were the epitome of normalcy in post–World War II America. According to cultural critic David Brooks, more than half of the respondents in a 1957 survey said that unmarried people were "sick," "immoral," or "neurotic."[13] At the end of the 1950s, nearly three-quarters of American adults were married. During that fifteen-year reign of the nuclear family, divorce rates fell and fertility rates rose. In 1960 nearly 90 percent of children under eighteen were living with their married parents.

Eighteen of the nation's top twenty-five cities lost population between 1950 and 1980. By 1980 more people—40 percent of the total population—lived in the suburbs than in either the central cities or the rural areas. Those suburbs of the 1950s, or "packaged communities," as Whyte called them, were sufficiently alike that a relocated corporate family could quickly pick up where it had left off. In November 1948, *Fortune* reported on the plans of developer Philip Klutznick, former commissioner of the Federal Public Housing Authority, for a new community called Park Forest, about thirty-five miles south of Chicago. Klutznick planned about three thousand rental units, a shopping center, four thousand houses for sale, and some "non-nuisance" industrial uses on a 475-acre tract.

Within four years Park Forest was an established community, with enough organization men and their families to make Whyte embed himself there for weeks on end. Whyte's access to the town and its residents was supported by the community pastor, Hugo Leinberger, who invited the reporter to stay several nights a week at his family home at 16 Fir Street, one of the two-story units on a courtyard. After spending the day interviewing housewives and community leaders, Whyte would join the family for dinner, often talking religion with the pastor and his wife. Even the church helped promote the belongingness of the community. About two-thirds of the Park Forest families were Protestants, split among a half dozen denominations. Having that many separate churches, some residents believed, would splinter the community. So the townspeople formed the nondenominational Faith United Protestant Church. Attracting new congregants was made easier by the fact that the frequent company relocations of many incoming residents had weakened their ties to any particular denomination.

The family's eldest child, Paul, then an elementary school student, recalled accompanying Whyte on walks through the town, with the journalist even then scrutinizing the interactions of people on the street.[14] (Thirty years later Paul Leinberger would write a follow-up to Whyte's work—see chapter 15.) Whyte's visits continued for several weeks at a time from December 1952 until June 1953. "After a deep breath," Whyte wrote, he returned for another visit to Park Forest in 1955.

Taking advantage of this immersion, Whyte picked up the subtle nuances of the Park Forest lifestyle, including, for example, the scene of an organization man and his family moving into town. Whyte described a prototypical couple—Dot and Charlie—and their children arriving at a residential court.

Soon the neighbors will come over to introduce themselves. In an almost inordinate display of decency, some will help them unpack, and around suppertime two of the girls will come over with a hot casserole and another with a percolator full of hot coffee. Within a few days the children will have found playmates, Dot will be Kaffeeklatsching and sunbathing with the girls like an old timer, and Charlie . . . will be enrolled in the Court Poker Club.[15]

If the women of Park Forest worked outside the home, it might have been as a receptionist or clerk. Whyte quoted an official from the National Association of Manufacturers who was urging liberal arts educators to include some practical skills that would be useful at work: "statistics, accounting, mathematics generally; for girls—typing."[16] A good typist, presumably, could be quickly put to work for the limited time between her graduation and marriage, when she would leave the workforce to tend to house and home. Discrimination against married female teachers in the United States was not terminated until 1964, with the passing of the Civil Rights Act.

During his extended stays in Park Forest, Whyte also became friendly with the developer, Philip Klutznick. By the time Whyte arrived in Park Forest, Klutznick knew that disorganized, scattered development was not only bad land use but also bad business. He had purposely developed Park Forest to include mixed uses so that he could control the growth of each component. Whyte saw firsthand the value of cluster developments as a means of combating urban sprawl. He also determined that the physical layout of the streets and housing units mattered. Whyte, an empiricist since his Marine Corps days, charted every social note in the local paper for a three-and-a-half-year period, from New Year's Eve parties to potluck suppers; the addresses of civic association leaders; and the areas where children chose to play (which often were not—interestingly—the areas designated for play). "The more central one's location," he wrote, "the more social contacts one has."[17]

Stay-at-home moms were a critical element in the equation. Whyte had written an article for *Fortune* before *The Organization Man* that described the screening of wives in the employment process and the advent of "wife programs" to help women fit into the corporate culture. One subject of the article was so upset by the depiction that she shook Whyte when she met him later. He stood by his description of organizational demands.[18] When women weren't inside managing the home, they were often on the road, shepherding children to and from school and husbands to and from the train station. When the husband was transferred, the wife would supervise the relocation from one suburb to another.

The institutions that existed in accordance with the social ethic were not always perfect. As Whyte proposed in the introduction to *The Organization Man,* "in our attention to making organization work we have come close to deifying it. We are describing its defects as virtues and denying that there is—or should be—a conflict between the individual and organization. This denial is bad for the organization. It is worse for the individual."[19] As Whyte reaffirmed in the final chapter, "The organization man is not in the grip of vast social forces about which it is impossible for him to do anything; the options are there." Whyte called for the individual to resist the tempting idea that his interests and those of his institution or of society at large "can be wholly compatible": "Like the good society, the good organization encourages individual expression, and many have done so. But there always remains some conflict between the individual and The Organization. Is The Organization to be arbiter? The Organization will look to its own interest, but it will look to the individual's *only as The Organization interprets them.*"[20]

Organizations were particularly susceptible to what Whyte called "scientism." The promise of scientism was that the techniques used in the physical sciences could now be used to create an exact science of human behavior. The proponents, Whyte noted, always claimed they were getting closer to an exact science, even if they still weren't there. "Already we have learned some useful social techniques; we can measure personality, can spot the obstacles to good group dynamics, and predict communication response. But these are merely the beginning; if only we provide the time and money, before long we can unwrap the whole enigma with a unified science of man."[21] Whyte would be as skeptical of that claim today as he was then.

The belief had a scientific and a moral basis (neither one of which Whyte believed). The scientific basis was derived from experiments purportedly showing that people working together can produce results that exceed their capabilities as individuals. There was also a moral value: people working together in a group were believed to be more likely "to sublimate their egos" and "create a *harmonious* atmosphere in which the group will bring out the best in everyone."[22]

This science of "group dynamics" studied the ideal size of a group, the relationship between group morale and productivity, and what effect the group could have on one who deviates from the norm. Whyte questioned how well scientists, geniuses, and innovators—people who might have led the American team in the space race—fared in the world of the social ethic. He wrote that "thousands of studies and case histories have dwelled on fitting the individual to the group, but what about fitting the group to the person?"[23]

Scientism was particularly blatant in the use of psychological tests for making personnel decisions. Whyte acknowledged that companies could use an aptitude test "to measure the specific, isolated skills a man had, and as far as his subsequent performance was concerned, it could predict the future only if the man was magnificently endowed or abysmally deficient in a particular skill." But companies wanted more. Personality tests promised to reveal which job candidates would fit in best with the group and which current employees would remain loyal to the organization. In the 1950s consulting companies pounced on these opportunities. The Bernreuter Personality Inventory sold one million copies in 1953 but was panned in the *Journal of Social Psychology* as "fruitless."[24]

Whyte was so opposed to such personality tests that he included several sample tests in *The Organization Man* and counseled readers on how to "cheat" on the tests. His advice to test takers was to give the administrators what they wanted to hear. Whyte's strategy boiled down to two points:

1. When asked for word associations or comments about the world, give the most conventional, run-of-the-mill, pedestrian answer possible.

2. When in doubt about the most beneficial answer to any question, repeat to yourself:

I loved my father and my mother, but my father a little bit more.

I like things pretty much the way they are.

I never worry much about anything.

I don't care for books or music much.

I love my wife and children.

I don't let them get in the way of company work.[25]

Few books, and even fewer book titles, have so encapsulated an entire generation. *The Organization Man* is still a rare piece of literature with a title that also serves as a tagline for the contents. But even now, more than a half century later, the "organization man" remains an easy—but not necessarily accurate—description of the businessmen (and the few businesswomen) and corporate ethos of the 1950s, 1960s, and 1970s. Whyte's best-selling book featured a call to action—resist, organization man, resist! But Whyte's portrayal of the people who did not resist was more striking. It became the lasting image of the man in the organization, dressed in the cliché gray flannel suit.

* * *

The Organization Man, essentially a sociological study by an author with no formal training in the field, soon became a cultural landmark. The first review was inauspicious, not quite Kaputnik but not a blazing liftoff, either. In the *New York Times* Sunday Book Review sociologist C. Wright Mills dismissed *The Organization Man* as offering nothing new and described Whyte as an "earnest" Boy Scout who just "really isn't prepared." Five days after that negative review, the *Times* printed a second review in its regular news pages, in which Orville Prescott, the newspaper's well-respected book critic, praised *The Organization Man* as "a truly important book."[26]

The book soon gained traction in literary and academic circles. By the end of March 1957, the hardcover edition was number three on the best-seller lists of both the *New York Times* and the *New York Herald-Tribune*. Whyte's book jockeyed for position on the lists with *Day of*

Infamy by Walter Lord, also a member of Princeton University's Class of 1939. By the end of 1957, *The Organization Man* had been reissued in paperback by Doubleday Anchor Books (with typography by Edward Gorey, later known for his surrealistic illustrations and books). With its multiple printings, paperback editions, and foreign sales, most recently in China, the book has been both commercially successful and culturally influential. Sales have been estimated at over two million copies.[27]

The public's interest in Whyte's book may have been fueled by several related books. Sloan Wilson's novel *The Man in the Gray Flannel Suit* was published a year before *The Organization Man*, and the movie, starring Gregory Peck and Jennifer Jones, came out in 1956. As was the case with Whyte's ideal organization man—the one not lulled into obeisance by his company's beneficence—the hero in the flannel suit was not a robotic conformist. In fact, he was the one man who earned respect by standing up to his boss. But the public's impression soon coalesced in a less flattering image: the gray flannel suit was a hopeless conformist.[28]

In 1959 another author piggybacked on Whyte's success with a roman à clef titled *Life in the Crystal Palace*. The author, Alan Harrington, made clear his inspiration in a blurb on the front of the hardcover edition: "This unusual book explores the personal lives of people who work for great corporations. It begins where *The Organization Man* left off, vividly reporting the author's experiences. It says to those who yearn for perfect security: 'I've had it, and I gave it up.' And it tells why." Harrington, a 1939 Harvard graduate, worked for several years in the 1950s in public relations for Standard Oil (one of the original top ten on the Fortune 500 list). Harrington wrote of the enticements offered by the 1950s corporate world, including medical benefits, life insurance, and retirement plans, as well as some perks that were precursors of Silicon Valley: Ping-Pong tables, television in the cafeteria, and Muzak piped into the offices.[29]

By 1960 Whyte's opus was even the subject of a *Mad* magazine parody edition, *The Organization Mad*. The blurb on the back cover proclaimed, "Are you an Organization Man . . . who's sick of his organization? . . . Are you a conformist . . . who's tired of conforming? . . . Join the growing army of clods who've discovered *The Organization Mad*."

But anyone who bought it soon discovered that the contents had nothing to do with Whyte's best seller. The back cover conceded, "You'll blow your tops when you discover . . . that those sneaky little devils at MAD are trying to make a fast buck." Enough "clods" fell for the title that the *Mad* magazine version went into a ninth printing in 1963.

Whyte the newsman became Whyte the newsmaker. The conference circuit beckoned. On March 2, 1957, Whyte appeared at a symposium on higher education at Sarah Lawrence College along with Frederick Burkhardt, president of Bennington College; Roy Wilkins, executive director of the NAACP; and Robert M. Hutchins, longtime president and chancellor of the University of Chicago. On April 15, 1957, with the book firmly on best-seller lists, Whyte appeared at a conference sponsored by a liberal think tank, the Fund for the Republic, with Hutchins and Adolf Berle, the Franklin D. Roosevelt adviser credited with influencing much of the regulatory structure governing the modern corporation.

In the 1957 graduation season *The Organization Man* was a convenient touchstone for commencement speakers. The theologian Paul Tillich told graduates at the New School that "we hope for nonconformists among you, for your sake, for the sake of the nation, and for the sake of humanity." A. Whitney Griswold, president of Yale University, where Whyte's research began with that study of the Class of 1949, worried about a "nightmare picture of a whole generation of yes men." IBM's Thomas J. Watson Jr., speaking at the DePauw University graduation, compared organization men to jellyfish. Abram Sachar, president of Brandeis University, decried the "growing cult of yesmanship."

In April 1961 Whyte participated in a two-day conference sponsored by the Advertising Council. The subject was "the common good" and a consideration of "moral attitudes and the will to achievement of Americans." The other panelists were indicative of the company that Whyte, the best-selling author, was now keeping: Thurgood Marshall, then a judge on the US Court of Appeals (soon to be a US Supreme Court justice), and Eugene J. McCarthy, senator from Minnesota (soon to be a presidential candidate), among others. Even then, more than three years after the event, *Sputnik*, and the national self-examination that it triggered, lingered in the air. Whyte argued that the self-examination should apply to journalism, as well, and commented that the press was "too soft, rather than too hard, on our institutions." The press, argued Whyte, needed to look more critically at "good" institutions that had thus far escaped serious criticism, especially institutions involved in education, city planning, and urban renewal. As the author of *The Organization Man*, Whyte had built a powerful platform.[30]

As late as the spring of 1965, Whyte's book was still being promoted by the paperback publisher Doubleday Anchor. An ad in college newspapers recommended it as one of three books for students' summer reading. "Whether or not *The Organization Man* describes the kind of life you want to lead," the ad stated, "it is absorbing, important reading for anyone interested in American society as it is today."

The Organization Man had also struck a chord among the employees of corporate America. When Whyte's book came out in 1956, Charles E. Little was working at a Madison Avenue advertising agency. He looked into the pages of *The Organization Man* and saw himself. Little quit the ad agency, went into the nonprofit world, and in the 1960s became executive director of an open space advocacy group. Whom did he discover on the board? Whyte. Over drinks at a Manhattan bar, Little found the moment to share Whyte's impact on his personal career path. "Don't ever say that again, Little," Whyte replied in his typically self-effacing tone. "I am not going to be responsible for whatever dumb choices you make."[31]

Amid all these reactions, the institutional establishment became defensive. At the annual meeting of the American Public Health Association on October 29, 1958, J. Donald Kingsley, executive director of the Community Council of Greater New York, accused Whyte of reversing cause and effect in his argument. Big organizations were simply reflecting broad social forces, not creating those forces. But Kingsley ended up agreeing more than disagreeing with Whyte's tenets. Human and public relations, Kingsley conceded, were both part of "scientific management" programs that were "neither scientific nor contributing to good management." Getting lost in this shuffle, Kingsley added, were "the productive individualist, the unusually gifted, and those who would rather be right than be loved." Just as Whyte did in *The Organization Man*, Kingsley concluded his case by calling on "productive individualists" to help create dynamic and creative organizations. "Institutions are only changed from within."[32]

In a book of essays published in 1959, *The Corporation in Modern Society*, a Harvard dean, Edward Mason, defended the fact that "innovation at the hands of the small-scale inventor and individual entrepreneur has given way to organized research." Mason, of Harvard's public policy school, added that "the rugged individualist has been supplanted by smoothly efficient corporate executives participating in the group decision."[33]

In 1963 a contributor to the *Harvard Business Review* attempted to spare big organizations from the charge that their size alone is the determining factor in producing the "cautious, conforming, security-conscious middle manager"—the epitome of the much-maligned organization man. The author, Lyman W. Porter, would eventually be a leading scholar in the field of organizational behavior. Acknowledging that Whyte's book "never says, in so many words, that the 'organization man' resides only in large companies," Porter noted that Whyte created the impression that "a disproportionate number of organization men are to be found in large rather than small companies." A better approach, Porter asserted, would have been to judge firms by their operational "work units." On the basis of various studies and surveys, Porter concluded that "big companies need not be apologetic either for their bigness or for their effects on their managers." If asked to respond, Whyte might well have agreed—subjugating the individual to the group was the real problem, regardless of the group's size.[34]

But some business analysts acknowledged that Whyte's arguments had merit. In 1967, writing in the *Academy of Management Journal*, Roosevelt University business professor Earl B. French noted that "perhaps no book has created more controversy in management and intellectual circles" than Whyte's *The Organization Man*. French found some truth in Whyte's allegation that "success within organizational life is more related to one's personality characteristics or interpersonal competence than to knowledge and technical skills." French cited a 1954 study of 149 firms hiring scientists and engineers straight from college. For 80 percent of those firms, personality was considered more important than training, work experience, or college grades. Another study, published in 1961, showed that highly productive bench scientists (as measured by published scientific articles) were rated as uncooperative and inflexible by their managers. French noted that several major technical break-throughs, including the US Navy's sidewinder missile, IBM's stretch computer memory, and Polaroid film, were achieved by individuals who had ignored management orders to stop work on the projects.[35]

In 1966 and 1967 the Motorola corporation ran a series of four-teen full-page ads in the student newspapers of Ivy League and other elite colleges featuring a dialogue with Motorola chairman Robert W. Galvin and somewhat skeptical college undergraduates. The ad cam-paign began with a Cornell University student citing the continued use of personality tests in the hiring process (a practice criticized in Whyte's book) as evidence that corporations were not really interested in their new hires as individuals. "Does business want the student for the creativity of his mind or for the conformity of his personality?" the student asked the executive. A decade after the publication of Whyte's book, Galvin did not attempt to wholly reject the thesis of *The Orga-nization Man*.

I think it's unfortunate that William Whyte's *The Organization Man* is often regarded by students as the final word on corporate life. It's not. . . . However, I do think Mr. Whyte sounded a valid warning. . . . We live in a complex society where technical advances tend to outrun social advances. At the moment, it may be easier to mass produce thinking machines than thinking men. . . .

It's a problem that concerns men everywhere. At the moment you're worried about what happens in a corporation. Many of us are worried about what happens to the computer-carded students at our over-crowded colleges and universities. There would be little constructive purpose to this dialogue if business wanted conformity. We don't. We want young men who will question the obvious, and the obsolete, and will back up their words with positive suggestions for change. We want men who won't accept the corporate structure just because it's there; who will know when it's time to reach out for a change.[36]

Galvin's response to the college student was remarkably nuanced, possibly because he himself was an example of an organization man who had taken a company that he was literally born into (his father and uncle cofounded Motorola) and shaped it into one of the leading technology companies of its time. "If it's intuitive, it's probably wrong," Galvin once said. He was clearly an example of the executive who knew, as Whyte observed, "there are times when he very well ought *not* to get along."[37]

Chapter 7

The Exploding Metropolis—
Discovering Jane Jacobs

I f you were a student at Harvard University in the early 1950s and wanted to major in urban design, Harvard might not have known what to do with you. There was not yet a program at Harvard in urban design. But change was imminent. In April 1956 the Harvard Graduate School of Design hosted a two-day conference to consider a "new science" of city planning. The school's dean, José Luis Sert, a protégé of the visionary French-Swiss architect Le Corbusier, invited a constellation of big thinkers, including architects and designers Richard Neutra, György Kepes, and Victor Gruen; planners such as Philadelphia's Edmund Bacon; landscape architects, among them Hideo Sasaki; and also architectural critics, led by the *New Yorker*'s Lewis Mumford and the editor of the influential Time Inc. publication *Architectural Forum*, Douglas Haskell.[1]

But just weeks before the conference, Haskell's schedule changed. He ran the name of a possible substitute past the design school's Jaqueline Tyrwhitt, who was organizing the event. Aware that Tyrwhitt (a rare female architect) would mean at least one woman in attendance, Haskell presented his suggestion judiciously (in the context of those male chauvinist times). "If another woman would not be out of place, might I suggest that a substitute be Mrs. Robert Jacobs—Jane Jacobs on our masthead."[2]

The invitation was sent to "Mrs." Jacobs, who was not just her husband's wife but also an accomplished writer with several pieces on city redevelopment already published in *Architectural Forum*. Jane Jacobs had recently realized that she had been "in very cozy with the planners and project builders." She soon recognized, however, that there was something wrong with the glistening new streets the planners and developers had created: they were devoid of people.[3] At the Harvard conference Jacobs did not cozy up to anyone. She asserted that many projects then underway threatened the creative core of the city. Some attendees were "unsettled." Many others were impressed. Lewis Mumford, the *New Yorker* critic, called Jacobs "a person to be reckoned with" and "a new kind of 'expert.'"[4]

William H. Whyte would later write that he "kept hearing about this Jane Jacobs." He met with her in New York and "was mightily impressed. I thought she was a real genius. But the curious thing was that she had never really written anything long. Originally, she said she wasn't up to writing a major piece."[5] Whyte may have leaped to that conclusion because until the Harvard conference, Jacobs had not been given bylines for her in-depth articles in accordance with *Architectural Forum*'s policy. But it soon became clear that Jacobs and Whyte were both willing to reexamine cities in a way that would run counter to a long-standing mindset at *Fortune* and elsewhere. In doing so they would be the prime contributors to a collection of essays published in the magazine in 1958 and later that year as a book titled *The Exploding Metropolis*. Living up to the provocative subtitle of its first edition, *A Study of the Assault on Urbanism and How Our Cities Can Resist It*, the book would lay out the challenges of the urban agenda that continue in the twenty-first century.

*   *   *

The Exploding Metropolis began, in characteristic Whyte style, with a simple declarative sentence: "This is a book by people who like cities." In 1958 it was a sentiment worth stating, since the prevailing mindset about cities—at *Fortune* and elsewhere—was not always so affectionate. In 1942 *Fortune* initiated an unusual series of pamphlets outlining how America should respond when the economy shifted back to a peacetime mode. *Fortune* identified Syracuse in upstate New York as a representative city with which the magazine could organize a postwar planning effort. *Fortune* commissioned a panel, including the president of the American Institute of Planners and an economist from the American Bankers Association, to consult with the city. The city in turn opened the planning process to the magazine's reporters. *Fortune* and its appointed experts concluded that Syracuse was beset by problems: "There isn't enough air, enough sun, enough open space in our big cities. There isn't enough privacy and what there is costs too much. There's too much noise. There is too much bustle and agitation, too little peace, dignity, and human warmth," the *Fortune* editors wrote in May 1943. One sign of the decline, according to *Fortune*: Sears Roebuck had relocated from downtown to the outskirts of town. The suburbs were beginning to rise.[6]

By the mid-1950s cities faced more problems. The postwar baby boom had triggered a housing boom in the cities' suburbs. Discriminatory lending practices helped create a White flight from the cities to those suburbs. The Interstate Highway System, launched in 1956, helped facilitate that flight. In many cities planners chose "urban renewal" as the quick and easy way to clear slums and blighted economic districts.

The Exploding Metropolis turned out to be in some ways a logical extension of Whyte's reporting for *The Organization Man*. For that book Whyte had immersed himself in the new "packaged community" of Park Forest, Illinois, and had met Philip Klutznick, a developer with an appreciation for the consequences of his work. Whyte's examination of cities and suburbs was also steeped in themes he had explored in his first two books: the importance of laymen interacting with the experts and the continuing inclination of the experts to be seduced by groupthink and "scientism."

The urban landscape also had all the elements of a good story: The field of study was so new that the experts were even wrangling over what to call it—"civic design" had been one phrase, but it was giving way to "urban design." The subject was already in the headlines. Urban renewal projects were in high gear, spurred by the Housing Act of 1954. Study of the urban landscape had also been based on alarming premises: density was bad, crowded cities were unhealthy; people on streets were to be feared; motor vehicle traffic had to be expedited. But most of these premises had never really been examined closely.

With cities, as with organizations, there was one view from the top down and another from the bottom up. Just as Whyte had gained insight into the corporate world by hanging out with the housewives of middle managers in their suburban neighborhoods, so too would he benefit by studying cities from the point of view of the people living and working in them, including passersby on the sidewalks, and not just from the point of view of planners sitting at their drawing boards.

Whyte's multipart series on urban issues in *Fortune* in 1958 challenged the assumptions and explored all possibilities of urban planning, including those not in favor with the experts. To write the articles that would become chapters in the book, Whyte turned to several *Fortune* colleagues: Francis Bello, who contributed "The City and the Car"; Seymour Freedgood, for "New Strength in City Hall"; and Daniel Seligman, for "The Enduring Slums." In addition, Whyte turned to two outside writers. One was Grady Clay, the highly respected real estate editor of the *Louisville Courier-Journal* (who would later be the editor of *Landscape Architecture* magazine). The other was that *Architectural Forum* writer who had "unsettled" the Harvard Graduate School of Design conference in 1956—Jane Jacobs.

By Whyte's account in the preface to the 1993 edition of *The Exploding Metropolis*, several of his *Fortune* colleagues did not think Jacobs could be trusted with the assignment. "She was a female, she was untried, having never written anything longer than several paragraphs. She lived in the West Village and commuted to work on a bicycle." Odder yet, she smoked a pipe in the office. But Whyte stuck with Jacobs, and she responded with a first draft of fourteen thousand words and then argued for "not a word to be cut." (It ended up running at about six thousand words.) "Our lamb had become a tigress," Whyte observed.

The appearance of the Jacobs article in *Fortune* shocked the magazine's publisher, C. D. Jackson. He was particularly upset by Jacobs's criticism of the recently announced Lincoln Center redevelopment, a pet project of the Rockefellers and other wealthy patrons whom the *Fortune* publisher would not want to alienate. Jackson called the *Fortune* office while traveling back from Washington, DC. "My God, who was this crazy dame?" the publisher demanded to know.[7]

But Jacobs's unconventional thinking turned out to be remarkably in line with Whyte's. They both championed the involvement of the layman as much as, or more than, the expert. An unbylined *Fortune* editorial (with an unmistakable Whyte tone) in February 1958 identified the role of laymen in city planning.

> In preparing its articles on "The Exploding Metropolis" . . . FORTUNE has had reason to become impressed with the job the many different kinds of experts—the architects, the city planners, traffic engineers, and the like—are doing to reshape the U.S. city. It has become even more impressed, however, with the layman. As any student of the city can find out by walking its streets, there is a surprisingly close relationship between the appearance of a city and the degree to which the layman has been involved in its plans.
>
> Not so many years ago . . . [i]f something needed doing in the city, the layman knew very well it wouldn't get done unless he saw to it himself, and he was not inhibited by a lack of expertise. In these seemingly more complex times, however, the citizen is apt to feel it's all too much for him and that anyway, what with the great number of planning commissions, study groups, and professionals of one kind or another, the job is best left to experts. This is not, alas, the case.[8]

Jacobs, who just a few years before had reported on the experts' view with a mixture of awe and admiration, had revisited her views. When she wrote her April 1958 essay for *Fortune* titled "Downtown Is for People," she expressed grave reservations about the experts' work and called for the citizenry to become involved.

> This is a critical time for the future of the city. . . . Great tracts, many blocks wide, are being razed. . . . Almost every big city is getting ready to build, and the plans will soon be set.

What will the projects look like? . . . They will be clean, impressive, and monumental. They will have all the attributes of a well-kept, dignified cemetery.

The remarkable intricacy and liveliness of downtown can never be created by the abstract logic of a few men. . . . Planners and architects have a vital contribution to make, but the citizen has a more vital one. It is his city, after all; his job is not merely to sell plans made by others, it is to get into the thick of the planning job himself.[9]

Fortune printed Jacobs's piece along with a sidebar by Clay, the real estate editor, titled "What Makes a Good Square Good." The criteria for a livable city, as set forth by Whyte and his *Fortune* colleagues in 1958, were almost diametrically opposed to what had been set forth by *Fortune* in its feature on Syracuse, New York, in 1943. Then the editors had talked about seeking dignity. In 1958 Jacobs feared that cities would end up with dignity in the manner of a well-kept cemetery, not a vibrant social center.

Doubleday published *The Exploding Metropolis* just six months after the final magazine article appeared in *Fortune*. As was the case with Whyte's first two books, *The Exploding Metropolis* received a double dose of reviews in the *New York Times*. In the Sunday Book Review, Harrison E. Salisbury, who had won the Pulitzer Prize in 1955, called it "an inquisitive and iconoclastic study" of both the "expansion and disintegration" of the metropolis and the land around it. Salisbury praised the book's inventory of the problems facing the country but had less praise for the remedies offered. On the other hand, Salisbury conceded, some of the problems were virtually intractable. He quoted a line from Whyte's introduction: "More and more, the city is becoming a place of extremes—a place for the very poor, or the very rich, or the slightly odd."[10]

Four days later *New York Times* reviewer Charles Poore had a different take. "This is a memorable, matched set of probing, hard-hitting . . . articles by the editors of *Fortune*." The book, Poore continued, "should cause blood pressure to rise in groups of city planners who, in the opinions of the editors, think more of the geometric proportions of their dreams than of the human beings who must live and work and try to play in their bleak arrangements of monumental filing cases." While *The Exploding Metropolis* gave an "exhilarating sense of manifest—and unmanifest—destiny to life on our cluttered, dynamic share of the planet," Poore wrote, it was also likely to seem "quaint" in a hundred years.[11]

Other critics viewed the book as alarmingly relevant. British architectural critic Ian Nairn compared *The Exploding Metropolis* to "the first blink of the fire-warning light in the aircraft cockpit."[12] Even though Grady Clay had written a sidebar for *The Exploding Metropolis*, he nevertheless reviewed the finished book in the July 1959 issue of *Horizon* magazine. "As can be well imagined, in these days of near-compulsory suburban migration, the city-proud are passionate advocates of what they believe to be a just but lonely cause. Perhaps for this reason, their most eloquent spokesmen have been found, not among city planners, but among sociologists, architectural critics, and journalists. Some of their most powerful statements can be found in an outspoken little book, *The Exploding Metropolis*."

Thirty-five years later, in 1993, writing the foreword to a reissued version of the book, Sam Bass Warner Jr., an urban historian and professor at Brandeis University, called *The Exploding Metropolis* "the spearhead of today's counter movements for urban preservation and environmentally sound urban design." To Warner a section called "The All-Class Community" was an "urban manifesto." In that section Whyte asserted that, despite the negative image of the city, "many couples maintain that the city can be a *better* place to raise children than suburbia. In the city, they believe, the children are brought up in an environment closer to reality; it is one geared to adults, not children, and unlike the one-class communities of the new suburbia, it exposes children to all kinds of people, colored and white, old and young, poor and rich." Whyte would repeat this theme in his work on the 1969 master plan for New York and in his 1988 book, *City: Rediscovering the Center*.

Then, as he would now, Whyte saw a need for the public to become more involved in the planning process. Writing in the mid-1950s, Whyte complained that newspapers were "generally uncritical of the institutional design." Critics then apparently had the same feeling as critics today when they question a developer's proposal that will impact the public realm. "Most of the civic leaders have been lined up to support the project and thus to question the design is bad manners at the least." The critic becomes the skunk at the garden party or is summarily dismissed as a NIMBY.[13]

Then, as he would now, Whyte saw the need for firsthand observation. "Looking at models and bird's-eye renderings gives no clues," Whyte wrote in 1958. "To borrow the refrain of the concluding chapter [Jacobs's chapter], you have to get out and walk."[14]

Reflecting Whyte's interest in the details of governance, *The Exploding Metropolis* included a chapter on the mechanics of municipal government by Seymour Freedgood. Here *Fortune* pointed out more issues that linger to this day: the conflicts between cities and suburbs; the relative benefits of mayor/council and city manager forms of government; the pros and cons of the civil service system; the challenges of funding mass transit; the need for a mayor or manager to work closely with a city planner if the latter is to accomplish anything. Well before Robert Moses became the favorite whipping boy of urban advocates, and a few years before Jane Jacobs joined the forces fighting Moses's plans for Washington Square Park and Lower Manhattan, *The Exploding Metropolis* identified Moses as the man who held no fewer than ten jobs in New York City and State, including chairman of two authorities. The New York Port Authority, Freedgood charged, did not set its policies on the basis of the interests "of the whole public, or of the interest of the whole area, including the needs of New York City. It makes its decisions in terms of its own, more limited public—i.e., the auto driver who keeps it going with his tolls, and the bond market."[15]

Today, more than sixty years after its original publication, *The Exploding Metropolis* seems far from "quaint," despite the prediction of the *New York Times* reviewer in 1958. If a modern-day advocate of sustainable urbanism wanted to create an action plan for his or her mission, *The Exploding Metropolis* would touch on most important strategies for dealing with both the cities and the suburbs. For a history course focused on urban issues in the second half of the twentieth century, *The Exploding Metropolis* could be a starting point. The book touches on most major issues in urban planning at that time, which are still relevant today.

Suburban sprawl. In the chapter titled "Urban Sprawl," Whyte pointed out that the Federal Highway Act of 1956 gave state highway engineers power to locate the forty-one thousand miles of new interstate highways, and their interchanges, wherever they wanted them to be. Coordination between the state engineers and the city planners, Whyte argued, "will be a positive force for good land use."[16]

The costs of urban renewal. Whyte decried the public housing projects towering over recently bulldozed neighborhoods. They were "the wrong design in the wrong place at the wrong time." The massive redevelopment projects in the nation's cities were "the concrete manifestation—and how literally—of a deep, and at times arrogant, misunderstanding of the function of the city." (The infamous Pruitt-Igoe housing project in St. Louis was completed two years before Whyte's comment. Demolition of the thirty-three towers began in 1972.)[17]

Unintended consequences of cars. "Redevelopers have taken the suburban shopping-center approach . . . and have planned for the driver, rather than the pedestrian," Whyte wrote. He forecast that the affordability of housing would be linked to its proximity to transportation, specifically highways. "As suburbia expands, furthermore, the journey to work is going to be a longer one for many people, new highways or no, and the compensations less."[18]

Long before "induced demand" came into vogue as a transportation planning term, Francis Bello, in his chapter "The City and the Car," described what he called the "most surprising" fact about car traffic: "Traffic seems to flow at just about the same speed everywhere, regardless of the size of the city, its age, its geographical assets or handicaps, the number of its expressways, or the cleverness of its traffic engineers." A similar reality concerned parking. "No city ever seems to have enough."[19] Bello's chapter could be reprinted word for word today and seem remarkably relevant.

Missing middle housing. The phrase did not exist then, but *The Exploding Metropolis* put its finger on the concept, which is still plaguing cities today: "The city is not for the average now; and the way things are going it is not likely to be so in the future. . . . In one key respect, 'middle income' projects are unsatisfactory: middle-income people can't afford them."[20]

The value of regional planning. Freedgood's chapter on city hall looked beyond the city limits, especially in terms of transportation planning. "Problems are area-wide, not city-wide," Freedgood argued, "and their solution, if there is to be a solution, will require cooperation between the city government and all other governments in the metropolitan area . . . and the cooperation of the state and federal governments as well."[21]

The Exploding Metropolis missed one issue. Critics, writing with the twenty-twenty hindsight created by the civil rights revolution of the 1960s, noted that *The Exploding Metropolis* failed to recognize the race issue in urban affairs. The book did acknowledge the disadvantages of non-White Americans. But it assumed that Blacks would do what immigrant groups had done in the past—assimilate, educate, and elevate themselves into the middle class. The root cause of the racial problem was believed to be more economic than racial. Raise the standard of living, through education and job training, and most of the problems would go away. The idea of institutional discrimination and racism was not foremost in the minds of Whyte, Jacobs, or the other contributors.

That blind spot notwithstanding, *The Exploding Metropolis* planted the seeds of urban thinking that would blossom throughout the rest of the twentieth century and into the twenty-first. As Warner pointed out in his 1993 foreword to *The Exploding Metropolis*, Americans may not have acted on every recommendation in the book, but the agenda had been set. And people certainly did begin to listen to the two leading contributors: Whyte and Jacobs.

Whyte's chapter on urban sprawl led to his next major area of interest, open space preservation. It also brought Whyte's work to the attention of the Rockefeller brothers, with whom he was about to begin a long-term relationship. And it established his credentials as an authoritative writer in the field of urban design. A decade later, when the New York City Planning Commission was looking for someone to stitch together a controversial and groundbreaking master plan, it turned to Holly Whyte. The author of *The Organization Man* had become the observation man, with an ability to recognize what worked and what didn't in urban spaces and to envision specific ways public policy could be tailored to meet the public need.

Jacobs's chapter, "Downtown Is for People," had been one of the high points of the *Fortune* magazine series. Shortly after it came out, Whyte corresponded with Douglas Haskell, her editor at *Architectural Forum*, who had "loaned" Jacobs to *Fortune* for the project. Whyte jotted a note by hand at the top of a seven-page collection of excerpts from thirty positive letters in response to Jacobs's article. "Look at what your girl did for us!" Whyte (a year younger than Jacobs) wrote to Haskell. "This is one of the best responses we have ever had."[22]

The best response of all, Whyte concluded in the preface to the 1993 edition of *The Exploding Metropolis*, was the call from the Rockefeller Foundation asking whether Jacobs would accept a grant to expand the chapter into a full-length book. "Yes, she would. Thus, *The Death and Life of Great American Cities*." Chadbourne Gilpatric, the associate director of the foundation with a special interest in urban issues, met with Jacobs a month after "Downtown Is for People" appeared in print. She told him of her hopes to take a leave from *Architectural Forum* and write a book that expanded on the themes in her *Fortune* article. She figured she would need nine months to complete the project and hoped that Rockefeller could support her with a $10,000 grant, about $85,000 in today's money.

Meanwhile Whyte joined sociologist and critic Nathan Glazer, who had just written a piece for *Architectural Forum* on city planners, in urging Jacobs to also get a book contract for her as-yet-untitled work. A few weeks later, in August 1958, Whyte provided another helpful endorsement. At the time Whyte was dealing with his career dilemma at *Fortune* and with the death of his father. Whyte also had taken on another writing project: an expansion of his *Fortune* piece on urban sprawl for the Urban Land Institute. Nonetheless Whyte took time to advocate for Jacobs's project: "I believe the result may prove to be one of the great contributions to the whole field of urban planning and design," he wrote to Gilpatric.[23]

In the summer of 1959, when the writing was taking longer than expected and she needed more money, Jacobs invoked her friend Whyte in her defense. In writing *The Organization Man*, she told Gilpatric, Whyte also had "got himself and the work bolluxed up at one point." Whyte gave another assurance to the Rockefellers: "Quite frankly I was happy to hear that she wants to spend more time on the book. . . . I wholeheartedly recommend the additional assistance for the extra time she wants to give the book. I believe a great and influential book is in the making." Jacobs got another $8,000.[24]

In June 1961, Random House circulated prepublication copies of the book to such literary figures as Gore Vidal, Dwight Macdonald, Edmund Wilson, and Whyte, who did not restrain himself in his praise. In a handwritten letter to Jacobs in October of that year he wrote:

> Jane—TERRIFIC! *You did it* and I can't wait to hear the . . . yells and churlish comments of the fraternity [no doubt referring to the professional planners and critics skewered by Jacobs's analysis]. I'm only part way through it but I can see that it's going to be one of the most remarkable books *ever* written about the city and probably the best in this century. (And it's fun to read!)[25]

Jacobs would write nine more books and be the subject of three biographies (including two published in 2016, a hundred years after her birth). Her magazine articles, interviews, and speeches have been the basis for two collections of writings. She appears at or near number one on lists of most influential urbanists. It is a rare book on urbanism or cities or twentieth-century history that does not have Jacobs's name in the index.

As Jacobs noted in the foreword to the 1992 Modern Library Edition of *Death and Life*, her book had become "subversive," exposing the "unworkability and joylessness of anti-city visions." But, she noted, she was not alone in that role. "Other authors and researchers—notably William H. Whyte—were also exposing the unworkability and joylessness of anti-city visions."

Whyte praised Jacobs and her work in a blurb that appeared on the back cover of the Vintage Book paperback edition of *Death and Life*, also published in 1992. "One of the most remarkable books ever written about the city, . . . a *primary* work. The research apparatus is not pretentious—it is the eye and the heart—but it has given us a magnificent study of what gives life and spirit to the city."

Whyte and Jacobs possessed remarkably complementary skills.

Jacobs's books soared with lyrical descriptions of physical spaces and theoretical ideas. Her example of the role an ordinary grocery store plays on an urban block captivated her highbrow audience at the Harvard conference on urban design. The "eyes on the street" in a mixed-use neighborhood and the "sidewalk ballet" below her Greenwich Village window became lasting and instructive images of good urbanism. But she balked at more rigorous empirical studies. At Whyte's suggestion, Jacobs met Herbert Gans; the sociologist showed Jacobs around Boston's North End, which became a focal point in *Death and Life*. While in Boston Jacobs also met with some faculty members from the Massachusetts Institute of Technology and Harvard. She later recounted that they treated her like a graduate student. "What they actually wanted me to do was make up some questionnaire and give it to people in some middle-income sterile project somewhere, to find out what they didn't like. Then I was to make tables of it." Jacobs was horrified at the thought.[26]

Whyte, on the other hand, reveled in tables, charts, graphs, and empirical studies, dating back to his days in Marine Corps intelligence. For *The Organization Man* he drew up diagrams of the street configurations in Park Forest, Illinois, and charted which units had the most social activities. In the 1970s his Street Life Project used detailed charts—and even questionnaires of the sort that horrified Jacobs—to plot the use of public spaces (chapter 13).

The book project that brought Whyte and Jacobs together, *The Exploding Metropolis*, also drove them apart in the eyes of some Jacobs followers. In the preface to the 1993 edition of *The Exploding Metropolis*, Whyte reflected on Jacobs's involvement. When Whyte first approached her, he recalled, "she demurred and told me she wasn't up to it. She had never written anything longer than a few paragraphs." As a staff member at *Fortune*'s sister publication, *Architectural Forum*, Jacobs mainly wrote captions, Whyte continued. Her "real work" was fighting the redevelopment efforts of Robert Moses and his Lower Manhattan Expressway project.[27]

The facts do not support Whyte's assessment in the 1993 account. Whyte could possibly be forgiven for writing that Jacobs's "real work" at the time was fighting Robert Moses and his many projects. In fact in 1958 she was only marginally involved in the celebrated fight to save Washington Square—a commemorative plaque in the square does not mention Jacobs. But she did move to the front lines in the late 1960s when she joined other protesters opposing Moses's proposed Lower Manhattan Expressway. By 1993 it might have seemed that Jane Jacobs had been fighting Moses forever.

As for Whyte taking a chance on an untested caption writer, Whyte himself (or his editor) would need only turn to the first chapter of the reissued *Exploding Metropolis* to find Whyte's reference to Jacobs's appearance at the 1956 Harvard conference. Whyte also quoted three sentences directly from her June 1956 article in *Architectural Forum*—far more than a mere caption—that presented the core of her viewpoint that so upset the establishment.

Whyte's apparent put-down of Jacobs has been a source of recurrent discussion by biographers of Jacobs, leaving a lingering impression that Whyte, the Princeton-educated and presumably privileged editor, and Jacobs, the self-educated Greenwich Village housewife, were rivals in the field of urbanism. It is true that while Jacobs was protesting Robert Moses's policies, Whyte might well have been at 30 Rockefeller Center, working with the Rockefellers, or socializing with other writers and artists at the Century Association club. While Jacobs was taking to the streets to advocate for her causes (and eventually would move her family to Canada to take her sons out of range of the Vietnam War–era military draft), Whyte was working within the system, rewriting land use polices, open space laws, and zoning codes.

But for all their style differences, Jacobs and Whyte came to their studies of urban life from similar backgrounds. Both grew up in comfortable middle-class homes in walkable neighborhoods in relatively small cities. Jacobs and Whyte were remarkably unified in their vision of an ideal city. They both looked first at the city as a pedestrian would. They both were leery of bird's-eye views and the experts who relied on them. They were complementary—not competitive—in the way they processed what they saw and the way they communicated their work to the world.

So how did Whyte get it so wrong in 1993, especially after being so prescient about Jacobs's work in 1958?

He possibly got caught up in the heroic dimensions of her public image as it developed after her landmark book. Peter Laurence, in *Becoming Jane Jacobs*, wrote that "the notion that Jacobs was primarily a housewife with unusual abilities" dates back to her arrival in the public spotlight in the 1960s.[28] That mythology was even stronger in the 1990s, when Whyte wrote the foreword to the 1993 edition of *The Exploding Metropolis*. By expanding on that myth, Whyte made himself a hero. Another biographer, Robert Kanigel, author of *Eyes on the Street: The Life of Jane Jacobs*, suggested that "perhaps depicting a callow Jane Jacobs made for a story more fun to tell."[29]

Whyte had a history of tailoring facts to fit a fun story. He reminisced that he had been beaten up as the "smallest and newest" boy at St. Andrew's, but a class photo shows him a head taller than many of the boys. At his commencement address at St. Andrew's School in 1946 he claimed to be a young man with no certain future (even though he was about to report to his new job in New York in a few days). As a young reporter at *Fortune* magazine, he liked to say, he was so unqualified that he was kept on only as an example for other reporters of how not to write. In fact, within ten years at *Fortune* Whyte was assistant managing editor and a best-selling author.

In addition to loving great stories, Whyte loved "characters," such as the black sheep of his extended family, his uncle Joe Price. Later Whyte celebrated the street people of New York and defended the rights of street musicians. So, when Whyte in 1993 recalled his interaction with Jacobs in the late 1950s, that was another part of her story that he could romanticize. She lived in the West Village and commuted to work on a bicycle.

But on the great questions of their time, from urban design issues to broad social concerns, Whyte and Jacobs echoed each other's work. In 1980 Jacobs created an iconic moment that resonated with both the feminist movement and the urbanist community. Jacobs and developer James Rouse appeared together at the Boston Great Cities Conference. Someone asked whether cities should be developed with inspiring visions and sweeping plans or with incremental change and small steps.

Rouse answered by quoting the legendary architect Daniel Burnham, who designed the 1893 world's fair in Chicago and the plan for the National Mall and Union Station in Washington, DC: "Make no little plans, for they have no magic to stir men's blood."

Jacobs had an immediate retort: "Funny, big plans never stirred women's blood. Women have always been willing to consider little plans." The audience erupted in applause.[30]

Jacobs's response also registered with the growing army of men and women fighting to protect the urban environment. A similar point had been made more than twenty years earlier in *The Exploding Metropolis*: "Little plans, lots of them, are just what are needed—high-rise and low, small blocks and superblocks, and let the free market tell its story."[31] The author of that passage was Holly Whyte.

Whyte was no feminist, but he was clearly in tune with Jane Jacobs and—eventually—a growing tide of conservationists, environmentalists, and urbanists. In the 1960s, as Jacobs was energizing the urban movement, and continuing to maintain the barricades against the heavy-handed development of Robert Moses and his ilk, Holly Whyte was poring over regulations for open space easements, highway safety data, cluster housing ordinances, tax assessments, and zoning incentives offered in exchange for privately owned public spaces. Rather than fighting developers tooth and nail, Whyte on occasion met them halfway, often with an introduction from a powerful new ally and an eventual lifelong sponsor, Laurance Rockefeller.

Chapter 8

With Laurance Rockefeller, Conservationist Turned Environmentalist

y 1959 William H. Whyte had left the cozy confines of *Fortune*
magazine and Time Inc. Officially he was on a leave of absence
from the organization, which had hired him with no prior experience as a professional journalist and had given him so many opportunities in just twelve years' time. Unofficially he had no plans to
return. But one of Whyte's last articles for *Fortune*, "Urban Sprawl,"
reverberated for years to come. As a freelancer, Whyte expanded on
the subject in a *Life* magazine article, "A Plan to Save Vanishing U.S.
Countryside," published on August 17, 1959. In September the Urban
Land Institute issued Whyte's sixty-seven-page "technical bulletin"
based on a year's worth of research. Titled "Securing Open Space for
Urban America: Conservation Easements," the bulletin advanced the
idea that the common-law device of easements could be the linchpin
for preserving vast swaths of open space.

Holly Whyte was no longer just the celebrated author of the best-
selling *The Organization Man*. By the age of just forty-two he also had
impressive credentials in land use and conservation. Whyte's career
was at a crossroads. But which would he be: the expert on organizations and their inner workings or the advocate for open space? And,

equally important, who would underwrite his work? Two deep-pocketed choices loomed: the Ford Foundation and the Rockefellers.

An old friend at the Fund for the Republic, a foundation formed
in 1951 by the Ford Foundation to counteract the rampant propaganda
of the McCarthy era, recognized Whyte's multifaceted professional
life. In the fall of 1959 that friend, W. H. "Ping" Ferry, had an idea he
hoped would lead Whyte down the path of an organizational and institutional analyst. At the time the fund was changing its name to the
Center for the Study of Democratic Institutions and was relocating
from New York to sunny Santa Barbara, California. In November 1959,
Ferry wrote the following to Whyte:

Dear Holly:

Sorry you had to miss the party on November 19, far and away
the best yet. Arthur Burns [Columbia University professor, chair of
the Council of Economic Advisers during the Eisenhower administration, and later chairman of the Federal Reserve Board] was in
rare voice, full of revolutionary ideas.

What are you now, anyway? Private eye? Pundit? Consultant?
Are you available?

What I have most on my mind is getting a sharp profile of the
automobile industry. There is plenty of stuff on individual actors,
plenty on the separate companies. But no one yet has tried an appraisal of the entire industry. I can write quite a lot on this subject,
but I won't do so unless you betray at least a spark of interest. . . . The
job itself could be of historic importance.

If you are otherwise occupied, which I hope you are not, you
might send me some suggestions. . . . Several people at Harvard
Business School have been recommended to me, but I am afraid
they are infected with the Business History virus.

As long as you aren't writing for *Fortune* anymore, why live in
New York? Why not live in Santa Barbara?[1]

The Fund for the Republic had its sights on Whyte since at least
1957. While *The Organization Man* was still rising on the best-seller
list, Whyte received a hefty $5,000 award (about $45,000 in today's

money) from the American Library Association—an award under-written by the fund. At various foundation events Whyte had net-worked with Robert Hutchins, the University of Chicago president who served as the first president of the fund, and Adolf Berle, the New Deal economist who in 1957 had written a paper for the fund titled "Economic Power and the Free Society." The fund had also asked Whyte to consult on a study of the modern corporation's impact on freedom and justice.

When Ferry made his proposal to Whyte, the automotive industry sat on top of the corporate world. General Motors was number 1 on the 1955 Fortune 500 list, the first of *Fortune* magazine's now iconic annual surveys. Ford was somehow missed in the 1955 survey but appeared as number 3 on the 1956 list. Chrysler was number 6 in 1955. There was certainly "plenty of stuff" to report on. Earlier in 1959 Alfred P. Sloan Jr. had completed his two-volume memoir, *My Years with General Motors*, ghostwritten by Whyte's colleague at *Fortune* John McDonald. Fear-ful that its contents might spark antitrust litigation, GM suppressed publication of the book. It was finally printed in 1964, after an arduous legal battle by McDonald. A year later an even bigger book about the auto industry was published, Ralph Nader's *Unsafe at Any Speed*.

"A job on the auto industry could be quite an absorbing task but for this scrivener, who has set himself a two-year writing assignment, far afield," Whyte replied in a handwritten note to Ferry. "Wish I could think of some good candidates but aside from W. H. Ferry find it hard. Why don't you take it on?"[2]

Ferry's enticing invitation to relocate to Santa Barbara, coming as another winter was about to descend on New York City, must have been tempting to Whyte, then living at 131 East 61st Street in Manhat-tan. "This spring I expect to be gadflying about California for a week or so in a U-Drive-It," Whyte continued. "Would like to stop by and see the delights of Santa Barbara."

In the late 1950s and early 1960s Whyte appeared often as a pub-lic intellectual—a three-headed one—to speak variously on land use matters, organizational issues, and urban concerns. He reprised his thoughts about cities at a Goucher College conference titled "Human Values in the Emerging American Cities" in April 1960. In a two-week span later that spring, Whyte appeared twice in Princeton, New Jersey. The first time he spoke at the annual meeting of a regional conservation group. His audience was no doubt intrigued by the author of the *Life* magazine article called "A Plan to Save Vanishing U.S. Countryside." Then he addressed the Princeton University senior class at its annual banquet. Whyte, billed as author of *The Organization Man*, warned the Class of 1960 about complacency. "Mr. Whyte," a student reporter wrote, "feels that the blame for the decay of American individualism should not fall on Big Government but on Big Business which has created its own kind of 'social security' for millions of junior executives."[3]

On some occasions Whyte's reputation as author of *The Organization Man* clearly preceded him. On April 20, 1961, Whyte testified in Washington, DC, at a hearing on a Senate bill to help state and local governments preserve open space in and around urban areas. He was introduced simply as William H. Whyte of New York City. "My only competence," he began, "is that for the last four or five years I have been trying to follow up the progress of all of the different programs, local and state, which have as their aim the conservation of open space and the shaping of suburban development."

After lengthy testimony explaining various tactics by which government entities could preserve open space, Whyte was interrupted by Senator Harrison Williams of New Jersey. "The record should reflect that Mr. Whyte is a former editor of *Fortune* magazine and author of *The Organization Man*, and has written a chapter or two for the very useful book, *The Exploding Metropolis*, and now is working on this program for the Rockefeller Brothers special study fund. Is that right?"

Whyte affirmed the accuracy of his résumé. Then Senator Paul Douglas of Illinois weighed in. "I wondered whether he was the Whyte who had written *The Organization Man*. There are many William Whytes and I was curious whether we had still another one. I want to congratulate him on his book. I think it produced a good, healthy reaction that has been a sort of antibody, so to speak, to offset undue conformism in American life. I am delighted now that in addition to being a very sophisticated debunker, he is trying to preserve the land and nature for the people."

Whyte was pressed into writing an *Organization Man*–oriented profile of his Princeton class for its twenty-fifth reunion in 1964. His college class, Whyte determined from poring over 476 reunion questionnaires (a response rate of about 90 percent), was surprisingly entrepreneurial and felt strongly about individual responsibility. Whyte's personal listing in the reunion yearbook is revealing. He summarized his new interest in developing legal devices to help stem the flow of urban sprawl. "For a scrivener like myself, it's quite an experience to join in something like this. Meanwhile, I hope to get back to several long delayed books—none of which, I should note, is to be *Son of Organization Man* or anything similar."[4]

By 1964 Whyte had moved firmly in the direction of studying land use and misuse. The Rockefeller brothers—the five grandsons of the Standard Oil founder who had formed their own philanthropic arm, the Rockefeller Brothers Fund, in 1940—had become acquainted with Whyte through his work at *Fortune*. (The eldest Rockefeller sibling, Abby, the only daughter, pursued her own separate philanthropic interests, which eventually would also rely on Whyte's expertise; see chapter 14.)

Whyte's relationship with the Rockefellers probably began with that two-part series on foundations in *Fortune* in 1955 and its unflattering review of the big foundations, including Rockefeller, Carnegie, and Ford: "The record is unimpressive," Whyte had written.[5] John D. Rockefeller III, the eldest of the brothers, may not have liked that coverage in *Fortune*. But by January 1958 he had found another article in *Fortune* that merited his attention—Whyte's piece on urban sprawl. John D. III sent Whyte a thank-you note for sending along a copy.[6]

A few months later Congress established the Outdoor Recreation Resources Review Commission (ORRRC). In 1959 President Dwight Eisenhower appointed Laurance Rockefeller as chairman of the commission. The middle of the five Rockefeller brothers, Laurance was a philanthropist, a venture capitalist with an eye toward emerging technologies (an early investor in Apple, for one example), an entrepreneur, and a conservationist. In 1958 he had cofounded the American Conservation Association. Rockefeller wasted no time appointing a nonpartisan advisory council of twenty-five members to the ORRRC.

To help write the final report, Rockefeller picked Whyte, author of the *Fortune* article on urban sprawl and the technical bulletin on conservation easements for the Urban Land Institute. When Whyte referred to a two-year writing assignment in his letter to Ping Ferry of the Fund for the Republic, he was no doubt referring to the upcoming work with Rockefeller. The "gadflying" to California was also probably in support of that ORRRC project.

When they began working together Whyte and Rockefeller were not exactly birds of a feather. Whyte had commissioned the article in *The Exploding Metropolis* that questioned the wisdom of the huge redevelopment of the Lincoln Square neighborhood that would create what is now known as Lincoln Center. "Six thousand families, mostly low-income Negroes and Puerto Ricans, will be displaced by the project," wrote Daniel Seligman of the *Fortune* staff. "When the area is redeveloped, it will have 4,400 housing units. Scarcely any will be occupied by the neighborhood's old residents—the monthly rent . . . will be too high for them—so they will inevitably pile into other areas of west Manhattan and create new slums."[7] The Rockefeller family had donated more than 40 percent of the cost of the Lincoln Center. Laurance would personally provide $2.5 million in 1962 to keep the project on track.[8]

There were other potential chafing points. In his 1959 bulletin on conserving open space, Whyte had noted the special case of "the gentry," who he described as "the third or fourth generation to hold the property, gentlemen farmers or ranchers, older executives who have bought a country estate, retired generals, or, simply, people who are rich." And they were likely to think of open space as "farmland, streams and meadows, white fences, and barns"—but not as parks. The gentry's open space would be "untainted by public access" and "inaccessible to most everyone but the very rich."[9]

Whyte could easily have been referring to Laurance Rockefeller. One of his entrepreneurial ventures, RockResorts, was launched in 1956 to create luxury resorts bounded by large tracts of preserved open space at remote locations in Wyoming, Vermont, several of the Hawaiian islands, Puerto Rico, and the Virgin Islands. They were all a long way from West Chester.

Beyond the difference in their socioeconomic stations, however, Whyte and Rockefeller had some things in common. Rockefeller, who preceded Whyte at Princeton by seven years, was also an organization man but not a cowering conformist. Rockefeller majored in philosophy at Princeton, he explained in 1931 to his father, in order to understand "conflicting desires and actions."[10] He was ready to resist the beneficence of even the most beneficent organization—he did just that in the 1970s as a conciliator among his brothers, reconciling conflicting aims of the family.[11] Like Whyte, Rockefeller had demonstrated his appreciation for oddball, unorthodox scientists. Rockefeller underwrote research into the controversial science of extrasensory perception. He also supported research into unidentified flying objects. In the 1990s he helped establish the UFO Disclosure Initiative at the Bill Clinton White House.

Beginning with his work on the ORRRC, Whyte soon became part of Laurance Rockefeller's circle of intellectual confidants. He would remain in that circle for the rest of his life. In an authorized biography published in 1997, Yale University historian Robin W. Winks wrote that Laurance Rockefeller "sponsored a dizzying array of research, generally indirectly through foundations and other institutions, sometimes quite directly. This research almost always had to do with what would come to be called 'the quality of life' debate. Interesting thinkers would pique his curiosity, he would read some of their work, invite them to meet with him, learn more about them and how they thought, often ask them to mull over some problem which intrigued him, and then remain in touch with them for life, his intellectual loyalties being as firm as his social and familial ones. A case in point is the 'urbanologist' William H. Whyte."[12]

Money, of course, was also part of the Rockefeller relationship. Friends of Whyte later in his life would worry that he wasn't charging enough for his consulting services. With Rockefeller, however, the remuneration seemed to be at the top end of the pay scale. A 1966 letter to Whyte from Laurance spelled out what appeared to be an annual agreement. It called for Whyte to be on call for the American Conservation Association (founded by Laurance) for up to 25 percent of his time for "service on boards, Commissions, and committees in which ACA has an interest." In addition, Whyte might be called on for specific writing duties "and other undertakings." Billing for such work would be prorated at an annual rate of $40,000 (the equivalent of about $320,000 in 2020). In addition, "the ACA will of course continue to provide you with office space, telephone, secretarial assistance, travel and incidental expenses for those projects under the retainer or those which may be assigned additionally." A note to the file a year later indicated that the ACA wanted to continue the arrangement on the same terms into 1968.[13]

Whyte also had ongoing royalties from *The Organization Man*. And in 1964 Doubleday had advanced him a hefty $20,000 for his next book. In this flush time Whyte planned to spend several months in England in 1965 researching greenbelts and new towns. And he planned vacations in Wyoming and Spain, including a "jaunt" in 1966 and six weeks in 1968.[14] Of course, that annual revenue would depend on Whyte being fully engaged throughout the year. And all the income would be subject to taxation. Whyte by this time had moved from 180 East 75th Street to a spacious brownstone apartment he purchased at 175 East 94th Street. He still needed to work for a living.

Whyte and Rockefeller joined forces at the ignition point for America's environmental movement. The conservation movement was broadening its scope from the pristine fields and streams of undeveloped America to the remaining land in the suburbs and the cities. Some in Congress wanted the ORRRC, for example, to review the country's national parks and wilderness areas but specifically not to study cities. But the commission did just that anyhow. "It had to," Whyte wrote later. "The simple, close-to-home activities, it discovered, are by far and away the most important to Americans. The place to meet this need, said chairman [Rockefeller], is where most Americans live—in the cities and suburbs." One section of the ORRRC's final report surveyed strategies for acquiring open space in rapidly developing regions. That report, noted Rockefeller biographer Robin Winks, "was the work of the imaginative William H. Whyte."

Whyte's next Rockefeller-supported project was the 1964 report *Cluster Development*, published by the American Conservation Association.

The 130-page book built on two findings from the ORRRC: that the basic need for outdoor recreation had to be met close to where the people lived, and that private land, including the "environment" surrounding people's homes, had to contribute to the land used for recreation. The report presented a new strategy for conservation groups. In the foreword, Rockefeller praised the conservationists' "fighting spirit" but then suggested a different tack.

> Historically, what conservationists have sought is *non*-development and for them the developer and his bulldozers have seemed the natural foe. . . .
>
> The time has come, however, for conservationists to take a much more positive interest in development—not just for the threat that it poses, but for the potentials that it holds. It is going to take place; and on a larger scale than ever before. But what will be its character? The answer to this question is critical to the whole problem of preserving the influence of the outdoors in American life.[15]

Members of the American Conservation Association, Whyte would later write, "believe that you have to meet the future halfway. They think conservation means wise use of our resources. Instead of taking a 'touch-not-one-blade-of-grass' position, they have been in the forefront of finding new ways of taking care of land and taking care of people, too."[16]

To take care of both land and people, Rockefeller and Whyte needed to be pragmatic and nonpartisan. Rockefeller, a Republican and the supportive brother of his politician brother, Nelson, was willing to work with the Democratic president, Lyndon Johnson. On May 22, 1964, Johnson presented his vision of the Great Society in a speech at the University of Michigan. Conservationists were thrilled by one of the three pillars of the society: protection of natural beauty. (The other two were cities and education.) In January 1965, President Johnson asked Rockefeller to coordinate the White House Conference on Natural Beauty. The conference put forth 190 recommendations on problems related—once again—to the city as well as the countryside

Figure 8.1 President Lyndon Johnson, center, turned to Laurance Rockefeller, second from left, and Holly Whyte, far right, to organize his 1965 White House Conference on Natural Beauty. (Rockefeller Archive Center.)

and highways. The whole event was comanaged by Whyte and Henry Diamond, a lawyer who worked on environmental issues with Laurance Rockefeller.

Rockefeller recruited Whyte once again in 1966, this time as a member of the new Hudson River Valley Commission. Other members included Alan Simpson, president of Vassar College (no relation to the former Wyoming senator by that name); W. Averell Harriman, the Democratic governor of New York who preceded Nelson Rockefeller; Henry T. Heald, president of the Ford Foundation; Lowell Thomas, the celebrated news commentator; Marian Sulzberger Heiskell, a director of the *New York Times*; and Thomas J. Watson Jr., chief executive officer of IBM.

Its roster of highly placed members notwithstanding, the Hudson River Valley Commission became embroiled in one of the most notorious environmental disputes of the 1960s. The New York public utility Consolidated Edison, backed by Governor Rockefeller, proposed to build a pumped-storage hydroelectric plant on the bank of the Hudson River at the scenic Storm King Mountain. Laurance, still believing that conservationists needed to look at both the perils and promise of development, went along with his brother—for a while. But as the opposition grew and Con Ed's response remained unconvincing, Laurance and the commission joined the opposition. In February 1966, the Hudson River Valley Commission reported its recommendation.

> The Commission strongly believes scenic and conservation values must be given as much weight as the more measurable economic values and that we should not necessarily destroy one value to create another.
>
> The immediate case in point is the plan of Con Edison to build a pumped storage plant at Storm King Mountain. The Commission believes that scenic values are paramount here and that the plant should not be built if a feasible alternative can be found.[17]

This bold statement from a group of such influential and establishment leaders helped transform Laurance from a conservationist into an environmentalist. Con Ed killed the hydroelectric project and donated its land for the creation of Storm King State Park.

At this same time concerns about the physical environment continued to increase. In 1968 the *Apollo 8* astronauts took a photograph of Earth that became an iconic image of an increasingly threatened planet. Paul Ehrlich's 1968 book *The Population Bomb* made any hope for the planet seem impossible. But that same year Whyte's book *The Last Landscape* was filled with hopeful action plans. Whyte knitted together a host of creative—even subversive—ideas for shaping the inexorable forces of development. *The Last Landscape* was not a conservation book; it was an environmental book (chapter 9).

But Whyte was no ordinary subversive. He was working from deep inside the system, from the Rockefeller complex known modestly as "Room 5600" at 30 Rockefeller Plaza. Room 5600 actually occupied three full floors at the top of 30 Rockefeller Plaza, interconnected privately via interior staircases. Working out of a small office on the fifty-fourth floor, Whyte and others in the Rockefeller in-crowd enjoyed a prime Midtown Manhattan location, splendid views, original art on the walls, and access to an outdoor dining terrace.

For the Rockefellers, especially Laurance, the new environmental movement seemed like a winning issue. But the Rockefellers, a Republican crowd, did not see their ardor matched in the 1968 presidential campaign of Richard Nixon. Although there were two references to environmental concerns in the Republican Party platform, Nixon's campaign took little notice of the issue. Then "the suggestion was made from the Rockefeller corporate headquarters at Room 5600 that he should take an interest in the matter." The Rockefellers lobbied for a nonpartisan approach. Laurance Rockefeller's biographer reported, "To the surprise of many, candidate Nixon took a genuine interest in conservation matters. Just over two weeks before the election, he delivered a radio address on the subject, using material generated at 5600."[18]

Any small edge was important in the 1968 presidential election. Nixon eked out a 43.4 to 42.7 percent plurality over Hubert Humphrey—third-party candidate George Wallace had 13.5 percent. At his inaugural address, on January 20, 1969, Nixon mentioned environmental protection—the first American president to do so. While he derided environmentalists in private, calling them "enemies of the system" in conversations recorded on his secret tapes, Nixon realized their political clout and launched a spree of environmental initiatives: the National Environmental Policy Act (1969), requiring all federal agencies to produce environmental impact statements for any regulations; creation of the US Environmental Protection Agency (1970) and the National Oceanic and Atmospheric Administration (NOAA, 1970); the Clean Air Act (1970); the Clean Water Act (1972); and the Endangered Species Act of 1973.

Soon it was Whyte's turn to be nonpartisan. Whyte, who called himself a Democrat in his senior class book at Princeton and who was most likely sympathetic to the anti–Vietnam War movement, was pressed into Nixon's service. The president had created a fifteen-member Citizens' Advisory Committee on Environmental Quality with Laurance Rockefeller as chairman. The committee's major report, "Community Action for Environmental Quality," was delivered in 1970. Like other findings produced from Rockefeller commissions, this forty-two-page document included practical recommendations for action on open space and recreation, townscapes, zoning, clean air and water programs, and the training of people for environmental careers. Robin Winks, the Rockefeller biographer, noted, "Comments on how to capitalize on bad breaks, how to stage public meetings for maximum impact, how to use the media, were all surprisingly direct for a government-initiated document. The prose bore the acknowledged imprint of William H. Whyte once again."[19]

Perhaps even more surprising for a government-initiated document, this one was turned into a three-part made-for-television series titled *Mission: Possible* (a takeoff on the CBS television spy series). Xerox sponsored it in prime time on the ABC network and, a year later, presented it on some two hundred public television stations.

If Nixon had not been caught waging illegal warfare in his reelection campaign, he might have been known as the environmental president. Historians might have pointed to the behind-the-scenes lobbying of the Rockefellers to encourage Nixon to embrace environmental issues as a critical factor in the 1968 election. And someone digging deeper yet might have seen the hand of Holly Whyte helping to articulate the Rockefellers' view toward environmental action.

The Rockefellers encountered some negative publicity of their own, particularly in their real estate dealings at Rockefeller Center; their role in the redevelopment of the Lincoln Center site; and the elimination of thousands of small manufacturing firms to make way for the twin towers of the World Trade Center. Whyte's association with Rockefeller and Rockefeller's support of the Conservation Foundation in 1962 "led to some loose and ill-informed talk of a cabal."[20] But Laurance escaped the criticism heaped on his brothers for their role in "tenant removal." And Whyte was implicated only by association, characterized as a Rockefeller "wheelhorse."[21] As skilled organization men often do, Rockefeller and Whyte avoided the spotlight.

Throughout the 1970s and 1980s Whyte continued to work with Laurance and the Rockefeller family. When Abby Rockefeller Mauzé's pet project, the vest-pocket park known as Greenacre Park in Manhattan, was threatened by plans for an overshadowing skyscraper, Holly Whyte came to the park's defense (chapter 14). Whyte counseled Laurance on several landscape design projects for their alma mater, Princeton University (chapter 16). When Whyte's cousin's son Price Baum was paralyzed in a diving accident, Laurance and Room 5600 helped get him treatment at the Rusk Institute of Rehabilitation Medicine.[22] (Price Baum later became a proponent of the Americans with Disabilities Act and director of a center for independent living in Virginia.) As we will see in chapter 17, when Whyte's mobility became severely limited by various illnesses in the 1990s, Laurance Rockefeller's faith in his friend of more than thirty years did not waver.

The 1997 biography of Laurance Rockefeller was underwritten in part by Rockefeller and fact-checked by several of his aides. The description of Whyte's office in Room 5600 is unlikely to be hyperbole: "In Whyte's sparsely furnished office in Rockefeller Center are dozens of reports, drafts, and speculative papers from his hand, all of them still influential in the thinking of [Laurance]."[23] For Rockefeller, as for many others who worked with Whyte and followed him in the fields of open space preservation and urban design and planning, it was a lasting influence. For Whyte, Rockefeller's support was also lasting, and it is acknowledged prominently in the book that showed the transformation of the conservation movement into what some people would describe as the environmental crusade—*The Last Landscape*.

Chapter 9

Preserving the Last Landscape, Rural and Urban

If you were an avid conservationist in 1968, you might have eagerly picked up *The Last Landscape*, the new book by William H. Whyte, and looked forward with anticipation to chapters on land use, cluster zoning, and ways to "design with nature," a phrase coming into the popular lexicon. *The Last Landscape* would have delivered on all of that. But you also would have followed Whyte down roads you never expected to travel: failures of public housing, bleak prospects for most "new towns," ways small spaces could be made to seem bigger, and—reminiscent of Whyte's days peddling Vicks VapoRub—tactics for "selling" the idea of land preservation easements to hidebound farmers.

And then there was a long section devoted to play areas. Children's play areas. Really? Yes, but it all made sense—and a lasting impression.

The *New York Times* Sunday Book Review of *The Last Landscape* employed a classic cartoon from the *New Yorker* to illustrate its review of Whyte's new book. The cartoon shows a homeowner raking leaves toward the curb in his quiet suburban neighborhood. A horseman, riding as if he were Paul Revere, charges down the middle of the street, crying out, "To arms! To arms! The bulldozers are coming."

In *The Last Landscape* Whyte sounded the alarm about the

developers' bulldozers. More important, he plotted strategies to fore-stall the bulldozers' advances. His prescriptions for shaping the future were many, and some of the approaches were—in that Paul Revere mode—revolutionary. Charles Abrams, at the time a visiting professor of city planning at Harvard University and the author of *The City Is the Frontier*, called Whyte's book "the best study available on the problem of open space." Abrams wrote the following in his *Times* review:

> All the gimmicks for salvaging the open spaces are here . . . , for the nature lovers seem to be no greenhorns in the use of zoning and other techniques. They are procuring special tax exemptions for farmers to keep them from selling, gerrymandering land, manipu-lating income tax escapes and subsidy schemes, even using dummies to buy up strategic land and a "dirty tricks" project, by which the fish-and-game department of one New England state buys enough isolated coastal wetland areas to effectively seal much larger areas and prevent their development. All of which Whyte lauds as "splen-didly unreasonable." His and theirs is a crusade and if a crusade is to succeed it must have good lawyers and money "to obstruct specula-tors' plans." All the "foiling operations" are listed with colorful ex-amples of how to work them.[1]

At this point in his life, Whyte could be splendidly unreasonable. Whyte, after all, had advised the Episcopalian congregants at his church on the Upper East Side of Manhattan to "blow the lid off ev-erything" if necessary to challenge the status quo. As the best-selling author of *The Organization Man*, Whyte had shown job candidates how to cheat on personality tests. *The Last Landscape*, with its schemes and manipulations, was entirely in character:

Dirty tricks by a fish and game department? Whyte never identi-fied the state, but he reported that "the fish-and-game department of one New England state is especially adept at this kind of tic-tac-toe. In the absence of sufficient money to buy prime coastal wetland ar-eas, it has bought time with a spoiling operation. Its negotiators, who vastly enjoy what they call their dirty tricks project, have very skillfully picked up enough isolated tracts to effectively seal many thousands of acres against development that otherwise would be inevitable." Whyte noted further that wetlands, which often have cloudy titles dating back to colonial days, "are particularly suitable for this kind of operation."[2]

Gerrymandering land? Assembling odd arrangements of municipalities to create election districts in favor of a particular political party has long been a tawdry American political tradition. Whyte wondered why the land preservation forces couldn't use the same tactic. Planners, he noted, looked first to large regional networks. Whyte found one regional planner with an unorthodox approach and quoted him at length: "A non-system of scattered spaces . . . may not satisfy those who want to design urban regions in the grand manner, but it has every likelihood of success." Whyte wrote that "full continuity" was not critical, since most people seek out "locally useful" spaces.[3]

Dummies buying up land? Well, the Western Pennsylvania Conservancy wasn't exactly a dummy, but in the 1960s it did quietly acquire nine thousand acres of land crucial to the creation of Laurel Ridge State Park, about sixty miles east of Pittsburgh. Parcel by parcel, it acquired the land "so quietly that over the two years the acquisition took, speculators never caught on to what was happening, and prices remained stable."[4] Something similar happened in the Great Swamp area of New Jersey, where conservationists and residents teamed up to acquire ecologically sensitive land and get it declared a national wildlife refuge. That foiled the Port Authority of New York's plan to build a jetport there, Whyte reported with admiration.[5]

Obstructing speculators' plans? A nonprofit group called the Philadelphia Conservationist, blessed with access to good lawyers, was able to do just that as it acquired land along the New Jersey shore that it knew would be valuable as a seashore park. But a housing developer had been awarded the contract to purchase a two-and-a-half-mile stretch of barrier reef. Undeterred, the conservationists offered the town three times more than the developer and raised a ruckus in public about the city giving the developer a bargain. The city rescinded the deal. The developer sued. The conservationists aided in the defense. The city eventually sold the land to the state's new Green Acres program.[6]

The Last Landscape capped a decade of Whyte advocating on behalf of open space, including open space in the densest urban settings.

The Organization Man may have sold millions of books and raised the consciousness of many people, but it did little to change institutional practices. *The Last Landscape* resulted in fewer sales—about fifteen thousand copies in hardcover and thirty-eight thousand in paperback before it went out of print in 1977. The book may not have earned back its substantial $20,000 advance.[7] But *The Last Landscape* and Whyte's work leading up to it influenced public policy at the federal, state, and local levels. Largely inspired by Whyte, conservation groups across the country established hundreds of local land trusts and permanently protected millions of acres of land. Whyte, as we shall see, was often in the thick of the battle, sometimes literally so.

Whyte was no outdoorsman. His life revolved around his home and office on the Upper East Side of Manhattan. But his appreciation of open space went back to his childhood in West Chester, Pennsylvania, on the edge of the lush Brandywine Valley. He had appreciated it as a boy in the 1920s and had used it as a setting for several of his short stories for his college literary magazine. Even then conservationists were sounding alarms about the vanishing countryside. In 1930 a state senator from Somerset County in central New Jersey noted that "the milk pail and the plow are being replaced by the factory; the farmhouse is giving way to the commuter's home." Those changes were inevitable, he wrote, "the natural results of the extension of the metropolitan district of New York City."[8]

But when the troops returned from World War II, the natural extension of the city to the country turned into an avalanche. There was an immediate crisis: housing. As Whyte was starting at *Fortune* in 1946 and 1947, the magazine called for government initiatives to enable builders to overcome the housing shortage. "Let's have ourselves a housing industry," *Fortune* said in an editorial.[9] The housing industry responded to the shortage by deploying bulldozers that had been used on World War II battlefields to clear and grade thousands of acres of open space. Then the builders adopted mass production techniques to frame and finish houses in record time. Sales of drywall, for example, soared as builders cut costs by eliminating the plastering of interior walls.

In postwar America the term "urban sprawl" came into common usage. While some Whyte acolytes believe that he coined the term in his 1958 *Fortune* article, the phrase predates that by at least a decade. A 1947 article noted the deleterious effects of "urban sprawl, ribbon development, overcrowded streets," and other growth problems facing Oxford, England.[10] A 1948 letter to the editors of both the *Washington Post* and the *New York Times* referred to "the problems produced by urban sprawl or middle-aged spread of our large cities." In a 1950 article in the *New York Times*, titled "The Suburbs Are Strangling the City," the author declared that "if population shifts are planned for and intelligently balanced ... urban sprawl can be prevented, but not urban *growth*."[11]

If Whyte had coined the term, it might have been "suburban sprawl," not "urban sprawl." As he noted in a paper presented as part of Goucher College's seventy-fifth anniversary celebration in 1959 and 1960, "we tend to think of the city as sprawling, or oozing, over the landscape. But actually it is not the city that is spreading; it is suburbia."[12] When Whyte began studying the phenomenon in the 1950s, William Levitt had already founded namesake towns on Long Island, in New Jersey (now called Willingboro), and in Pennsylvania. In *The Organization Man* Whyte included a section on Levittown, Pennsylvania, and eight chapters on the suburban lifestyle in Park Forest, Illinois, another town that seemingly sprang up on an empty field.

In 1957 Whyte and Douglas Haskell of *Architectural Forum* assembled a two-day panel on "the city's threat to open land." Among the panelists were Catherine Bauer Wurster, an affordable housing advocate; Edmund Bacon, a Philadelphia planner; Charles Abrams, an urban planner who practiced some of what he preached by owning property in Greenwich Village (and who would later write the *Times* review of *The Last Landscape* quoted earlier); Charles M. Haar, a Harvard Law School professor specializing in land use; Carl Feiss, an urban planner who fought to save buildings from urban renewal's wrecking ball; and Henry Fagin, planning director of the Regional Plan Association of New York, New Jersey, and Connecticut. Jane Jacobs reported on the event for *Architectural Forum*.[13]

As measured by how often it was repurposed or reprinted, Whyte's 1958 *Fortune* article, succinctly titled "Urban Sprawl," may have been his most impactful piece at *Fortune*. In the article Whyte urged government entities to leverage their money by buying not entire tracts of land but rather development rights to the land, and then not developing it. In addition to being reprinted in *The Exploding Metropolis*, the *Fortune* article was reprinted in both general interest and professional journals, including *House and Home* (February 1958); *Planning 1958*, the journal of the American Society of Planning Officials; and *Recreation 51* (1959). Whyte's expanded article in *Life* magazine in 1959 suggested another new weapon in the fight against sprawl: the use of cluster zoning to create planned unit developments. The article struck a chord with *Life*'s mass-market audience.

> Take a last look. Some summer's morning drive past the golf club on the edge of town, turn off onto a back road and go for a short trip through the open countryside. Look well at the meadows, the wooded draws, the stands of pine, the creeks and streams, and fix them in your memory. If the American standard of living goes up another notch, this is about the last chance you will have.
>
> Go back toward the city five or 10 miles. Here, in what was pleasant countryside only a year ago, is the sight of what is to come. . . . Across the hills are splattered scores of random subdivisions, each laid out in the same dreary asphalt curves. Gone are the streams, brooks, woods, and forests that the subdivisions' signs talked about. The streams are largely buried in concrete culverts. Where one flows briefly through a patch of weeds and tin cans it is fetid with the ooze of septic tanks. . . . Here and there a farm remains, but the "For Sale" signs are up and now even the golf course is to be chopped into lots.[14]

In December 1959, Whyte followed up on the *Life* article with a sixty-seven-page "technical bulletin" based on a year's worth of research he had conducted for the Urban Land Institute. The bulletin, titled "Securing Open Space for Urban America: Conservation Easements," mapped a strategy that differed greatly from traditional open space acquisition plans. Previous efforts had focused on acquiring large tracts of land to be used as a public park or recreation area, or enacting zoning ordinances that would force developers to leave unused acres of space around each new home—space usually turned into vast but seldom-used lawns.

Whyte described how easements could preserve tracts of open space. Much cheaper than outright purchases, easements could preclude future development on a prime tract. A conservation group could acquire the easement, which essentially curtailed the development of the land, and the owner could continue to use the land (and bear the costs of maintaining it). The easements ran with the land, regardless of who might own it in the future. The bulletin included eight appendices on subjects ranging from a sample scenic easement deed in the state of California to a reservation agreement, used in Ohio, that would reserve a conservation group's right to purchase a tract of land for a certain period—a way to buy time while conservationists arranged a permanent defense against potential development.

More than just a policy wonk, Whyte also included some practical advice for dealing with landowners. The very rich landowners, Whyte noted, did not always like the idea of their land turning into a public park, with signage, benches, and other public amenities. In the 1959 technical bulletin Whyte wrote: "The simple fact is that these people do have this bias and that they happen to own the best land just beyond today's suburbia. The job is to understand their inclination and to exploit rather than deplore it."[15]

Whyte was pragmatic about dealing with government parks officials who might take an all-or-nothing approach to land preservation:

> To think of open space acquisition only in terms of full title and formal park development is to leave unexplored the great chances for saving a complementary, and no way less important, kind of open space. It is a kind of open space, furthermore, that will not strain operating budgets. As has long been known, gifts of land can often be troublesome unless there is going to be money to develop the property and to maintain it. Land that is conserved with easements however is maintained by the owner, and economics aside, aesthetically this provides something a park cannot.[16]

The colorful prose of the *Life* magazine article on saving America's scenic landscape had an emotional appeal that one would expect of an advocate. The technical talk about easements, property deeds, and other legal instruments in the Urban Land Institute bulletin reflected an informed overview that one would expect of an expert analyst. Throughout the 1960s Whyte played both roles in the land preservation movement.

A bill that Whyte co-wrote for the state of Pennsylvania, though delayed when the state commissioned a large-scale study of the issue, nevertheless became a model for conservationists in California. In 1959 there had been a "breakthrough" in Monterey County. Outraged by the open land vanishing before their eyes, citizens decided to act at the county level. Inspired by the county law, the California legislature passed a bill that allowed any city or county in the state to "buy land or buy interests in land, easements, or buy land and lease it back for the purpose of open space conservation and for the shaping of urban development." The key element, Whyte said, was the preamble, a "statement of legislative finding that this conservation of open space was a valid public purpose" and was not restricted to the traditional concept of "immediate public use."[17] In other words, an easement could preserve a scenic view, not just set aside land for an access road to an adjoining piece of property or for a sewer line.

In 1960 Whyte went to bat for a Long Island–based developer, Norman E. Blankman, who hoped to use the principles of cluster zoning to redevelop the 516-acre estate of Cornelius Vanderbilt Whitney in Old Westbury. Under the existing zoning, with a two- to three-acre minimum lot size, Blankman would have been able to build 236 single-family homes on the property. Most of the trees on the property would be removed and an existing golf course bulldozed into building lots. Blankman, citing Whyte's articles on urban sprawl in *Fortune* and *Life*, proposed instead to construct 283 new townhouses in clusters concentrated on about seven acres, reserving the rest for woodlands and recreational space and saving the golf course. To implement this approach, Blankman retained the noted architect Victor Gruen, already known for his design of suburban shopping malls and for a plan for Fort Worth, Texas. Blankman also hired Whyte and Hugh Pomeroy, the director of planning for Westchester County, New York, to testify at the climactic public meeting.

That 1960 meeting was a developer's nightmare. Angry residents of Old Westbury viewed Blankman's idea as revolutionary and danger-ous. What if the $60,000 houses did not get sold? If they did get sold, what kind of people would buy them? If the deal was so good, what was the catch? What if Blankman changed his mind about the open space? "Tempers flared, and at about 11 p.m. the meeting was on the verge of breaking up into fisticuffs," Whyte reported.[18] Even though town offi-cials eventually voted against Blankman's proposal, *Architectural Forum* devoted three pages to renderings for Gruen's striking design for the Whitney townhouses. In 1963 Blankman sold 280 acres of the estate to the New York Institute of Technology—land that would no longer be subject to property tax. The institute has since repurposed Sonny Whitney's magnificent stables for offices.

In 1961 geographer Jean Gottmann took note of cities and suburbs blending together into one almost continuous urban band from Boston to Washington, DC, and called it the "megalopolis." That same year the California open space acquisition law became a model for New York, Maryland, Connecticut, Massachusetts, Wisconsin, and—hap-pily for Whyte—Pennsylvania. New Jersey enacted its Green Acres program, using matching grants to help counties, municipalities, and nonprofits acquire land. In the early 1960s at the state level, Whyte wrote, measures that would have seemed "wildly socialistic" only a de-cade or so before were being approved by legislatures "with remarkably little controversy."[19]

Also in 1961 Senator Harrison Williams, a Democrat from New Jersey, proposed a federal grant program for acquiring urban open spaces. The bill called for $50 million in seed money that could be multiplied fivefold by state and local governments. As Illinois sena-tor Paul Douglas marveled at the committee hearing, Whyte was "a very sophisticated debunker." Whyte, presumably, would not advance some "wildly socialistic" land-grabbing scheme. Whyte was his typi-cal self: empirical and pragmatic. The police power of zoning, which could be considered a socialist act, was not the solution to preserving open space, Whyte believed. Rather than curtail sprawl, Whyte told the senators, large lot zoning of one or two acres or more per house led to a "horrible scatteration" of development. Whyte also told the senators that open space programs had been held up, in part, because of the lack of regional planning authority. Some planners "say it is fine to do this, but we first must have an overall metropolitan authority and then go out and sell this idea to the people." But local communities, Whyte added, were ahead of the planners and ready to begin acquiring land on their own.

Whyte soon realized that "open space proposals have a certain sleeper quality." In his 1962 report for the Outdoor Recreation Resources Review Commission, Whyte noted that open space proposals "start slowly, but they gather support more quickly even than their proponents expect. Open space, in short, has political sex appeal—and one of the best ways of speeding up action is to get documentation of the fact to the right people."[20] Political sex appeal was matched by popular appeal. In 1962, for example, a seven-year-old boy from California made national news when he wrote to President John F. Kennedy after discovering that development was destroying his favorite place to hunt for lizards. The quirky punctuation and spelling added to its authenticity.

Dear Mr President.
    we Have no Place to go when we want to go out in the canyon. Because there are going to Build houses So could you set aside some land where we could Play? thank you four listening
        love scott[21]

A year later the folk singer Pete Seeger recorded a hit song that still reverberates today: "Little Boxes." Both Whyte and Laurance Rockefeller realized that the conservation movement was becoming more than preserving wilderness and wildlife. But in terms of grabbing the public's attention, the image of a beautiful landscape being bulldozed to make room for ticky-tacky housing developments was most effective.

Acquiring open land was half of the land use equation. The other half was developing land more efficiently. Whyte's 1964 book *Cluster*

Development, underwritten by Laurance Rockefeller, brought the cluster concept and all its ramifications into sharp focus. In typical style, Whyte jumped headfirst into the policy details, including the text of the New York State Cluster Enabling Act, and local ordinances for planned communities and subdivision open space plans in Virginia, Maryland, Missouri, and California. He also included sample homeowners' association forms for communities in Ohio, California, and Connecticut. The book included twenty pages of charts detailing the size and scope of dozens of different cluster developments, with columns for size of the project and the raw land cost, the density of the project, the names of the architects and planners, description of open space and recreational facilities, and—perhaps more important for would-be investors and developers—the price and number of completed transactions in which buyers had received mortgage approval.

Cluster Development also paid attention to the politics of the issue. Whyte recounted the contentious hearing over the Whitney estate in Old Westbury, and another Norman Blankman venture that also ended in rejection, this time in Tenafly, New Jersey. Ready to make lemonade from lemons, Whyte concluded that "one by-product of this unhappy affair is a virtual syllabus of the objections laymen can raise about cluster. . . . They are the kind that developers and planners must be prepared to answer, or, ideally, anticipate so well they won't have to be asked at all." He then proceeded to list twenty-two such questions, all taken verbatim from the records of the public meetings, some of which will sound familiar today.

> Would the demands on borough services be greater in the cluster plan or by conventional subdivision?
>
> Will the total tax return to the borough of the "cluster plan" be equal to the return from individual homes?
>
> What assurance is there that these individual residential units are a saleable commodity, and that they can compete with rental apartments and individual dwellings in the housing market?
>
> What provisions could be made to ensure the prevention of any buildings on the rest of the land?[22]

Despite his setbacks in Old Westbury and Tenafly, Blankman fought on against urban sprawl. Still somewhat ahead of his time, he formed a nonprofit advocacy group, Housing All Americans, and lobbied for residential projects close to rail corridors, the concept now known as transit-oriented development.

The public's interest in land conservation continued to grow. The first list of endangered species, released in 1967, included the national symbol of the United States, the bald eagle. More than one real estate broker took on a slogan that has been variously credited to Mark Twain or Will Rogers: "Buy land; they don't make it anymore." Saving a piece of open land from development or despoliation was a highly visible goal. Compare the open space issue with the environmental damage caused by DDT. Rachel Carson's 1962 book, *Silent Spring*, ignited a public furor. But the solution to that crisis was beyond the reach of ordinary citizens. In fact, a nationwide ban on DDT was not enacted until December 31, 1972, more than ten years after the book was published (and more than eight years after Carson's death). Saving open space, in contrast, could be accomplished—quickly—at the federal, state, or local level.

Close to his boyhood home, in the Brandywine Valley in eastern Pennsylvania, Whyte worked with a University of Pennsylvania environmental law professor, Ann Louise Strong, to promote conservation easements, "compensable regulations," and other measures short of outright purchase to protect the farmland and scenic qualities of the valley. "Holly, then as always, was an articulate, informed, and vigorous proponent who energized a groundswell of enthusiasm," Strong said. Their effort failed to gain sufficient municipal support, but it was a model for work later carried out by the Brandywine Conservancy, a private nonprofit group. The conservancy secured easements on more than thirty-five thousand acres. It also built a museum in Chadds Ford with a substantial collection of works by Andrew Wyeth, whose paintings celebrated the Brandywine Valley's scenic richness. Whyte praised the Brandywine Conservancy's work as "ingenious."[23]

In West Chester in 1969, Whyte's mother objected to a proposed expansion of the old Hartshorne estate next door to the house where Whyte and his younger brother had been raised. She feared that the construction would damage trees that dated back to the 1700s. Echoing her son's plea for urban environmentalism, Louise Whyte wrote to the local paper, "We seem only to be aware of conservation in the big open spaces!"[24] Whyte's "splendidly unreasonable" gimmicks for saving "the last landscape" had found an eager audience.

*   *   *

In *The Last Landscape* Whyte tied all these strands together with his usual zest for detail. The average rooftop of 1,200 square feet, for example, produces 750 gallons of runoff in a one-inch rainfall. A suburban subdivision's rooftops create "a veritable flood-producing mechanism." Engineers, Whyte pointed out, had long calculated the benefits of highway construction for cars. There were also environmental costs. Whyte noted that the National Shade Tree Conference had placed a value on the trees destroyed by a highway—$6 per square inch of cross section in 1968 dollars.[25]

In studying organizations, Whyte had exposed folklore masquerading as scientific thought. In land use he quickly discovered similar forms of "scientism" creeping into the discussion. Whyte cited a traffic safety committee of the American Association of State Highway Officials, working in concert with the Bureau of Public Roads, which had determined that "to increase safety when vehicles leave the pavement, a clear recovery zone . . . should be provided along the roadway thirty feet or more from the edge of the traveled way in rural areas. Corrective programs should be undertaken at once." The result was the wanton felling of trees throughout the country. But Whyte, ever digging into the weeds, noted that the committee's own research cited a study of 507 vehicle accidents. Trees were involved in only 13 of those accidents. In the vast majority, 326, out-of-control vehicles had struck a man-made highway structure of some sort.[26]

Whyte always reacted cautiously to clichéd images captured by photographers with telephoto lenses. In *The Last Landscape* the images were of new suburban developments. "These were the little boxes that so outraged people of sensibility and means," Whyte wrote, referring to the song recorded by Seeger in 1963. "Photos of their rooftops and TV aerials, squeezed together—the telephoto lens again—became stock horror shots. But critics drew the wrong conclusions. What was wrong, they thought, was that the houses were too close together, when what was really wrong was that they were not close enough."[27] Even Whyte admitted that the subdivision design practiced in the new suburbs was better than the previous model of houses scattered here and there. Levittown in Bucks County, Pennsylvania, accommodated seventy-five thousand people—about three houses per acre or four thousand people per square mile. But it could have been better. Many of the projects Whyte studied for his 1964 book, *Cluster Development*, had ten or twenty units per acre, along with substantial tracts of undeveloped land.

As in his other writing, Whyte reveled in exploring the counterintuitive. The challenge was not that there was too little open space; it was rather that there was too much—so much, in fact, that there had been no incentive to create a discipline for how best to use it. "The less of our landscape there is to save, the better our chance of saving it," he wrote. Whyte also refused to accept the common wisdom. Some proponents of open space lobbied for "preferential" tax assessment of open space land, so that owners of large tracts of land—farmers, for example—could continue their current use without being forced by economics to sell the land to a developer who would wring a higher value out of the land. By the mid-1960s seven states had passed such provisions. Connecticut asked Whyte to prepare a similar open space assessment bill. But he was skeptical. Maryland, a state that had enacted a system of preferential assessments, seemed to be losing land to development as quickly as any other state. To find out how the practice worked in the real world, Whyte spent several weeks in Maryland, visiting assessors' offices and checking the property records of large landowners. Whyte concluded that the public was "being had." The farms still enjoyed the low assessments, but the owners often were not the farmers. The owners were real estate speculators, quietly waiting for an opportune time to develop their tract of land.[28]

Whyte's discussion of new towns in *The Last Landscape* was, as Jane Jacobs wrote in a blurb for the 1970 paperback edition, "*the* definitive discussion of the subject." In that discussion Whyte made clear his skeptical view of the disciplines of planning and architecture. "The possibility of working with a blank slate is what most excites planners and architects about new towns. Freed from the constraints of previous plans and buildings and people, the planners and architects can apply the whole range of new tools."[29] The new tools included esoteric approaches (by 1968 standards) such as game theory and systems analysis enabled by the computer age, but not, in Whyte's estimation, the old tool of common sense.

The idea of a self-contained new town, Whyte wrote, was "a contradiction in terms." For one thing, he noted dryly, "there's to be no sin in them." The "raffishness" of a real city was missing. Even the bars were designed to be "genteel," almost always adjoining restaurants, with Muzak in the air. "Urbanity is not something that can be lacquered on; it is the quality produced by the great concentration of diverse functions and a huge market to support the diversity. The center needs a large hinterland to draw upon, but it cannot be in the hinterland; it must be in the center."[30]

Whyte believed that the critical elements of a city could not simply be repackaged "in tidy communities somewhere else." Some of the seemingly unsuccessful parts of a city—unused loft buildings, or once elegant neighborhoods that had deteriorated—in fact become the "incubator" for new enterprises and the homes of "new bohemians," a catchall term for the artists, musicians, actors, and writers of Whyte's time.

Whyte had some hope for the new town of Reston, Virginia, in part because the developer, Robert E. Simon Jr. (whose initials were part of the town's name), did not impose a single master plan but instead planned the town section by section, with adjustments based on lessons learned and new market conditions.[31] He also commissioned different architects for different neighborhoods, thereby avoiding a monolithic institutional design. And Simon insisted that apartments be placed on second and third stories above retail stores in the town center. But, as Whyte pointed out, "the very constraints that architects and planners deplore can be a virtue. Architects seem to do their best work when they are faced with impossible situations—eccentric sites, ornery topography, buildings from another era to be encircled, abandoned pits." And people living in these towns would help make them more amenable, "in large part by doing that which the plans did not expect or wish them to do."[32]

But Whyte wasn't counting on the dream of a truly self-contained community ever being built from scratch. In not one of the new town plans he studied had he ever seen space allotted for a cemetery.

Commenting on the vast array of unsightly images one could encounter along so many miles of American highways, Whyte offered the following observation, a precursor to his next major book, *City: Rediscovering the Center:*

> Where there is waste, there is opportunity, and this applies to almost every aspect of the urban landscape—the ever burning pyres of rubbish, the town incinerators which do not incinerate very well, the lots piled with junk cars and stoves and refrigerators, the lots that are not used for anything. . . . That we have so much of it is almost encouraging. It is the area of second chances.[33]

The final lines of *The Last Landscape* are as relevant today as they were when written in 1968. "The land that is still to be saved will have to be saved in the next few years. We have no luxury of choice. We must make our commitments now and look to this landscape as the last one. For us, it will be."[34] The book's practical suggestions for saving open space, from dirty tricks to gerrymandering and various other obstructions, are all still applicable and still effective today. And the results are measurable. As author and environmentalist Tony Hiss wrote in his foreword to the 2002 edition, Whyte's strategy of using easements rather than outright purchase of open space was "a huge success, particularly in the last couple of decades." Hiss cited the Land Trust Alliance, a national umbrella organization that estimated in the previous twenty years some 1,200 new local land trusts across the country had permanently protected 6.4 million acres of land. That total included 2.6 million acres that had been preserved by employing Whyte's "genius" concept of easements.[35]

Environmental historian Adam Rome took note of Whyte's role in the open space movement in a 1998 essay for the *Geographical Review* and again in his 2001 book *The Bulldozer in the Countryside.* Rome called Whyte "more important than anyone else in forcing new thinking about open space and sprawl." Rome contrasted the success of the easement program, suggested by Whyte, with the effort of the Kennedy administration in the early 1960s to establish land banks "at the frontiers of metropolitan settlement. In addition to preserving open space, the land banks would allow citizens to exercise more control over the timing and location of development, since public officials could sell or hold the fringe properties in accordance with public plans." But the idea was derailed by home builders and real estate interests who viewed the idea as "a dangerous, untested meddling with the market." Whyte's "splendidly unreasonable" approach required a less heavy hand on the part of government.

But that approach was not a panacea. Whyte, according to Rome, "also held out the appealing hope that Americans could solve the open-space problem without fundamentally changing the structure of the real-estate market and without rethinking the rights and responsibilities of property ownership." Ultimately, Rome asserted, the pace of development outstripped the best efforts of the proponents of conservation easements and cluster zoning. Land use regulation was the ultimate deterrent. "Whyte was unwilling to challenge the basic premises of the [home-building] industry." The movement he helped create eventually did challenge the industry, but without Whyte at the forefront.[36]

Whyte's attention was indeed diverted from open space preservation to other, equally pressing issues in the urban landscape. And in that work, as pointed out in chapters 12 and 13, he not only embraced the regulatory powers but also helped to strengthen them.

*   *   *

Amid all of these original and important insights into the relationship between people and the environment around them, *The Last Landscape* also featured a chapter titled "Play Areas and Small Spaces." In many cities, large parks and open spaces had already been designed to their full potential. But, Whyte believed, many cities had small, unused spaces with great potential for outdoor uses—"tremendous trifles," Whyte called them. To put them to their best use, cities had to challenge the accepted wisdom of "old-line" park officials, who considered such spaces too small to be useful and too expensive to maintain. Whyte praised "vest-pocket parks," some of which might be no bigger than a single-family house. Paley Park, built in 1966 at 3 East 53rd Street in Manhattan, thrived in part because of movable chairs—"comfortable chairs, the kind you can pick up and move."[37] All of these considerations laid more groundwork for Whyte's subsequent book and film, *The Social Life of Small Urban Spaces*, and his subsequent design for the renaissance of Bryant Park.

Whyte saw several lessons in his observations of children's play spaces. "In most housing projects, private as well as public, the play areas appear to be designed by administrators. Administrators who dislike children," Whyte wrote in *The Last Landscape*. Whyte proposed that children be allowed to play in areas that are deliberately left "undesigned and underdeveloped." Some "adventure playgrounds" beginning to appear in England in the 1960s seemed like a good model. Whyte noted similar "free-form" playgrounds, including one at Jacob Riis Houses, a public housing project on the Lower East Side of Manhattan. The new playgrounds looked dangerous. "There are numerous places to fall from, and with all the jostling and clamoring about, children have to exercise a radar-like perception to keep from banging themselves up. Maybe this is why they don't bang themselves up much," Whyte wrote. "Apparent danger is a safety factor."

Always prodding planners and architects to get up from their drawing boards and visit the physical spaces they designed, Whyte advised them to "follow children . . . there are lessons to be learned. They like clutter, forbidden clutter, best of all, and they show a marked antipathy to barriers and signs telling them what not to do." The way children use or misuse play areas could be "cues for future designs. But the designers rarely see them. They do not, as a practice, go back and study how children actually use their projects, or how adults do, for that matter."[38]

Whyte devoted only two pages to small spaces but allotted ten pages to his examination of play areas. Why so much? One reason could have been that he was spending more time in play areas than usual. As he was pondering the vanishing landscapes in the countryside and the increasing importance of small spaces in urban areas, the organization man had become a family man as well.

Chapter 10

Organization Man to Family Man

A s William H. Whyte's stepbrother, Jim Perry, wrote in a memorial, "Holly liked characters, no doubt because he was one himself."[1]

Whyte, an avowed policy wonk who could bury himself in land use laws and zoning ordinances, nevertheless had a soft spot in his heart for people who ran against the grain of conventional standards. In his memoir Whyte waxed poetic about his mother's ne'er-do-well brother, his uncle Joe. When Whyte wrote about the Marine Corps, he expressed fondness for his slightly dysfunctional commander, Lieutenant Colonel "Wild Bill" McKelvey. When researching the "organization families" who populated the suburb of Park Forest, Illinois, Whyte highlighted one housewife who formerly had been a "burlesque stripper." Her presence, Whyte reported, "thoroughly confounded" the other housewives. He quoted her as she and her husband prepared to leave town: "They're just jealous because I'm theatrical folk. All these wives think I want their husbands. What a laugh. I don't even want my own. The bitches."[2]

In *City: Rediscovering the Center*, Whyte devoted an entire chapter to street people, including odd people with odd names—Moondog, Mr. Magoo, Captain Horrible, Aztec Priestess, and the like. Their presence, Whyte believed, was an index of a place's vibrancy. Above all, they were characters. Whyte liked characters.

Not surprisingly, then, in the fall of 1964 Whyte married a character, and a celebrity in her own right, Jenny Bell Bechtel. Whyte's college class-mates quickly took notice of the wedding via an item, with photographs, printed in the Class Notes section of the *Princeton Alumni Weekly*.

> Our organization man Holly Whyte has finally got himself or-ganized. After many years of careful and imaginative pursuit, he brought down a bird of paradise on Oct. 17; namely Jenny Bell Bechtel shown twice above, courtesy of *Time* magazine in which she was recently featured.
>
>   Jenny, who was here for our 25th Reunion is well worth the wait-ing. As a college student at Sweet Briar, she made the cover of *Ma-demoiselle*. After a few years modeling in New York, she began de-signing dresses and is now a most attractive leader in the industry, specializing in exotic designs from Africa. It is to Holly's everlasting credit that while all of the rest of the Dark Continent shouts for freedom! Jenny sweetly surrenders hers to him (and vice versa).[3]

At the time of this first marriage for both parties, Holly was forty-seven. Jenny Bell was less than a month away from her thirty-eighth birthday. The only daughter of Adelaide and Clarke Bechtel, Jenny Bell was raised in the Germantown section of Philadelphia. Her father, the second-generation owner of a wholesale jewelry business in Philadel-phia, was able to send her off to Sweet Briar College, a private women's college in rural western Virginia. It was a time of separate education for men and women and some odd social interactions that resulted from that reality. Those socials included Princeton University's annual Houseparties Weekend hosted by the all-male undergraduate eating clubs. In the spring of 1946 young women from the "seven sisters" col-leges and other women's schools descended on the Princeton campus. The student newspaper ran a front-page banner headline proclaiming that 561 "girls" were arriving for the big weekend. The paper also listed every young woman by name—Jenny Bell Bechtel was among them.[4]

Many of those house party guests had husband hunting on their agenda. Some of them may have ended up as stay-at-home moms in suburban enclaves such as Park Forest, Illinois. But Jenny Bell already was pursuing a career of her own. She had done some fashion modeling at Sweet Briar, appearing on the cover of *Mademoiselle*'s 1946 back-to-college issue. The modeling led to a career as a fashion designer. What appeared to be her first pieces, petticoats that Lord & Taylor carried, were not in fact designed by Jenny Bell. Her mother designed the petticoats to protect her daughter from prying eyes as she disrobed in front of strangers on modeling assignments. But mother and daughter pretended Jenny Bell had designed them. "No one liked to think they'd been designed by some lady in her 40s from Germantown, Pennsylvania," Jenny Bell said later.[5]

Through the 1950s Jenny Bell continued to model and design clothing. In June 1954 a *Glamour* magazine cover featured a model wearing a dotted white organdy dress with a sailor collar—"designed by Jenny Bell." By then she had dropped Bechtel from her professional name. In 1955 an advertisement for B. Altman's Junior Circle line featured Jenny Bell modeling one of her own designs. In 1962 she designed a combination sweatshirt and nightshirt with college colors—it became a fad item on men's college campuses.

Jenny Bell also dabbled in writing. In 1954 she created a children's book called *Jenny Bell's Jingle Book*. It was spiral-bound, with a tiny bell attached by a string to the binding. The sixty-page book featured a potpourri of whimsical poems based on childhood fantasies (a girl finds a tiny man in her basket), the colors of the rainbow, and the letters of the alphabet. For each letter Jenny Bell wrote an intricate four-line stanza. The letter "X" was a challenge, cleverly met by the young author:

X is for Xenophon, Xerxes, and Xavier,
For xylophone, xyster, and X marks the spot,
Xmas and X-ray and xanthic and xanthin,
Xebic and xylic—for x that's a lot.[6]

The book was illustrated with whimsical line drawings by a family friend, Peter Cook, who graduated from Princeton in 1937, two years ahead of Whyte. Cook excelled at hockey, earned a degree in architecture, and then pursued a career as a farmer and as a fine artist. Cook's wife, Joan, was the daughter of John Follinsbee, a prominent artist in the Bucks County school of painting.

Jenny Bell dedicated the *Jingle Book* to, among others, Paula and Stevie Cook, two of the younger children of the Cooks. Steve Cook, now a retired physician, remembers various suitors of Jenny Bell showing up at Heathcote, the Cook family home just outside Princeton. Soon enough there was just one, Holly Whyte, who, like Peter Cook, was a member of the Century Association in New York.[7]

By then Jenny Bell was already a world traveler. In 1963 she visited Kenya, where family friends owned a farm. She took an interest in traditional Kenyan dresses, particularly brightly colored wraps called *kikoi*. Upon her return she marketed the dress design through Lord & Taylor in New York. *Time* magazine breathlessly reported in a story that appeared a month before her marriage to Whyte, "She was allergic to the sun, terrified of snakes and never met an elephant she couldn't do without, but Jenny Bell Bechtel came home from her first safari with big game under her belt and a blazing career in the bag."[8]

The "blazing career" featured the Jenny Bell label showing up in the racks at B. Altman, Wanamaker's in Philadelphia, Marshall Field's in Chicago, and Neiman Marcus in Dallas. Not even her late-in-life pregnancy, at age thirty-eight, took Jenny Bell off her career track. If stay-at-home moms were the rule of American society in the middle of the twentieth century, then Jenny Bell Whyte was a harbinger of things to come. She took advantage of her pregnancy to design a line of maternity clothes, acquired by Lord & Taylor. A *New York Times* article announced the deal with the headline "Maternity Styles Draw Eyes to Legs—Designer Believes That Short Skirts Are Most Flattering." As Jenny Bell explained in the article, "When you're pregnant all you have to offer, really, is legs."[9]

Even after the birth of their daughter, Alexandra, Jenny Bell continued to work—as a designer and a writer. Her marriage was grist for a first-person article in *Mademoiselle* magazine in January 1967. The article, titled "The Case for Marrying Later," with the byline Jenny Bell, was said to have sparked the most subscription cancellations in the magazine's history. By today's standards the premise seems hardly controversial.

> I myself married late and happily, but that is beside the point. I think I would be as happy today if I could have married the same man at 18. But where I was at 18 I wouldn't have met him, and as I was he wouldn't have liked me. . . .
>
> Sex is no longer an excuse for early marriage. Perhaps it never should have been, but that is now an obsolete question. The current generation ought to consider itself liberated by frankness and reliable contraceptives. Two people deserve to be respected if they are in love. Weekends and holidays spent together should be spent *together*, indeed. A first love affair *may* lead to marriage, yet it certainly doesn't *have* to for it to be beautiful and memorable.

The legendary Betsy Talbot Blackwell edited *Mademoiselle* in the 1960s "for the smart young woman," as it said on the cover. The January 1967 issue could function as a time capsule of those smart women in transition. Jenny Bell's forthright approval of premarital sex was tempered, several paragraphs later, by admonitions against "trial marriages" and promiscuity. "Society, and her peers, are not going to excuse the promiscuous girl now, any more than she was excused before," Jenny Bell wrote. "She remains, as she has always been, a loveless creature to be pitied."[10]

Another turning point in Jenny Bell's career came in the early 1970s when an early American woven coverlet—or quilt—"fell into" her hands. The piece of fabric that prompted her business was available only because it was no longer suitable for its original use. "My daytime length skirt would never have been made if the coverlet had been found in good condition," Jenny Bell wrote in a richly illustrated feature in *Americana* magazine. "Generations of laundresses had been at it with lye soap and washboards. Stains discolored it, moths had lived in it, mice had nibbled away most of the fringe. . . . Yet some areas were still bright and strong and beautiful. It was the earliest kind of American weaving—Overshot—and there were interesting borders on three sides."[11]

Given her husband's interest in repurposing pieces of the urban infrastructure, the "tremendous trifles" that he referred to in *The Last
Landscape,* it would be tempting to suggest that Holly influenced Jenny
Bell's resourcefulness. But given Jenny Bell's strong-willed nature, it
might be just as tempting to say that she opened his eyes to the promise of small pieces, once valued but later discarded. In any case, to Jenny
Bell that first piece of material was as much an opportunity as an old
factory building or unused public space would be to her husband.

She soon found a trove of available materials—yards of textiles that
had once been on display at the Brooklyn Museum but were being
sold off to make more room. Whyte offered $2,000 for the entire lot.
With that material she started her own label, Museum Pieces to Wear,
in 1971. She eventually found sources of other antique Asian, American, and European fabrics at auctions and museums. Some material
came from clients themselves, who might want, for example, a dress
fashioned from an old fabric that had been a wall hanging. From such
used material Jenny Bell designed garments that ranged in price from
the hundreds to the thousands of dollars. If the prices seemed high,
she noted that "the fabrics are museum quality—and who knows, they
could even end up back in a museum."[12]

Jenny Bell's enterprise was the subject of several substantial articles
in the *New York Times.* For one client she made a dress from a French
tablecloth dating back to the late eighteenth century. She used an early
nineteenth-century Mandarin robe to create a skirt and decorated it
with "the forbidden stitch," an embroidery technique that had been
used only by the Chinese court and later was considered a lost art.
In one instance a woman from Washington, DC, sent her a box of
nineteenth-century fabrics that she had been given by her parents,
missionaries in China. "I nearly died with delight when I opened the
box," Jenny Bell told the *Times.* She turned the fabric into a wedding
dress, with a pleated panel in front and gold embroidered dragons on
the sides.

Jenny Bell took one look at a mid-nineteenth-century Chinese wall
hanging, which came from the Isabella Stewart Gardner Museum in
Boston via the Parke-Bernet Galleries, and envisioned a dress. From
the material in a red brocade Mandarin coat, she fashioned a skirt. "It's

Figure 10.1 At his thirtieth college reunion, Whyte, here with Jenny Bell and Alexandra, was honored for his writing accomplishments, including putting his "unmatchable imprint" on the 1969 plan for New York City. (Seeley G. Mudd Manuscript Library, Princeton University.)

much better for these things to come out of the closet and be worn," Jenny Bell said. "I always hate to part with them."[13]

By the time Whyte wrote *The Last Landscape*, his daughter, Alexandra, may have been a field tester for his informal studies of play areas referred to in the 1968 book. A few years later Alexandra was certainly an observer when Whyte organized young people to assist him in charting the flow of pedestrians through public spaces. But Alexandra was also exposed to her mother's career, on several occasions modeling her mother's creations. Whyte noted with pride his daughter's varied background in a statement for his fiftieth class reunion at Princeton in 1989. "What all this preparation led to was enrollment in the Harvard Divinity School [after graduating from Barnard]. The cause and effect I cannot figure out." (Alexandra is now a teacher and administrator at a Friends school in Maryland.)

In 1978, when the *New York Times* came calling for a holiday season feature on Christmas decorations, Alexandra and Jenny Bell took center stage. The Whyte family Christmas, the *Times* reported, was as homemade as possible. Reflecting Jenny Bell's Pennsylvania German Quaker background, the family urged friends to limit their gifts to items "made from scratch." Their own gifts in return were often both handmade and recycled. Jenny Bell and Alexandra created evening bags from textile fragments and baked cookies and cranberry loaf. Alexandra made her own paper envelopes for mailing a Quaker calendar that doubled as a greeting card. Brimming with a thirteen-year-old's conviction, Alexandra told the reporter she did not believe in "bought Christmases."

As for Holly Whyte, his participation in the holiday crafting was limited to encouraging words. "He doesn't like to work so hard, at least at this kind of work," declared Alexandra. "So he gives us his opinion." That opinion was to the point. "Less is more," he would tell his wife and daughter under the Christmas trees (there were sometimes two to accommodate all the hand-crafted decorations).[14]

Whyte applied the "less is more" maxim most often to the process of planning. In that endeavor, Whyte thought, action that preceded— rather than followed—planning would always be valuable. That point of view notwithstanding, Whyte would play a key role when the city of New York attempted to create a master plan after more than thirty years of inaction. The result, the *Plan for New York City 1969* and the film that accompanied it, was as idiosyncratic as the character who wrote it.

Chapter 11

From Men in Suits, a Radical Plan for New York City

I f there had been a personality test in 1969 to screen candidates for a job writing a long-range city master plan, William H. Whyte would have flunked it. And he might have taken some quiet pleasure in that fact. Whyte was not a fan of personality tests, and he already looked skeptically at planners and their master plans to guide open space preservation efforts. The planning, as he wrote in *The Exploding Metropolis*, was all "very orderly and logical; the trouble is the land may be gone before it works."[1] In the mid-1960s, when Whyte was working on *The Last Landscape*, he and the chief planner of the Regional Plan Association, Stanley Tankel, had lunch at the Harvard Club in Manhattan. Whyte lectured Tankel, the planner, on the importance of action, and not letting endless planning sidetrack it. Tankel seemed eager to stop the lecture.

"Well," Tankel retorted. "You know what planners think about that."

Whyte responded: "Okay, what?"

"We say, action drives out planning."

"Exactly," Whyte replied, with a beaming smile.[2]

As Whyte would later observe, planners would prefer "to go to hell with a plan than to heaven without one."[3] New York City in the late 1960s was heading for hell, with or without a plan. The city charter of

1938 had mandated a new city master plan, but the city had deferred to its own one-man planning department and wrecking crew, the power broker Robert Moses. There was no need to hire expensive planners when plans for New York were being sketched out, as the *New York Herald Tribune* reported in 1947, "on Moses' personal drafting board, in camera."[4] But in 1962 Governor Nelson Rockefeller stood up to Moses and ended his reign.

When reform-minded John V. Lindsay was elected New York mayor in 1965, the city seemed on the brink of collapse. *Time* magazine put Lindsay on the cover of its November 1, 1968, issue. The headline: "New York: The Breakdown of a City." Lindsay tried to change the narrative, promoting "Fun City," banning cars from Central Park on Sunday mornings, and encouraging "happenings" in city parks. The mayor extended his turnaround efforts to the planning department, advocating for a bottom-up rather than a Moses-style top-down approach. Within the department Lindsay created "an architectural and infrastructural brain trust," the Urban Design Group, to advance innovative zoning tactics to "create public benefits, not just restrict harms."[5] But the city still needed a master plan, in part because various federal agencies required municipalities to have a master plan to qualify for housing aid.[6]

So why pick Whyte to play a critical role in the plan for New York City? The chapters titled "Townscape" and "The Case for Crowding" in *The Last Landscape* hinted at Whyte's urbanist views. And he was friendly with at least one elected member of the New York City Planning Commission, Elinor Guggenheimer, who asked Whyte in 1967 for tips on how to organize a successful conference. Whyte, not shy about sharing his insights, responded with a four-page "Dear Ellie" letter. His ten key factors included a brisk opening, no luncheon speaker (an informal lunch was shorter and gave participants a chance to mingle), and five-minute speaking limits for each panelist (he had a red light on the lectern that turned on after four minutes). And, he concluded, "Coffee: Yes, Yes, Yes."[7]

Whyte had another qualification. Donald Elliott, the planning commissioner since 1966, insisted that the plan be engaging. "The staff at the planning department was a dedicated group, but they couldn't put two words together that anyone could understand. Elliott wanted a sophisticated plan that people would want to read," says Peter S. Richards, a former producer at WGBH public television in Boston, who served as editor of the project.[8]

In the end, Whyte figuratively and literally found his voice as an urbanist through the *Plan for New York City 1969* and the accompanying film, *What Is the City but the People?*, which he narrated. In finding his voice he also discovered what he considered an injustice in the New York City planning process, the squandering of opportunities to create valuable public open spaces in the heart of the city. That discovery was the genesis of Whyte's next major urban initiative in 1970, the Street Life Project, and it became the basis of his 1980 book and film, *The Social Life of Small Urban Spaces*.

Whyte's challenge was not only to make the proposed *Plan for New York City 1969* readable; it was also to make it politically palatable. Lindsay faced a difficult reelection campaign in 1969, running as an independent after losing the Republican primary in June. A passage from an early version of the plan had already angered some White middle-class residents who felt they were being unfairly blamed for the problems of minorities. The controversial passage: "The plight of New York City is not unique. . . . It has developed from the callous disinterest of our prosperous, mostly white, middle-income citizens in the widening gap between their lives and the desperate condition of the growing group of urban poor, mostly black or Spanish-speaking." The revised and more nuanced section in the final version of the plan read as follows:

> One of the major discontents of many middle-class neighborhoods is the feeling that blacks and Puerto Ricans are having too much done for them as it is. . . . We do not minimize the problems involved, nor the length of time it will take to meet them. But we strongly believe that programs opening up opportunities for blacks and Puerto Ricans will in the long run reduce the divisive tensions in the city.

According to the *New York Times*, the writer executing this deft shift from harsh reality to nuanced political correctness was Whyte.[9]

The first volume of the plan, a 182-page, ninety-thousand-word statement called *Critical Issues*, was finally released on November 15, 1969, at the fortieth anniversary meeting of the Regional Plan Association at the New York Hilton. It was conveniently eleven days after the election, in which Lindsay the Independent defeated Republican John J. Marchi and Democrat Mario Procaccino. The plan generated instant controversy—even the RPA meeting was protested by "black militants," as the *New York Times* would describe them (without identifying the reason for their protest).[10] One thing everyone could agree upon was that the plan was unconventional, both physically and in terms of content. Each of the six volumes was published in large format, seventeen by seventeen inches. The introductory *Critical Issues* volume and the five additional books addressing each of the five boroughs collectively weighed twenty-eight pounds—literally a weighty tome. The printing bill was reportedly $425,000.[11]

Sparing no promotional effort, the *Plan*'s film accompaniment, *What Is the City but the People?*, was shown on Channel 13, the New York public television station, a few days after the release of the plan. The movie and Whyte's narration, as we will see, was as unconventional as the plan itself.

"Any resemblance to the Master Plan visualized at the time the City Charter called for it in 1938 is purely coincidental," architecture critic Ada Louise Huxtable wrote in her *New York Times* appraisal. "Its renewal strategies are not the familiar redevelopment schemes in which the city is divided into neatly mapped areas with before and after pictures of blight and beauty and a vision for the year 2000." The strategies enunciated in the 1969 plan, she wrote, "deal with the renewal of people—their education, job opportunities, standards of living, participation in the governing process, and chances to 'make it' in a city where the supporting middle class has been drawn from a continuous stream of immigrants and migrants, the oppressed, and the talented."

Huxtable continued: "There are no elaborate 'trend projections' and there is no 'ultimate grand design'; in short, none of the traditional paraphernalia of the standard master plan."[12]

Huxtable's assessment was spot-on. The *Plan for New York City 1969* stated, "This plan is not a conventional master plan ... not a physical plan ... Our primary concern is with the processes for the city's growth." Even setting specific phases for implementation was "paper boldness" and "intellectually preposterous," the plan stated. "Our plans are going to be influenced by forces that the city can neither forecast nor control." The authors of the plan—officially the planning commissioner, Donald Elliott, with Whyte listed as "consultant"—admitted at the outset that they did not know if the recent decline in the birth rate would continue or not, or if a guaranteed national income would ever be adopted, or what technological advances lay ahead. "We advocate a step-by-step process that will allow us and our successors to adapt to the unforeseen."[13]

The plan began with a brutally honest assessment of the city and its prospects: "It is obvious that a great deal is wrong. The air is polluted. The streets are dirty and choked. The subways are jammed. The waters of the rivers and bays are fouled. There is a severe shortage of housing. The municipal plant is long past its prime. Greatest of all is the problem of the slums. Traditionally they have offered a route to something better in life, but they no longer seem to."[14]

The introductory text was followed by nine pages of black-and-white photographs showing the city in its glory and despair. One of the two-page spreads presented a quotation from Henry Wadsworth Longfellow: "We should find in each man's life sorrow and suffering enough to disarm all hostility." The sorrow and suffering on the pages included a photo of a lone person hunched against a blank wall, with a caption that said simply, "Mental illness." Photos from an emergency room showed a victim of an auto accident and the arm of a person who had attempted suicide. A vertical photo identified as a "tenement staircase in the Bronx" showed a small Black boy sitting at the bottom of the frame amid a pile of litter. His eyes were the brightest points in the image. You could see sorrow or suffering, or maybe even a glimmer of hope.

Whyte's literary touch was evident throughout the *Critical Issues* section.

Backhanded compliments: "It is astonishing that we have managed to create a system that is such an affront to the senses," the plan noted, with respect to the New York subway system. "But it works."[15]

Wry damnations by faint praise: regarding the design of vehicular approaches to bridges and tunnels, the master plan noted that "engineers managed to contrive the railings and abutments at just the angle to blot out for people some of the most spectacular vistas in the whole world."[16]

And the trademark Whyte observation of taking a jar half empty and portraying it as three-quarters full: "The primary need is more small parks, greatest where there seems to be no space left. But there is space, a surprising amount, and where there is none we can create it." He took a similar tack with the city's crowded streets and sidewalks. "To some observers this concentration of activity is what is most wrong." But, the plan contended, "concentration is the genius of the City. . . . We are not afraid of the bogey of high density."[17]

As in his other writing, Whyte reveled in plainspoken declarative sentences: "Public corporations have a way of being unaccountable to the public" and "When organizations are empowered to do as they damn well please, the temptation is strong for them to do just that." The plan argued that vocational students should get a broader basic education than that represented by a general diploma, which signals to prospective employers that "the holder was too dumb or too lazy for vocational or academic work."[18] In a section on parks that echoes Whyte's message in *The Last Landscape*, the master plan declares that "most of the city's playgrounds appear to have been designed by people who hate children."[19]

Richards, the project editor, and the Planning Commission staff labored on the report at its offices at 2 Lafayette Street, near New York City Hall. Whyte worked mostly from a one-room office at 131 East 61st Street, where Richards would occasionally confer with him. Though there is no record of this issue being raised, Room 5600 would have been inadvisable as a site for Whyte to engage in Planning Commission work—the Rockefellers were promoting controversial development that would favor financial, insurance, and real estate (FIRE) interests at the expense of small manufacturing firms still operating in Manhattan.[20]

"Holly provided the structure and a lot of verbal ideas," recalls Richards. At one point a half dozen planners and Whyte spent several days at a retreat at the riverside home of Chester Bowles, then ambassador to India, in Essex, Connecticut. Bowles's daughter Sally, a member of Lindsay's "cabinet," hosted the gathering. Architect Jonathan Barnett, part of the Urban Design Group, recalls arguing about, among other things, the readability of a document that was going to be printed in an oversized seventeen-by-seventeen-inch format. Whyte did not say much about any of the issues raised. "He mostly listened and smiled," Barnett recalls. "Of course, he knew he had the last word."[21]

Whyte put fifteen months into the effort, producing drafts in longhand and pressing Jenny Bell into service as a typist. She reportedly changed a word or two here and there, which made him, she claimed, "very angry."[22] The plan reflected—and no doubt refined—Whyte's thinking in several areas that were the foundations of his subsequent writing and advocacy work.

The authenticity of the urban experience. The *Plan for New York City 1969* admitted the city's problems, but it did not apologize for them. The city was not a blank canvas—as a rural landscape might be to a suburban housing developer, for example—but a teeming enterprise with idiosyncrasies that were part of the charm. The plan noted:

> We pursue no illusory utopia. New York could never be an ideal city. It has too great a dynamism and its problems are immense because they are in part the consequences of it. The slums are a terrible problem, but the blacks and Puerto Ricans came to them because they were looking for a better life, and their new militancy, disturbing as it may be, is a sign of hope and not of despair. The fierce competition for land, the crowding, the dislocations of demolition and rebuilding, are vexing problems but they are also problems of vitality.[23]

Zoning. The city's code "told developers what they can't do, but has done little to suggest what they should do." The *Plan for New York City 1969* recommended high-density districts in areas close to mass transit routes and making a floor area ratio of two square feet of developed space for every one square foot of land a minimum instead of a maximum.[24] "Current zoning," the plan stated, "permits either housing or industry, not both together. . . . This is too rigid." Echoing the arguments made in *The Last Landscape*, the *Plan for New York City 1969* called for industrial land to be "used more efficiently. Much has been squandered in the post-war emphasis on one story plants, and this has been the city's own fault. By requiring large parking areas and low ground coverage, zoning practices have enforced horizontal sprawl. This is wasteful, even in suburbia; in the city, it is profligate."[25]

Redevelopment. The plan cited "major opportunities for redevelopment of old industrial areas" including sections of the Bronx and along the East River in Brooklyn. It looked approvingly at the conversion of lofts in Manhattan south of Midtown into residential units. But it warned that the conversion process should not force small firms to go out of business prematurely. The repurposing of the Brooklyn Navy Yard had created "an almost instant industrial park."[26] According to the plan, finding new uses for the old boats and ferries lining the city's waterfront could be a profitable undertaking. Every new school, the plan recommended, should be designed as a potential recreation center in itself and accessible to neighborhood people, instead of off limits.

Diversity of uses and of people. All those redevelopment opportunities notwithstanding, the plan rejected "the concept of wholesale demolition and barrack-like projects. Instead of clearing away neighborhoods we must work with the fabric of them and put as much emphasis on maintenance and rehabilitation as on new construction. Instead of one fixed static plan we must follow an incremental step-by-step approach and involve the people of the neighborhoods from the first steps on." The plan recommended a mixture of housing types and encouraged "architectural experimentation." Retail and commercial uses should be mixed in with projects, the plan continued. "In some cases we think it would make sense to mix industry in too and are recommending vertical zoning as a way of making it compatible." The thinking could be boiled down to a single goal: "Downtown will stay open after 5 p.m."[27]

Mixed-use designs would have their own risks. "But mixture and diversity make the character of this city and they ought to be encouraged in our plans. For homogeneity there is suburbia."[28]

Proactive reviews. The city was already being marred by "huge new buildings, often brutal and graceless." Signs and street furniture, the details that represent the city to the person on the street, "ought to be vastly improved." The plan called for "enlightened visual review" before final plans for a project were set in stone. In general, the city needed to become more responsive to the needs of the local neighborhoods. "It is not enough for us to hold a public hearing on a project. It is too late in the game. It is yea or nay then."[29]

Incentives. The plan cited the recent Times Square Theater District as a shining example of what could be accomplished through development incentives. But, mindful of the need for proactive review, the plan also referenced a 1961 ordinance that provided incentives for developers to devote space to public plazas or arcades in exchange for extra building space. The revised code had led to substantial redevelopment, especially along Third Avenue and Avenue of the Americas. "The total environment produced, however, ... is nowhere near the amenity that there could have been."[30] Within a year Whyte would begin a crusade to force developers to design these bonus plazas for the public they were intended to benefit (chapter 13).

Several passages in the plan would raise the hackles of substantial constituencies. Motorists, for example, would cringe (as we know they still do today) at the notion that "the use of cars in the business districts should be limited to the few people for whom they are a necessity, and to those who are willing to pay handsomely for the privilege." In today's terminology that would be the controversial "congestion pricing."[31] Another section of the plan bemoaned the difficulty of assembling tracts of land from various owners and the price gouging by owners of small properties standing in the way of big developers (including one 250-square-foot plot in Lower Manhattan that sold for $1 million—in 1960s dollars). To turn Manhattan into the "national center" that the plan envisioned, it recommended that the city be permitted "to complete assemblages for private and nonprofit developers, even if the existing use conforms to the zoning and is not a nuisance."[32] Those two items alone would be a tough sell in any city, then or now.

After the plan's publication, the Planning Commission held no fewer than sixty-two public hearings, one at each of the local community districts that the plan had identified. "It was a herculean effort," Elliott recalled many years later. "Almost no one talked about what we had put into the plan. They talked about the local problems they faced."[33]

The *Plan for New York City 1969* came to an ignominious end. In 1973 John Zuccotti succeeded Elliott as planning commissioner. Zuccotti dismissed master plans as "glossy brochures," with an assumption of "vision and controls" that run counter to "a free and pluralistic society." On that note Zuccotti announced that the 1969 plan was being set aside.[34]

Neither glossy nor controlling would seem to describe either the printed plan or the movie that went with it. And though the plan was set aside, it was not forgotten. A half century later the *Plan for New York City 1969* and the film continue to be studied, largely for the unconventional point of view and visual imagery of the printed document and the harsh urban reality presented in the movie.

The written plan's accompanying film, *What Is the City but the People?*, proved to be as unconventional as the plan itself. The movie dramatically portrayed the city at its worst as well as at its best, and it boldly suggested that solutions would have to come as much from the city's residents as from its professional planners. If you wanted a world of happy endings you could go to Hollywood, the film suggested, or if you wanted perfect order, you could go to the suburbs (which the film presented in a segment with Pete Seeger singing "Little Boxes" in the background).

But if you wanted to appreciate the juxtaposition of rich and poor, blessed and damned, you could do it only in a city such as New York. It was no accident that the opening scene of the movie was reminiscent of the opening scene of the 1948 movie *The Naked City*. And if viewers of the 1969 film classic *Midnight Cowboy* wondered if the people shown sleeping on the sidewalks of Midtown Manhattan were truly homeless or just actors, they could get their answer by viewing the *Plan for New York City 1969*'s film. It was all too real. (The cinematographer for *What Is the City but the People?*, Arthur Ornitz, also worked on *Midnight Cowboy*.)[35]

For the first thirty seconds of *What Is the City but the People?*, helicopter rotors blare in the background. Then sirens wail. The camera flashes from one off-putting sign to another: "Danger: Keep Out"; "Warning: Do Not Enter." Another sign: "Police Dogs Inc." A pedestrian crosswalk sign is shown at the "Don't Walk" phase.

The first human voice that is heard hollers, "Get out!" Later someone shouts, "The city stinks!" The film shows a cop slapping a ticket on a windshield. "Goddamit!" a voice shouts off camera. In what appears to be a sidewalk altercation over a parking spot, a man is shown hitting a woman with a piece of wood. An antiwar protest is shown for a few seconds, with chants of "Power to the people" on the soundtrack. Some Black Power signs flash on the screen. The film flashes in a split-second pace from one gritty scene to another.

The camera lingers at the scene of one vagrant attacking another. The apparent winner smashes a bottle over the head of his victim. The victor looks into camera, and the frame is frozen. At that point, more than two minutes into the film, the calm voice of a narrator is heard for the first time, introducing the counterpoint to all that has just been presented: "New York. Every morning two million people pour into Manhattan below 60th Street. . . . They work in advertising agencies, corporate offices, clothing factories, and department stores. . . . This is the national center. . . The very concentration is precisely what makes it all work." The calm voice belongs to Holly Whyte, who also makes an appearance at the end of the one-hour film. A lanky six-footer, Whyte strides across the green landscape of Prospect Park in Brooklyn, dressed in his signature tweed sports coat and tie, with dress shoes. His walk ends in front of a brownstone on a tree-shaded street a few blocks away. As with the text in the printed plan, Whyte's narration in the film ends with can-do resolution: "There's a tremendous reservoir of old brownstones in the city. They are being discovered by young people who otherwise might move to the suburbs."[36]

Both the plan and the film became the subject of academic criticism. In 2013 and 2014 the Art Institute of Chicago and the Princeton

University Art Museum presented an exhibition that raised the question, What role do images play in engaging citizens? The exhibition and companion book, titled *The City Lost and Found*, included photographic and cinematic elements of the *Plan for New York City 1969* and *What Is the City but the People?* In the book that accompanied the exhibition, Greg Foster-Rice, a photography professor at Columbia College in Chicago, described the "iconic role that images of the city played at all levels of urban reimagining in the 1960s and 1970s." Foster-Rice continued, "The density of imagery was so uncharacteristic of earlier city plans that it was frequently noted by reviewers and seemed to mirror the density of the urban experience itself, visually reinforcing the plan's promotion of density."[37]

In 2015 another academician explored the intersection of media imagery, architecture, and urban development in New York in the late 1960s and early 1970s. In *Imaginary Apparatus: New York City and Its Mediated Representation*, McLain Clutter, now chair of architecture at the University of Michigan, carefully considered Whyte's assertions, such as "concentration is the genius of the city" and that density and the dynamism it generates make New York "jump and hum with life": "Such ebulliently anthropomorphic language initiates the recurrent trope of naturalizing the city's dynamics, describing New York as a kind of quasi-organic entity whose ecological processes are an object of near sublime wonder."

To Clutter, the still photographs in the plan and the raw imagery of the movie constituted parts of the "mediated representations" of the city that needed to be understood by architects and urban designers. "In each photograph there is something to be augured. It is undefined, too confusing to be immediately apprehended. The photographs beg contemplative engagement with the viewer. . . . If the reader harbored some predetermined vision of the density and dynamics that the plan's authors advocated, these images seem placed to prompt a radical rethinking of these expectations."[38]

Could any of these intellectual conceits have been on the mind of Elliott, Richards, or Whyte, the wordsmith, as the *Plan for New York City 1969* and the accompanying film were being produced? This may be a propitious time to invoke Whyte's "face-value technique."[39] Most likely the authors of the plan were trying to make a direct point: that the plan was about the people of the city, for those people, and dependent on the people for its realization. It was 1960s participatory politics, not early twenty-first-century academic musings.

Those politics should not be overlooked. In the turbulent 1960s, architecture students at various universities were leaving their ivory towers and creating "people's workshops" in inner cities. In the 1960s even some gray flannel suits became agents of change. Princeton's bow-tied president Robert F. Goheen, who quoted Holly Whyte to exhort students to be ready (figuratively speaking) to blow the lid off everything, successfully transformed the university into a coeducational institution and greatly expanded the presence of minorities. The Yale University chaplain William Sloane Coffin Jr. became a leading antiwar and civil rights activist (and may have been the most celebrated member of that once vaunted Class of 1949 at Yale). And Whyte, by then, was an accomplished practitioner of "splendidly unreasonable" acts. As Huxtable wrote in 1971, "don't write off the revolution because it is being made by men in business suits at City Hall."[40]

What Is the City but the People? depicts the planners themselves coming under direct fire from the residents. The portrayal at times is harshly realistic. The architect Jonathan Barnett speculates now that the filmmakers may have unilaterally created a final cut of the film that dramatized the conflicts they observed, rather than the parts of the planning process Elliott and the Planning Commission would have emphasized. But Elliott, mindful of an "urban underground" that had developed among young planners on his staff who criticized the department's lack of transparency,[41] may have allowed the unflattering film to be aired as a sign of his openness to criticism. In any case, the establishment that paid for the film also allowed it to be shown.

After the opening montage of horrific—but undeniably authentic—urban scenes, the film introduces Mary McCarten, a resident of the working-class neighborhood of Hell's Kitchen in the west Midtown area. "It's got everything you want for a good community," McCarten says. "We have a complete economic and ethnic mixture—that's what you need." She walks through the neighborhood, stopping to ask a resident about her recent stay in Long Island. The woman has been there and come back. "I like the city," she tells McCarten. "If only you had a better apartment to live in it might make it more pleasant," McCarten says. "Oh no, I love it here," the woman says. McCarten responds, "Alright, we're trying to see that you stay here."

The scene then shifts to two men in business suits visiting the site of a major redevelopment project proposed in the Midtown area, a project that could bring—they claim—150,000 additional office workers to the area. Whyte's assuring narrator's voice is heard: "Donald Elliott and Jaque [pronounced "Jack"] Robertson understand McCarten's concern. Elliott, chairman of the New York City Planning Commission, and Robertson, an urban designer, want to resolve the inevitable conflict between office expansion and neighborhood residents."

Elliott, a 1954 Carleton College alumnus with a law degree from New York University, had served as counsel to Mayor Lindsay before being appointed chairman of the Planning Commission in 1966. Jaquelin T. Robertson, an architect (Yale, 1959) and a Rhodes scholar, had been appointed by Lindsay to his Urban Design Group. That committee, working with the Planning Commission, had forged the incentives for the Special Theater District in 1967.

In the film these two planning officials review blueprints. Robertson, speaking in a patrician tone, waxes enthusiastic about the potential synergies that can be created. "What's really exciting, Don, is that we're going to be able to do something that's never been done before in New York, which is rather than parcel-by-parcel building, where you really get no joint benefits after you have built up a whole street individually. . . . We're really talking about a new town in the middle of New York City."

It all sounds like the Robert Moses approach of just a few years earlier. But the film does not end there. Rather it shifts to a candid exchange with residents—an exchange that most public officials would seek to erase from the record rather than present for posterity. The camera again shows Elliott and Robertson, this time at a community meeting, explaining a drawing titled "Clinton Park Housing—Urban Renewal Area, Acquisition Stage 1." Even in 1969, the mere mention of urban renewal must have drawn raised eyebrows throughout New York, whether or not you had read Jane Jacobs or William H. Whyte.

The dozen working-class people in the room, whose families probably include longshoremen whose jobs are being inexorably lost, are skeptical.

A resident asks: "What provisions have been made for relocation of tenants?"

Elliott answers: "Relocation is the most difficult thing about any development. . . . The improvement in the way we do relocation is actually quite dramatic."

A man sounds anxious: "I feel we are being neglected . . . in the way we are being more and more commercialized and not having the residential part of the community preserved in any way. Commercialism will come in and wipe us out."

The camera shifts to Robertson. He says nothing but takes a long—and presumably thoughtful—drag on his cigarette.

A woman speaks: "When is something going to happen?"

Elliott answers: "We don't move as fast as private people. I wish we did. We've got to go through this elaborate procedure. In the long run I think it's going to work."

Another man cites some recent history: "When you took that 50th Street site for a school—was it five years ago?" Voices in the audience say "Yeah." "And you dislocated all those tenants. And we've even had to come and beg to you, at least make it a playground."

The camera shifts to Elliott, who rests his head on his hand. Robertson doodles with pen on paper. For a painful sixty seconds, neither one speaks as various residents do all the talking.

A woman with a vision problem, who needs four separate keys to get from the street to her apartment, complains that she can no longer go out after dark. "I wanna get out of there the worst way."

Another woman gets the last word: "What is the matter? The city really has to start to think in terms of the people. . . . Is it any wonder that our city is in the condition it's in?"

McCarten's voice is heard again. "We want progress, but they can't forget the people. Let them build before they tear down anymore. That's my hope."

In this scene the power belongs to the people. The Planning Commission, along with its plan for New York, clearly does not have all the answers. Whyte says in his narration several minutes later: "Experts are full of ideas. Residents sometimes come up with better ones."

The report and the film were precursors of an ecological approach to environmental problems, an approach that would soon be applied from wilderness and rural areas to suburbs and cities. Just months after the *Plan for New York City 1969* was released, *Time* magazine launched its Environment section, with scientist-activist Barry Commoner on the cover. During the organizing for the first Earth Day on April 22, 1970, Whyte met Fred Kent, one of Whyte's first disciples and the man who for more than forty years would lead the Project for Public Spaces, still one of the leading legacies of Whyte's urbanism (chapter 18).

The *Plan for New York City 1969* may not have had a vision for the year 2000, as some in 1969 may have hoped. But for Whyte it was a call to action—to figure out how the public had been shortchanged in so many privately owned public spaces and to examine more closely the city and its urban landscape.

Chapter 12

Preservation Tactics in the Urban Landscape

After his fifteen-month assignment working in the public sector on the *Plan for New York City 1969*, William H. Whyte could have continued building on (and profiting from) his newfound status as author of *The Last Landscape*. Whyte, by then, was a commanding voice in the land preservation movement.

As a consultant to the New Jersey Open Space Policy Commission in 1970, for example, Whyte played the role of éminence grise and morale booster. One member of the commission, William A. Haffert Jr., confessed to Whyte that the meetings "are boring me to death" and implored him to help formulate some recommendations, including the formation of a land use authority with civilian representation, if not actual control. "Your own excellent books and articles contain statements which, I believe, could help capture popular attention," Haffert wrote. The commission's work "could use some good civilian clout" and the interim report needed a stronger tone, "as only *you* could draft it."[1]

When Whyte, who was being paid $200 per day for his consulting (roughly in line with what the Rockefellers were paying around that time), revisited the Open Space Policy Commission, he expressed "amazement" at the group's efforts. "Normal procedure is to study and study and study and as one who has watched many promising ideas researched to death, I salute your impatience," Whyte told the New Jersey commissioners. "You say you don't want big studies. You want proposals for action."[2]

Plenty of other public and private open space agencies would have welcomed Whyte's wisdom. But two distractions soon vied for Whyte's attention. That 1961 New York City zoning amendment that failed to deliver the public amenity that it promised would become an obsession for Whyte in the 1970s and 1980s (chapters 13 and 14). The other distraction was the growing concern about losing New York City landmarks to the wrecking ball. Whyte saw an opportunity to apply the tactics of the land preservation movement to the urban landscape—specifically to preserve landmarks that had only minimal protection afforded by the traditional landmark designation process. This was the time to act.

Battles to save New York City landmarks had been fought building by building through the first half of the twentieth century. In the late 1950s Carnegie Hall, which opened in 1891, faced competition from the new Lincoln Center for the Performing Arts being built nearby. The music hall's owner, the real estate developer Robert E. Simon Jr., announced that it would be sold, most likely as a teardown. The New York architecture firm Pomerance & Breines had designed a forty-four-story office tower for the prospective new owner. But that owner ran into financing problems. Simon, a music lover himself, dropped the price by a quarter million dollars to enable the city and a private fund-raising group led by violinist Isaac Stern and his wife to save the building.[3] (Simon used the proceeds to assemble the land for his new town of Reston, Virginia, a project Whyte discussed in *The Last Landscape*.)

Pennsylvania Station, the pink granite Beaux Arts structure in Midtown Manhattan completed in 1910 by McKim, Mead, and White, was also targeted for demolition. Jane Jacobs, the modernist architect Philip Johnson, Eleanor Roosevelt, and other luminaries protested—in vain—to save it. The loss of Penn Station, as well as other elegant structures, was "so wanton," Whyte wrote, that it triggered a "vigorous counterattack."[4]

One counterattack began in 1965 when the city formed the New York City Landmarks Preservation Commission. As Whyte would later describe it, the commission could "designate all sorts of places as landmarks . . . but otherwise the definition of a landmark was whatever the commission thought should be a landmark. Once a structure was so designated, the owner could not change the exterior without the commission's approval. Demolition of a landmark building was forbidden unless the owner could prove there was no economic alternative. To help provide just such an alternative, the city's zoning stipulated that the owner could sell his air rights to an adjacent property owner."[5] The air rights stipulation helped the commission win its historic US Supreme Court battle in 1978 with Penn Central Railroad over the preservation of Grand Central Terminal. The railroad claimed that the landmark designation deprived it of making a fair profit. The Supreme Court noted that Penn Central could still make money by selling its air rights.[6]

The New York City Landmarks Preservation Commission did come to the rescue of some notable buildings. At its first public hearing in 1965, it designated the Astor Library on Lafayette Street—built as a free lending library in 1854—as a landmark. The building eventually became home to the Public Theater. But there were limitations to the commission's scope. Structures had to be at least thirty years old to be considered. The commission's decision could be overturned on appeal. Some preservationists thought the city was too cautious in its application of the law and too mindful of powerful property owners. "It didn't take the preservation community too long to recognize gaps in the new landmark preservation law," says Anthony C. Wood, preservationist, historian, and author of *Preserving New York: Winning the Right to Protect a City's Landmarks.* City officials essentially said that if the law created too many adverse consequences for property owners, the law would have to be changed. "Their No. 1 goal was to conserve the law, so they were very conservative in its application," Wood says.[7]

A second counterattack was needed to help strengthen the city's resolve. In 1969 Simon Breines, the Manhattan architect whose firm had designed the possible replacement for Carnegie Hall in 1960, suggested the creation of a private nonprofit landmarks conservancy to augment the official city commission. Breines ran his idea past the Municipal Art Society, as well as Whyte and Brendan Gill, the *New Yorker* drama critic who would later cover architecture for the magazine. Whyte's description of the conservancy's role sounds like a page out of *The Last Landscape*. Some of those "splendidly unreasonable" tactics for saving land could also be applied to the urban environment. "We thought a lay group such as ours could be helpful in supporting the commission, needling it, and doing a number of things the commission could not—such as buying old buildings and recycling them, or conserving the scores of buildings and blocks that did not rate landmark status but were nonetheless of architectural or historic significance."[8]

The Landmarks Preservation Commission at first wanted nothing to do with this upstart group. "I can see no advantage to setting up a new 'Landmarks Conservancy' whose functions, as you described them, would duplicate and perhaps compete with those already established. What we all need is money," the chairman of the Landmarks Preservation Commission, Harmon H. Goldstone, wrote to Breines on December 1, 1970.[9]

But these "practical preservationists," as Whyte called the new landmarks conservancy group, persisted. The wisdom of working with developers rather than treating them as natural foes, as Laurance Rockefeller and Whyte had advised conservationists in 1964,[10] was not lost on these urban preservationists. The board members eventually included, among other influential New Yorkers, Breines, the architect who would later write *The Pedestrian Revolution: Streets without Cars*; Simon, the developer who was using his Carnegie Hall proceeds for his new town of Reston, Virginia; Richard Buford, an executive with the Uris development company who was also president of the South Street Seaport Museum; and attorney Michael Gruen, son of the architect Victor Gruen. Whyte, who signed the certificate of incorporation along with Breines and Gill in 1973, described the new preservation movement as one "of outstanding effectiveness, dedication, and [perhaps most important to Whyte] guile."[11]

The nonprofit New York Landmarks Conservancy made no effort to compete with the established New York City Landmarks Preservation Commission. Instead it worked to protect buildings that required more than landmark status to be saved, or other buildings that would not qualify for landmark status but that were significant nevertheless.

To save some structures, for example, the Landmarks Conservancy accepted donations of "façade easements," stipulations that there would be no structural changes to the exteriors. The potential donors' zeal for preservation often was matched by their awareness of the income tax deduction they could claim. Whyte compared the process to what was already being done successfully by land preservation groups, "including the Brandywine Conservancy in my home county—an extraordinarily ingenious program for so conservative an area."[12]

The Landmarks Conservancy also rescued the United States Custom House, designed by Cass Gilbert and completed in 1907 at the foot of Broadway in Lower Manhattan. When the New York City Landmarks Preservation Commission was formed in 1965, one of its first designations went to the Beaux Arts Custom House. But the United States Customs Service vacated the space in 1973 to relocate to the new World Trade Center. The General Services Administration was placed in charge, and—to its credit—looked for ways to reuse the building. The GSA enlisted the New York Landmarks Conservancy to develop plans for the preservation and reuse of the building. In 1994 the space became home to the National Museum of the American Indian.

To preserve the Romanesque revival Federal Archives building on Christopher Street in Greenwich Village, the Landmarks Conservancy essentially played the role of a private developer. When the federal government vacated the late 1890s-era building, it donated it—with preservation restrictions in place—to the city. A private developer of luxury housing paid into a new Landmark Restoration and Rehabilitation Fund, managed by the Landmarks Conservancy and used to create a revolving loan fund for the purchase of historic properties.

The saving of Fraunces Tavern, the site where George Washington gave his farewell address to the troops in 1783, illustrated the Landmarks Conservancy's creativity. The tavern, at 54 Pearl Street, had been designated as a landmark in 1965—one of the first to gain that designation under the new landmarks law. Good news. But the bad news was that the five buildings flanking it on either side had not been so designated. In 1974 a developer began to demolish them. The Landmarks Conservancy convinced the city to issue a temporary stop work order and then won designation for the buildings on the National Register

of Historic Places. After successful lobbying for special zoning legislation, the conservancy purchased the five buildings and leased them to
a private developer for conversion to residential and commercial use.

Whyte also worked with the city's Landmarks Preservation Commission on occasion. From a historic preservationist's point of view,
Madison Avenue on New York's Upper East Side was an ugly duck-
ling. No individual building appeared worthy of historic designation.
As Whyte described it, the street had "no uniform cornice line," and
the facades and the signage featured "a jumble of styles."[13] But people,
especially shoppers, loved it. The street offered retail shops on both the
ground floor and the second floor. Cafés placed tables and chairs on the
sidewalks. The threat was that developers would replace the modestly
priced retail spaces with high-priced office and residential developments. In 1981 Whyte helped to convince the Landmarks Preservation
Commission to include Madison Avenue as part of its Upper East
Side Historic District.

The inclusion helped forestall the development, but it did not attempt to prohibit the somewhat garish signs that helped the Madison Avenue retailers survive. "[We weren't] going to make them have
pretty little storefronts," recalled Lorna Nowvé, who worked at the
Municipal Art Society at the time and was one of the founders of the
Historic Districts Council. "It helped people understand what historic
preservation needed to be, in terms of the fact that it was not to freeze
things in time. . . . Holly [was] one of those people who said Madison
Avenue can change appropriately. It also meant the Landmarks Commission had to be a little more flexible."[14]

Essentially the strategies devised to save the boondocks now proved
valuable to the Upper East Side. "Looking back, I think we were much
too slow to realize how relevant these rural easement strategies were to
the city," Whyte wrote later.[15]

*   *   *

Busy with this new landmark preservation work and just beginning his
lengthy study of small urban spaces, Whyte by 1972 had moved to the
sidelines of the open space movement. One telltale was evident that
year when Laurance Rockefeller organized yet another environmental

commission, this one an initiative of the Richard Nixon administration. The Task Force on Land Use and Urban Growth, like earlier Rockefeller-led commissions, was not timid. It advanced one specific proposal that was sure to be considered controversial by the Republicans. Until that time, legislative policy had been built on US Supreme Court precedents that required a balancing of "public benefit against land value loss" when considering the protection of natural, cultural, or aesthetic land resources. Instead, the task force argued, "a mere loss in land value" should "never be justification for invalidating the regulation of land use."

The report influenced the wording of Nixon's proposed national land use policy law. In his final review, the president paused when he reached the language on weighing the public benefit versus the property value. Before signing off on it, he asked pointedly, "Who's the SOB who wrote this?"[16]

The son of a bitch in this case was not William H. Whyte. After serving on three different Rockefeller-organized commissions in the 1960s and being responsible for some "imaginative" reports, Whyte this time was not the editor. In fact, he was not even on the commission. The SOB was William K. Reilly, chairman of the task force, who also wrote the draft of the proposed land use policy law. That law, as Adam Rome wrote, moved Republicans to rethink the rights and responsibilities of property ownership.[17] A few years later, as president of the Conservation Foundation, Reilly would view Whyte as a mentor and become a major supporter as Whyte moved into the next phase of his career. By then Whyte was following up on that unfinished piece of business from the *Plan for New York City 1969*: the study of small urban spaces.

Chapter 13

The Art of Small Urban Spaces

In the 1970s William H. Whyte recalibrated his critical thinking, turning from the land preservation movement to the study of the urban landscape. Whyte's counterintuitive approach would pay off in this pursuit, just as it had with other issues he had tackled earlier in his career. The urban streetscape was too congested, everyone said. Really? Whyte asked. Was that congestion necessarily bad? There's not enough open space. Really? It's too noisy. There's not enough light. Really? Really?

In working on the *Plan for New York City 1969* Whyte had marveled at the tax incentives that had helped save the Theater District. But he looked less favorably at incentives in the 1961 zoning code that offered a developer an additional ten square feet of commercial (and lucrative) floor area for each square foot of public plaza created. A developer who was allowed to build a forty-story office tower under the regular zoning code, for example, could build up to forty-eight stories in exchange for putting a public plaza at the base of the building. By the late 1960s every single developer in Midtown had taken advantage of the incentive. No one had balked at the terms. Hundreds of new public plazas covered about twenty acres of prime New York real estate.[1]

The incentive was a good deal for developers. But how good? Whyte soon discovered some empirical data that told the story. Jerold S. Kayden, who was studying both urban planning and law at Harvard University, had written a research paper on incentive zoning in New York. His research showed that developers had reaped nearly forty-eight dollars' worth of extra floor space for every dollar invested in a plaza. After Kayden's research was published by the Lincoln Institute of Land Policy, Whyte placed a call to Kayden, then just a graduate student. Whyte, eager to learn more, treated Kayden "as a colleague." And the young graduate student quickly saw the basis of Whyte's concern—a concern that Kayden maintains to this day (chapter 18).[2]

The incentives, Whyte concluded, resulted in "several fine individual buildings," but most of the public spaces were seldom used for any normal activities, not even for reading or people watching. Many sat empty—congestion was no problem at all. The only requirement for the plazas, according to the 1961 zoning code, was that the plaza be accessible to the public at all times. "That, as it turned out, was about all they were," Whyte wrote. The city was "being had."[3]

But what made the plazas so bad? At the conclusion of his work on the *Plan for New York City 1969*, Whyte had suggested to Planning Commissioner Donald Elliott that the city create a unit to evaluate the outcomes of various planning initiatives, including the plaza incentives. When such a unit failed to materialize, Whyte plunged into the subject on his own and quickly generated some considerable support. Hunter College appointed him a "distinguished professor," a position that enabled him to hire student interns to assist in the research. Then he won an "expedition grant" from the National Geographic Society. The story of how he won that grant varies, but by one account Whyte ran into an old friend, Conrad Wirth, a member of the society's board, and described his research. Wirth asked Whyte how much money he needed. Whyte said $25,000. Wirth said, "Make it $35,000."[4]

Whyte formed the Street Life Project in 1970 to coordinate the work. At the time, he wrote, there was no good role model: "Direct observation had long been used for the study of people in far-off lands. It had not been used to any great extent in the U.S. city. There was much concern over urban crowding, but most of the research on the issue was done somewhere other than where it supposedly occurred. The most notable studies were of crowded animals, or of students and members of institutions responding to experimental situations—often valuable research, to be sure, but somewhat vicarious."[5]

Whyte practiced direct observation. Drawing on his Marine Corps belief in inductive reasoning, he began with no foregone conclusions. His first target was a place that he found puzzling: the plaza in front of the Seagram Building at 375 Park Avenue between 52nd and 53rd Streets. He had cited Seagram in the *Plan for New York City 1969* as an example of a space, "either by design or happy accident," that had become a popular gathering place despite its "austerely elegant" design and lack of benches for sitting. "We were curious to know why." The architects of the 1958 modernist office tower, Mies van der Rohe and Philip Johnson, had not intended the plaza to be anything other than a grand pedestal on which their building would stand. One early plan called for the entire plaza to be a pool, with a lone walkway leading from the street to the main entrance.[6] Johnson later remarked, "We designed those blocks in front of the Seagram Building so people could not sit on them, but, you see, people want to so badly that they sit there anyhow. They like that place so much that they crawl, inch along that little narrow edge of the wall. We put the water near the marble ledge because we thought they'd fall over if they sat there. They don't fall over; they get there anyhow."[7]

But part of the plaza's attraction to the public was its sun-drenched open space, the shimmering pools on the northwest and southwest corners, and the sense of enclosure created by its across-the-street neighbor, the Renaissance-style five-story Racquet and Tennis Club. Just as Jane Jacobs had her second-floor window on Hudson Street in the West Village to view the "street ballet" below, so Whyte used the Racquet and Tennis Club roof as the perch from which he filmed the "action" at the Seagram plaza.

"The architects had valued simplicity," Whyte wrote later of the Seagram plaza. "There were no fussy railings, no shrubbery, no gratuitous changes in elevation, no ornamentation to clutter spaces. The steps were made easy and inviting. The place was eminently sittable, without a bench on it. The periphery includes some 600 feet of ledge and step space, which is just right for sitting, eating, and sunbathing. People use all of it."[8]

Armed with that information, Whyte again petitioned Elliott, the planning commissioner, to consider the costs and benefits of the incentive zoning. "I entrapped him into spending a weekend looking at time-lapse films of plaza use and nonuse. He felt that tougher zoning was in order. If we could find out why the good plazas worked and the bad ones didn't, and come up with hard guidelines, we could have the basis of a new code. Since we could expect the proposals to be strongly contested, it would be important to document the case to a fare-thee-well."[9]

Whyte himself had expressed doubts about the efficacy of zoning in the past, believing it to be an ineffective tool in the land preservation movement. So when asked, essentially, to try his hand at writing a zoning ordinance, Whyte prepared like a marine. He began with painstaking observation and created a disciplined process to chart the movements of people in and out of public spaces as well as within them. And he charted those movements not just for an hour or so but throughout an entire day, day after day. "I suppose nothing I have done demonstrates the lessons I learned on Guadalcanal as much as the Street Life Project," Whyte wrote in his memoir.[10]

Ann Herendeen, one of the youngest members of the observation team, was hired to work for a gap year between high school and college. "I had no qualifications, just a new high school graduate, and that was apparently all Holly needed, someone who could observe and take accurate notes," she recalls. Training was minimal. "Holly explained the basic premise. We were observing to see what worked and what didn't, with the goal of making recommendations for future construction."[11]

The methodology was straightforward: Whyte assigned observers to monitor specific places. At one point Herendeen had a route of plazas to visit daily at lunchtime, between noon and 2:00 p.m. On a hand-drawn map, the observer would indicate who was present. An "X" represented a man; an "O" indicated a woman; an "S" next to an "X" or an "O" designated someone standing. Circles around letters indicated that those people were part of a group. The observers updated the chart on a regular basis.

Whyte strove to be unobtrusive. He placed his camera at hip level as he filmed or took photographs at street level. And he usually wore a coat and tie, dress shoes, and a small-brim fedora, looking like an ordinary organization man rather than a streetwise urban anthropologist. As one of his interns, Paco Underhill, later wrote, "No vampy loafers for someone who walked the streets, no sneakers, no business-casual Polo shirts. I must have seen him at least once without a tie, but I can't remember when."[12]

Initially the Street Life Project interns met with Whyte at his small office on East 61st Street. Later his base moved to Room 5600 at Rockefeller Center. One of his office neighbors, Bill Moody, a program officer at the Rockefeller Brothers Fund, recalls tagging along on some lunchtime expeditions as Whyte and his team observed and charted movements in and out of a public space. "The sites seemed so simple. But he would always take extra time to look deeper at every place," says Moody. "I was amazed at how much time they spent at a location."[13]

Whyte would use the word "monomaniacal" to describe the work. One chart of just one day's activity at the Seagram plaza took the Street Life team more than one hundred hours to produce, much of it in front of film viewers. "I think that chart was worth the effort. But the time spent was simply too much for the technique to be reproducible," Whyte wrote. "Since then, we have learned to cut the time by over half, and with no loss of accuracy."[14]

Like the vanishing landscape, the rites (and rights) of people in public spaces turned out to have some "sex appeal." Whyte played to that appeal in a December 1972 *New York Times Magazine* article titled "Please, Just a Nice Place to Sit." As the headline suggested, there were not enough places to sit, "and not entirely by accident, either," Whyte charged. "Some builders genuinely and sincerely mistrust people. . . . They instruct architects to design features that will discourage 'loitering'—what a Calvinist tract is in that word—and sometimes there is a show of active hostility." Whyte's photographs accompanying the article showed sawtooth railings on a ledge outside the Regency Hotel on East 61st Street. The following were among his other findings.[15]

People sit most where there are places to sit. As Whyte would later write, "This may not strike you as an intellectual bombshell, and, now that I look back on our study, I wonder why it was not more apparent to us from the beginning." Simple places—ledges, for example—were often the best places for sitting. Steps, "if they are broad enough," also work as seating. He cited the steps of the New York Public Library and the Metropolitan Museum of Art as good examples.

Front-row seats are prime spots. But rear spaces should be visually accessible to the front. The best of both worlds is a secluded, cavelike place under a tree, yet with a view of the action out front. Steps and ledges offer freedom of choice, allowing people to sort themselves out in a variety of groupings. Benches and fixed seats might be more comfortable, but they limit choice. The best solution of all, Whyte would eventually conclude, was movable chairs.

Women are a good barometer of a space's popularity. Women "are choosier than men—watch them confer when they're figuring where to sit and eat." A low proportion of women is a sign "that things are wrong" with a particular space. Whyte noted also that within a plaza "men will favor the front locations; women, the rear. Lovers, incidentally, are quite regular. Contrary to plaza lore, they do not tryst mostly in the secluded places. They're right out front."

Sidewalk food vendors are critical. The vendors, selling "Italian ices, hot dogs, knishes, chestnuts, and soft drinks are its caterers, by default." They meet a demand in the neighborhood that had previously been met by small restaurants, luncheonettes, and sandwich shops—the places demolished to make way for the office towers and the plazas.

People naturally gather at street corners. The same is true of the corners of a plaza. "You'll see satellite groups and conversations at the curb and the corners. Plazas should tie into it." Whyte concluded his 1972 piece with a call to action that would reverberate in his later writing.

> Throughout the city we can vastly increase the amount of useful space for people, with more plazas, more street space, more nooks and small oases; and for merchants and businessmen as well as everyone else, it would be a lot better if we did. It wouldn't be paradise—New Yorkers would be miserable in such a place. But there'd

be more of what gives the city its edge—more shmoozing, more picnicking, more kooks and screwballs and pretty girls to look at.

And there'd be a place to sit. Not a bad test for city planning.

A year and a half later Whyte shared some additional findings from his study, this time playing directly on sex appeal. In 1974 *New York Magazine* featured a memorable cover image: two young urban professionals—a man with his suit coat thrown over his shoulder and a blonde woman looking up at him. They are embracing, inches away from locking lips. In the background passersby and people sitting on benches pay no attention. A cover headline declares, "A four-year study shows there's more shmoozing, smooching, noshing, ogling, milling, and mingling than ever, and why it's getting better all the time." As detailed in the following paragraphs, Whyte, author of the study, had plenty to report to the magazine's audience.[16]

On the usage of plazas and small parks: Whyte offered empirical evidence that it was increasing. Comparing "across the board" averages from the summer of 1972 to the summer of 1973, the number of people sitting in these spaces had increased by around 30 percent. The counts for the summer of 1974 were about 20 percent higher. "The center city is about the last place one would think of for outdoor recreation," Whyte wrote. "It may be the most important."

Cars versus pedestrians: Whyte's research corroborated the impression of most New York pedestrians—they were given short shrift. Whyte targeted the east sidewalk of Lexington Avenue, between 57th and 58th Streets, as "possibly the most congested one anywhere in the world." The sidewalk's width was twelve feet, but the effective width for moving pedestrians was only about half that because of various impediments such as trash cans, signposts, news vending boxes, and the like. Nevertheless, Whyte's team recorded some thirty-eight thousand people passing by an observation point during a period from 8:00 a.m. to 8:00 p.m. on a weekday. During that same period the nine-and-a-half-foot-wide parking lane was occupied by a total of twelve parked cars, which had carried a grand total of fifteen people.

Closing streets to cars: New York had turned Madison Avenue from 61st to 72nd Streets into an all-pedestrian mall on Tuesday evenings for about eight weeks in the spring of 1971. The closing was fought bitterly by some merchants, who were convinced the area would "be overrun by hippies, students, and other undesirables." Whyte's time-lapse photography showed that the crowds were "overwhelmingly" office workers and shoppers. In a letter to the *New York Times*, Whyte presented (in vain, as it turned out) more empirical data to support the mall. During the operation of the mall, foot traffic was about double the average flow of nine thousand people per hour. As for the alleged predominance of hippies descending on Madison Avenue, Whyte challenged "anyone to examine the 72,000-odd frames of our photographic record and find more than a handful in which hippy types can be spotted."

When Whyte extended his study from Manhattan to Brooklyn, he needed an observation perch. He sought advice from Margot Wellington, at the time working for the Downtown Brooklyn Development Association (and soon to be executive director of the Municipal Art Society, which would become a major supporter of Whyte). She pointed him toward the Abraham & Straus department store, eight stories high, and then got him permission to go to the roof.[17] Such rooftop perches were not comfortable for everyone on Whyte's team. Paco Underhill, an early member of the Street Life Project, discovered he was afraid of heights. He quit the project and applied Whyte's observational techniques to the study of customers in retail stores—a profitable endeavor that became Underhill's lifelong occupation.[18]

Whyte, obviously years behind the emerging feminist movement, offered several observations about "girl watchers." The most demonstrative of the lot were the hard hats, ready to "whistle and shout when pretty ones go by." One notch below the hard hats on the demonstrative scale were white-collar Wall Street workers. The girl watchers uptown, Whyte observed, were more subdued. That was puzzling to Whyte since, in his judgment, "uptown has the prettiest girls." In a qualification that might have passed for political correctness at the time, Whyte added that the girl watchers were not offensive: "It is all machismo, and passive. Never have we spotted a girl-watcher picking up a girl, or trying to."[19] (At least one of his women interns from that period now recalls Whyte's language as that of a harmless dinosaur and says she appreciated the thoroughness of his observations, even of men with roving eyes. Whyte ignored no one.)

Whyte, the dedicated empiricist, looked for ways to judge the validity of the Street Life Project findings. "Social science courses generally put observation on the bottom of the technological ladder and expose students to it briefly before taking them onwards to the more quantitative techniques. Because of this bias, most research tends to be once or twice removed from the reality being studied; on subjects like urban crowding, it is not apt to be of people on the streets, but of data on responses to questions about people on the streets. For students of street life, as a consequence, there are few counterpart studies to provide a base for comparison."[20]

Whyte and his team of student researchers, however, found just such a counterpart when they crossed paths with some veteran urban analysts from the Regional Plan Association (RPA) of the metropolitan New York area. Boris S. Pushkarev, a Yale University–trained architect and the RPA's senior vice president, and Jeffrey M. Zupan, a registered professional engineer, were studying pedestrian crowding on sidewalks and at intersections. On several occasions the two groups studied the same blocks at the same time. The RPA engineers used aerial photography to chart pedestrian flows; Whyte relied on time-lapse photography. Notwithstanding their different styles, Pushkarev and Zupan's findings "matched closely" the results of the Street Life Project.[21]

Whyte enjoyed more good news in 1975. The city used many of his recommendations in its new zoning incentives for public plazas. The wording reflected Whyte's view that "most incentive zoning ordinances are very, very specific as to what the developer gets. The trouble is that they are mushy as to what he is to give, and mushier yet as to what will happen if later he doesn't. Vague stipulations, as many cities have learned, are unenforceable. What you do not prescribe quite explicitly, you do not get." The paragraphs that follow detail some of the explicit provisions in the revised 1975 code.[22]

One linear foot of seating space was to be provided for every thirty square feet of plaza. Whyte saw a special advantage to movable chairs as opposed to stationary benches. "Chairs enlarge choice: to move into the sun, out of it, to make room for groups, move away from them. The possibility of choice is as important as the exercise of it. If you know you can move if you want to, you feel more comfortable staying put." For that reason, Whyte recommended that the new zoning guidelines for public plazas credit each movable chair with thirty inches of linear seating, even though they usually measure only nineteen inches in width. The building department objected, raising the fear of chairs being stolen. In the end it compromised: no more than 50 percent of the seating requirement could be met with movable chairs, and they could be put in storage between 7:00 p.m. and 7:00 a.m. (As of 1974, when Whyte took note of the chairs for his *New York Magazine* article, not a single chair had yet been stolen from either Paley Park or Greenacre Park, the heavily used vest-pocket parks in Midtown Manhattan.)

Trees at least 3.5 inches in diameter should be planted along every twenty-five feet of sidewalk. A plaza of five thousand square feet should have a minimum of six trees.

At least 50 percent of ground-floor frontage of a new building must be devoted to retail or food uses in order for the building to qualify for an open space bonus. Retailing, Whyte believed, was critical to street life.

The elevation of a plaza was often critical to its success or failure. "The level of an urban plaza shall not at any point be more than three feet above nor three feet below the curb level of the nearest adjoining street." Stairs "shall have closed risers, no projected nosings, a maximum riser height of 7.5 inches, and a minimum tread width of 11 inches."

Some Whyte ideas didn't make the cut. "If you want to seed a place with activity, put out food," Whyte asserted. He couldn't find a way to quantify the presence of food, but he did recommend that the new zoning law require "basic food facilities" in all new plazas and parks. The Planning Commission rejected that, but it did allow up to 20 percent of an open area to be set aside for food kiosks and outdoor cafés without their being counted as floor area obstructions. And the provision was made retroactive so that existing plazas could make room for food vendors.

*   *   *

At this point in his life, Whyte had been preaching for more than twenty years that changing the status quo requires skepticism, questioning, and curiosity—and the willingness "to blow the lid off everything" if needed. He had tailored his message to employees in business, to citizens trying to save open space, and to nonprofits protecting historic landmarks. But now he was challenging the status quo on city streets, essentially practicing urban planning without a license. But Whyte's lack of training in architecture, landscape architecture, or planning may have been fortuitous. As a layman with no architectural reputation at stake, Whyte could look at the public spaces adjoining a building without needing to pass judgment on the building. The Street Life Project appeared "to benefit from a non-designer's viewpoint," noted Miriam Fitzpatrick, an assistant professor of architecture at University College Dublin, Ireland, who has studied Whyte and the Street Life Project extensively and continues to use Whyte's work in her courses (chapter 18). "Because the Street Life Project was based on fieldwork and hard evidence," she wrote, "it remained relatively independent of aesthetic judgment about the Modernist spaces it examined."[23]

Whyte himself saw the advantage in not judging the space by the buildings surrounding it. In fact, Whyte concluded, there seemed to be no correlation between the "elegance and purity" of the building's design and the user-friendliness of the plaza adjoining it. As Whyte wrote in *The Social Life of Small Urban Spaces*, "the designer sees the whole building—the clean verticals, the horizontals, the way Mies [van der Rohe] turned his corners, and so on. The person sitting on the plaza might be quite unaware of such matters."[24]

Fortunately for Whyte, several architects welcomed social scientists (and laymen such as Whyte) into their realm. As Whyte's Street Life Project progressed, the architecture dean at Princeton University, Robert Geddes, was looking for an addition to his advisory council. At that time, Geddes recalls, "the idea of architects being interested in the social sciences was almost nonexistent." The dean appreciated Whyte as a layman who "saw architecture as an interactive process, not just getting something built. . . . What Holly Whyte assumed was what we had could be improved. The purpose of art was not the object itself, but what it does to the person who experienced it."[25]

Whyte's work was further validated by other architects and academicians pursuing similar approaches in studying cities. Kevin Lynch of the Massachusetts Institute of Technology had done empirical studies of people's movements in three urban settings for his influential 1960 book, *The Image of the City*. On the basis of five years of studying the ways in which people use, perceive, and absorb the city, Lynch categorized the urban landscape as paths, edges, districts, nodes, and landmarks. In 1961 Gordon Cullen, an English architect and urban designer, published his book *Townscape*, in which he identified and analyzed the characteristics of successful British towns and developed them into lessons for architects and planners. Cullen was well known to Whyte. As the editor of *The Exploding Metropolis* in 1958, Whyte had commissioned Cullen to draw illustrations of American townscapes "from the way people actually see them, from eye level."[26]

A decade later sociologist Erving Goffman scrutinized the "voluntary coordination of action" between pedestrians crossing paths on the sidewalk and the "civil inattention" that allows strangers to sit quite close together without infringing on the other's right to privacy.[27]

The Danish architect and urban designer Jan Gehl came closest to matching Whyte in the thoroughness of his studies of urban centers. Whyte hosted Gehl on a visit to New York in 1976, advising him in a letter that he had secured a reservation for him at the Barbizon-Plaza Hotel at a "special faculty rate of $29 a night. It is not cheap, perhaps, but a bargain in comparison to prevailing rates." As reported in *People Cities: The Life and Legacy of Jan Gehl*, Whyte and Gehl discovered in their meeting that "many of their findings about human behavior in public space seemed universal, whether in Italy, Copenhagen, or New York." Gehl thought that discovery surprised Whyte, who seemed to believe the behavior he observed was idiosyncratic to New York and New Yorkers.[28]

If Whyte actually believed that, he would soon have reason to change his view. The Japan Society in New York and the International House of Japan sponsored Whyte and family on two visits to Tokyo to study street life there in 1976 and 1977.

In his New York surveys Whyte was surprised at the self-congestion created by pedestrians. On the busiest sidewalks of Manhattan, Whyte assumed, pedestrians stopping to chat would move off to the side, away from the flow of traffic. Instead they would stand their ground in the middle of the flow and sometimes move even closer to the center of the flow. Street Life Project intern Madge Bemiss charted the Tokyo pedestrians, keeping a log of conversations on the sidewalk outside the entrance to a major Tokyo department store. She compared it with a survey of pedestrian interactions outside Alexander's department store on 59th Street in Manhattan. In both locations the pedestrians' behavior was remarkably similar—people tended to cluster in the middle of the pedestrian flow. (A Yale graduate who knew the Whytes through family friends, Bemiss discovered architecture as a Street Life Project intern. She now practices in Richmond, Virginia, and credits Whyte for lessons that define her approach as an architect.)[29]

"What attracts people most in an urban space is other people," Whyte concluded.[30] In Tokyo as in New York, there were almost no pedestrian collisions, despite numerous close calls. "By rights, people should be bumping into each other all over the place," Whyte observed. "They don't seem to."[31]

Many of the principles that applied to successful urban places, Whyte discovered, also applied to suburban settings. In 1976, on the twentieth anniversary of publication of *The Organization Man*, Whyte returned to speak in Park Forest, the town just outside Chicago that had been his petri dish for his study of organization men and their families. Mostly he talked about the community's downtown center and how it was failing. A proposal to cover the Plaza, as it was called, and create more parking to rival the big new covered mall outside of town was "asinine." Whyte urged instead that the center develop more "functional activities," including a restaurant and possibly a municipal office. "The heart of any good shopping center is pedestrian use," Whyte told the Park Forest audience.[32]

As "fascinating" as all this research was (as well as "a wonderful reason to travel"), Whyte knew that the research had to be presented in a book. And he knew he owed a book to Doubleday, which had published *The Last Landscape*. In April 1973, Whyte handwrote a note to Geddes at Princeton, declining to renew his term on the architecture school's advisory council and alluding to a 1974 deadline. "My research work on urban space should be winding up this fall and thereupon I plan to hole up for at least a year to pull the material together and complete a book. To do it I must foreswear any other commitments and stick monomaniacally to my task."[33]

But Doubleday was under a different impression. Managing editor Pyke Johnson Jr. told Whyte in October 1976 that the business department had come across some old contracts and realized his deadline had been March 1969—suggesting that Whyte might have signed a deal for a new book (and the advance that would go with it) as soon as he submitted *The Last Landscape*. But Johnson's tone was casual: "This constitutes no particular pressure, just an effort to clean things up so that your conscience won't be bothering you and that we won't have to nag you."[34]

The project kept getting broader—from the United States to Japan, from the cities to the suburbs, from street vendors to shopping malls. As Whyte had written in the *Marine Corps Gazette* during World War II, "the transformation of information into intelligence requires no super-mind gifted with a mystical intuition, but one with sufficient humility not to short-cut sound procedure and jump to immediate conclusions."[35] Communicating the findings of the Street Life Project took far more time than arriving at them.

By the late 1970s, though Whyte had "not quite yet" made sense out of all of his observations from the Street Life Project and his subsequent consulting work, he did see "immediate applicability" to one element—"our study of spaces that work, don't work, and the reasons why."[36] The result was a 125-page "pre-book," *The Social Life of Small Urban Spaces*. "The little red book," as some urbanists call it, had thirteen printings through 2016.

Whyte discovered an old ally from his open space days to underwrite the book's publication. The Conservation Foundation, founded in 1948 (with support from Laurance Rockefeller), lobbied to protect undeveloped land and the wildlife it harbored. But in the 1970s, undoubtedly encouraged by Whyte, then vice-chairman of the organization's board, the Conservation Foundation had begun to address the urban landscape. Its president, as of 1973, was William K. Reilly, the "SOB" conservationist who had risked Richard Nixon's wrath by promoting the public good over private interests. "Why should conservationists care what the people in New York streets are doing?" asked Reilly in the foreword to *The Social Life of Small Urban Spaces*. "Quite simply, if people find cities uninhabitable, they will want to move out of them. So our challenge is to conserve both country *and* city."[37]

Whyte's 125-page pre-book came closer than any of his other writings to offering a prescription for creating better, that is, more livable, urban environments. Whyte offered a checklist for any city planner designing a public space: street access, seating, sun, water, trees, food, and an opportunity for triangulation, when strangers are prompted to talk to one another as if they were friends. Because seating is critical, Whyte provided some specific guidelines. The optimum height for seating is 17 inches, for example, but people will sit "almost anywhere between a height of one foot and three." A bench or a ledge can accommodate people sitting back-to-back if it is at least 30 inches deep, but 36 inches is "better yet." Benches bolted to the ground are not used nearly as much as movable chairs. Groves of trees are inviting spots for people to sit. The relationship of a plaza to the street is critical. "Ideally, the transition should be such that it's hard to tell where one ends and the other begins," Whyte wrote.[38]

In the book Whyte also tackled head-on the litany of common—but often unfounded—complaints about cities. These complaints were cited with so much certitude when Whyte started the Street Life Project that even die-hard lovers of the urban scene probably accepted them as harsh facts of life, the cold reality you had to accept in the big city. In contrast, Whyte sounded like an eternal optimist.

Too much congestion? Whyte created a way to measure the carrying capacity of a public place or—to put it another way—how many people is too many in a given space. To arrive at a number, Whyte made detailed studies of five places that appeared to be most intensely used. He recorded the number of people sitting at peak and off-peak hours. He then calculated the average number of people per 100 feet of available seating. The range was 33 to 38 people per 100 feet. That number, Whyte noted, was less than the actual physical capacity of the seating. If people sat as closely as they do on a bus, the average would approach 60 people per 100 feet. That number was lower supported a Whyte theory first noted at the Seagram plaza: capacity is self-regulating. "Many planning boards worry about carrying capacity and fear that more amenities, more sitting spaces, could stimulate too much use." But the real worry, Whyte noted, should be underuse. People "determine the level of crowding, and they do it very well."[39]

Not enough open space? Even in a densely developed city such as New York, Whyte believed, there were ways to "create" more open space—simply by making what already existed more amenable to people. "We know how," Whyte wrote. "In both the design and management of spaces, there are many ways to make it much easier for people to mingle and meet." In another year or so, Whyte would outline a plan for the 9.6-acre Bryant Park to be returned to the general public after a long run as a haven for pimps and drug dealers. In addition, Whyte suggested, some "felicitous spaces" could be created out of "leftovers, niches, odds and ends." Such small places "are right in front of our noses. If we will look."[40]

Too noisy? People's perception of sound in a public space and the actual noise level can be two very different things. Visitors flocked to Paley Park, a 42-by-100-foot space with a waterfall perpetually flowing over the closed end opposite the street. Whyte measured the sound level of the waterfall at about 75 decibels, louder than that of the street outside. When he played tapes of the waterfall alone, people thought it was the sound of a subway car or truck passing by. Inside the park, however, visitors described the experience as quiet and restful.[41]

Not enough light? The new zoning for New York in 1975 required that new plazas and open spaces be given a southern exposure. But even plazas stuck with a northern exposure could bask in reflected glory—sun that bounced off glass and stainless steel, travertine tile, and mirror walls into places that were formerly in the shadows. How could Whyte tell the difference? Over the course of eight years of filming on several streets he had to change the exposure settings on his cameras by a half-stop to adjust for increased light.[42]

By the 1970s reporters and commentators often described Whyte as an urban sociologist or anthropologist. Whyte himself must have viewed with great irony the description of his work as scientific and the inclusion of his name in the ranks of the social scientists. In *The*

Organization Man, Whyte had called out "scientism" as one of the most pernicious elements of organization life. Scientism was "the promise that with the same techniques that have worked in the physical sciences we can eventually create an exact science of man." And one particular branch of that scientism was "social engineering," a set of beliefs that could easily corrupt "social science." In fact, as Whyte wrote, social science would be better off if it were called, simply, social studies. "The study of man and society is quite worthy enough an occupation without being saddled with the task of hammering out a finite, embracing science, and the ultimate test of a social scientist's particular way of looking at people cannot be absolute truth; only the arrogant—or the stupid—can so aspire."[43]

Whyte clearly aspired to no absolute truth. In his study of Tokyo crowding, for example, he cited the importance of context. "It is probably not happenstance that so many of the most popular walkways range between 15 to 20 feet in width"—broad enough to accommodate heavy flows, narrow enough that they don't feel empty when lightly used, and at either time allowing the pedestrians to experience both sides of the walkway. But Whyte added that he was not suggesting 15 to 20 feet as the optimum for city planners, or that there even was an optimum. "Context is all-important and this has to be studied just as much as quantitative factors."[44]

And while specific guidelines were necessary, Whyte also knew they were not sufficient to create the most successful public places. Such places have their own idiosyncratic context. Whyte stated the point in the book. He also showed it visually in the fifty-eight-minute film, also called *The Social Life of Small Urban Spaces*.[45]

Unlike the film that accompanied the *Plan for New York City 1969*, which was the work of cinematographers John Peer Nugent and Gordon Hyatt, the *Social Life of Small Urban Spaces* film was mostly an amateur effort. Whyte wrote it and also narrated it. Whyte and one of his interns, Marilyn Russell, filmed the scenes with a handheld 16-millimeter camera. The graphics were produced by hand with white press type on black poster board. To show a paragraph of the city's new zoning ordinance, Whyte trained the camera on the text in the zoning book. The background music was credited to an ensemble called the

Bainbridge Brass Quintet, which appeared to be a somewhat informal group of street musicians visible in the film. The credit for the soundtrack went to a home-based recording studio in Princeton, New Jersey, not far from the Cooks' residence, where Whyte was a frequent guest.

While it was not the product of a skilled film documentarian, the *Social Life of Small Urban Spaces* movie clearly benefited from a prolonged evolution, with many screenings and much editing. From the beginning of the Street Life Project, Whyte spoke before community groups in New York and other places, sharing the results of his observations. He personally narrated the otherwise silent film clips he showed, and he always gauged the reaction of the audience. Ralph Widner, running a think tank for state and local officials in the 1970s, employed Whyte and his film to document what some developers were doing to kill street life in downtown areas. He remembers Whyte screening film clips in Columbus, Ohio, in 1979. "He tailored his pitch perfectly and won a rousing ovation," Widner says.[46] Margot Wellington of the Municipal Art Society in New York was an early backer of the film. "This was before he had a soundtrack," she recalls. At first Whyte just talked over the film as it ran. "He loved to enlighten people. You couldn't be more original than Holly."[47]

Ann Herendeen, one of the Street Life Project interns, remembers Whyte constantly "tinkering with the film, editing and re-splicing it. Like any good performer, he tailored each performance to the specific audience, and he learned from each performance to improve for the next one."[48] Fred Kent, working with both the Street Life Project and the successor organization, the Project for Public Spaces, watched the film through its many iterations. Kent appears in one scene, jotting down notes on a clipboard. "Holly was a master at creating a moment of insight," Kent says. "He set up the moment [in the film]. Then you see it."[49]

Whyte's daughter, Alexandra, has recalled her father coming home from a public appearance and announcing, "It's happy hour." That meant that Whyte had received a standing ovation for his presentation. The former college playwright and prep school actor knew that was a moment to savor. "Holly—let's admit it—was a ham," his stepbrother, Jim Perry, observed.[50]

Eventually, backed in part by the Municipal Art Society and the J.M. Kaplan Fund, Whyte gathered enough support to have the film edited with his own narration included in the soundtrack. Whyte's observations in the film reflected the idiosyncratic aspects of urban life. The film shows the flows of city life that could never be explained by a planner's checklist or a zoning amendment. Two businessmen are on a collision course as they cross the Seagram plaza. One holds up and adjusts his course slightly, and they pass without incident. The vitality of a public plaza depends as much on its entrance to the sidewalk as it does on the space itself. Whyte catches people taking notice of Paley Park with no intention of walking into it, and then, in some cases, veering off their course and into it anyhow. Water is meant to be enjoyed and touched. Whyte's camera lingers on a woman's bare foot dangling above a reflecting pool at the Seagram plaza. "You know she is going to dip her toe in," Whyte announces. In a few seconds she does just that.

The film celebrates the serendipitous delights of the urban scene. While most of its brightest moments were filmed on the streets of Manhattan and a few other metropolitan centers, some variation of the joys experienced there can be found in just about any place where people gather. One of Whyte's more intriguing settings is an ordinary block of 101st Street in Manhattan, in Spanish Harlem. Families sit on stoops, kids play under an open fire hydrant, men chatter while they wash their cars on the street. "It turns out," says Whyte in his narration, "that every attribute of a successful urban place can be found right here. We just didn't realize it at first."

Now four decades old, Whyte's observations stand the test of time. Fashion-conscious viewers might find the clothes out of date. Otherwise most of the scenes could have been filmed yesterday. The film was—and still is—authentic. It is also proof that Whyte's urbanism was as much art as it was science.

Chapter 14

From Small Spaces to the City: Rediscovering the Center

In the early 1980s Random House had the bright idea to reissue *The WPA Guide to New York City*, a relic from Great Depression–era America. The original authors of the seven-hundred-page guide-book, members of the Federal Writers' Project of the Works Progress Administration (WPA), were not content with merely describing the many points of interest in all five New York boroughs. The writers also sought, according to the preface of the 1939 guide, "to indicate the human character of the city, to point out the evidence of achievements and shortcomings, urban glamour as well as urban sordidness."[1]

Random House reprinted the guide verbatim, including the dated listings ($7 per night at the Plaza, for example, and $3 and up for a room with private bath at the Barbizon Hotel for women). To provide some modern-day context for this quaint opus, Random House enlisted William H. Whyte to write an introduction. Clearly relishing the assignment, Whyte first took a rhetorical jab at his longtime foil, the *New Yorker*, which in 1939, Whyte claimed, had intimated that the guide was so detailed that it would be impossible to ever update it. But thanks in large part to the landmarks preservation work in the 1960s and 1970s, Whyte contended, many buildings that "gave the streets scale and character" were preserved. "The wonder is that so much of what the *Guide* describes remains." One example in 1982 was the West Village. Whyte attributed its continuity to Jane Jacobs and her allies spoiling Robert Moses's redevelopment plans. "The West Village today is just about what it was before—mixed up, a bit tacky, and full of life," Whyte wrote in the WPA introduction.[2]

Then he took on the doomsday proponents who believed that the turmoil and chaos of the 1960s and 1970s were the city's death throes. There had been some doom and gloom in 1939 as well. New York City, like the rest of America, was still in the Great Depression. Even the Rockefellers had to do some belt-tightening, abandoning plans for a new opera house and instead building the eleven-building Rockefeller Center complex in Midtown Manhattan. The critics called it "wasteful and useless." As the 1939 *WPA Guide* noted, the center was saddled with the "world's largest" mortgage.[3]

More problems for the city lay ahead. Even the *Plan for New York City 1969*, written by Whyte and commissioned by the city, began by acknowledging the problems. By 1971 Jane Jacobs and her family, including two draft-eligible sons, had left New York for Toronto. She appeared that year in a Canadian television documentary, *City Limits*, in which she observed that New York once "was a marvelous city for solving problems . . . [but it] isn't doing that anymore. It's a very sad thing to see this happen to a great beautiful city. It's the classic way a great city dies."[4] Jacobs's pessimistic view may have constituted New York's rock bottom. Whyte summed up the city's decline in the 1982 introduction to the revised *WPA Guide* as follows:

The city lost even more of its manufacturing. Top management began moving corporate headquarters closer to home, in suburbia. Office vacancy rates crept up. Building construction collapsed. The subway system that made the city work began itself not to work. . . . The city's deficits went up. Its credit rating went down. On the verge of bankruptcy, the city asked Washington for help and was scorned. (*Daily News*: "Ford to New York: 'Drop Dead.'"). Moralists across the country could take heart; for this wicked and profligate city the end was surely at hand.

But not quite yet. New Yorkers are a resilient lot, and they responded to the contumely with something like patriotic fervor.[5]

Whyte possessed some of that patriotic fervor. In the 1970s he documented the day-to-day vitality of the city in his *Social Life of Small Urban Spaces*. In the 1980s Whyte applied the lessons he had learned in the heart of New York City to other urban centers, from Bellevue, Washington, to Dallas, Texas. He even applied those urban lessons to smaller towns in suburban areas, including his own hometown of West Chester, Pennsylvania, and his frequent summer destination, Princeton, New Jersey. The best days of cities—large and small—were ahead. Whyte's capstone book, *City: Rediscovering the Center*, raised the flag of what would soon be called the new urbanism.

Some of the city's biggest problems, Whyte believed, were fleeting. Consider that corporate exodus, for example. Whyte had identified the outflow when it was at its peak in the mid-1970s. Close to forty major companies had moved out, or had announced they would move out, including General Foods, IBM, Olin, PepsiCo, Texasgulf, Continental Can, and Union Carbide. The state of Connecticut ran ads showing subway tokens in lush green grass, with the headline "Turnstile or Life-style?"[6]

But Whyte argued that the exodus would soon reverse itself. First, the lifestyle being compared to the turnstile was that of the corporate chief executive officer, not the average worker. Of thirty-eight corporations that had recently departed, thirty-one had relocated to within a short drive of the CEO's home, Whyte's research revealed. The average CEO commute was about eight miles. In addition, the suburban locations had their own disadvantages. For workers there was less access to the job market, which reduced potential mobility and bargaining power—"as the company damn well knows." And in the suburbs, the company did not have access to the city's talent pool. It is the density of cities that makes them work so well. "Stand on a busy street corner and watch for a while; you'll be struck by the frequency of chance encounters and impromptu conferences. The high probability of these easy meetings is an asset of no little importance—particularly so for people in communications and finance. They need edges—the opinions they didn't solicit, the screwball idea, the grapevine news—and this is what they get in the center."[7]

To test his hypothesis, Whyte in the 1980s compared the stock market performance of the companies that had left in the 1960s and 1970s with the performance of the companies that remained in the city. For thirty-eight companies that had left New York (reduced to twenty-two because of buyouts and mergers), the overall stock valuation had increased on average by 107 percent. For thirty-seven major corporations that had stayed in New York, the overall valuation had increased on average by 277 percent—"downright startling," Whyte wrote. He also found corroborating evidence: Regina Belz Armstrong of the Regional Plan Association studied productivity, profitability, and growth records for companies that had left the city for the suburbs from 1972 to 1975. They grew at half the rate of those that remained.[8]

"The street is a great place for business," Whyte wrote in the 1982 *WPA Guide.* "Watch a group of executives go through their post lunch good-byes and you will appreciate how functional the street is as neutral turf. No party has an advantage over the other."[9]

The lessons from *The Social Life of Small Urban Spaces* could help fix other problems. The 1939 *WPA Guide* described Bryant Park, the almost-ten-acre space between the New York Public Library and Sixth Avenue, as the library's outdoor "reading room" under the trees. By the late 1970s drug dealers and prostitutes had taken over the "reading room." Police entered the parks in pairs—for their own safety. Whyte was run out of the park at knifepoint on one occasion. Enid Haupt, chair of the library board, had been mugged on the library steps. At that time the New York Public Library board launched a fundraising campaign to renovate the library. The Rockefeller Brothers Fund was receptive to the idea but suggested that the improvements extend to the park surrounding it. And, the Rockefellers recommended, Holly Whyte could create an action plan for saving the park. In late 1979 Whyte submitted his plan, backed up by data collected from his Street Life Project and its successor organization, the Project for Public Spaces.

Back in 1971 and 1972—comparatively good years for Bryant Park
... the average number of people to be found at Bryant Park during
the noon period on a nice sunny day was about 1,000, with peaks up
to about 1,400. . . .

The figures are lower today. . . . Usage is off by a third to a half.
Interestingly, so is the proportion of females—always a valuable in-
dicator. . . . Conversely, the number of undesirables has risen, but in
absolute terms by not so very much. As a very rough estimate, I
would put the hard core of regulars at about 100. But they sure look
like more. They are the constant and when nobody else is in the park
they are very, and menacingly, visible.[10]

If the park could attract enough law-abiding people, they would
outnumber the undesirables. The park's previous redesign in 1934, under the direction of Parks Commissioner Robert Moses, was intended
to turn the park into a sanctuary. "The intentions were of the best and
the design was widely praised," Whyte wrote. "Now we know better."
The 1934 redesign of Bryant Park included a perfect combination of
elements that would keep people out: It was raised four or five feet
above street level with particularly steep steps on the Sixth Avenue
side. There was a wall built around it, topped off with a spiked iron
fence. Thick shrubs against the fence blocked views in or out—criminals found it most appealing. "The park will be used by people when it
is opened up to them," Whyte predicted.

Whyte recommended structural changes to open up access, events
programming, improved maintenance (with new public restrooms),
and increased policing. But, Whyte wrote, "First things first. A few
thousand dollars worth of chairs and tables and food facilities would
do more to liven up the front than hundreds of thousands worth of
marble and paving. And they can be immediate." He cited as an example the Metropolitan Museum of Art, which put out up to two
hundred movable chairs on either side of its main entrance—the area
became a magnet for street performers and pedestrians.

Great ideas, but how to implement them? "First things first" turned
out to be working with the Bryant Park Restoration Corporation, a

new private nonprofit charged with arranging financing, gaining approvals, and brokering the interests of the New York Public Library, the Parks Department, and the city government. Also involved in the restoration planning: a newly formed business improvement district (BID), a consortium of property owners in the immediate vicinity of the park who would be assessed a fee to help pay for the park's ongoing programming and maintenance.

The Rockefeller Brothers Fund oversaw the hiring of a person to oversee these entities full-time. The lead candidate was Dan Biederman, a 1977 graduate of Harvard Business School who had started his career at a New York–based consulting company. He also took an interest in urban issues as a volunteer on his Midtown Manhattan community board, which advised the New York City Planning Commission. Biederman knew of Whyte and *The Last Landscape*. Whyte had recently sent a handwritten note to Biederman regarding some issue before the community board. They met up when Biederman interviewed for the Bryant Park job. Whyte did most of the talking, apparently wanting to make sure Biederman bought into Whyte's plan for the park. After he was hired, Biederman went along with Whyte on "little expeditions" involving public spaces. "Holly didn't believe in delegating. If he had a report to give you, he would call first and then he would personally deliver it," says Biederman.[11]

The execution of Whyte's Bryant Park redesign was delayed when the New York Public Library decided it needed the space underneath the park for two floors of subterranean stacks. Finally, in 1988, the work began with the nationally prominent Philadelphia-based landscape architecture firm Hanna/Olin executing Whyte's vision.

The landscape architect, Laurie Olin, grew up in Alaska and studied at the University of Washington. He became interested in cities after reading sections of *The Exploding Metropolis* as they appeared in *Fortune* magazine, as well as *The Last Landscape*. Olin had seen the underside of urban life when he was assigned to study a skid row neighborhood in Seattle. "A group of us all came up through this radical moment," he recalls. "We were all opposed to sprawl and some of us were looking closely at the life of the city. Holly was the first to study that, and he was probably the smartest and wisest of the lot. *The Social Life of Small*

Urban Spaces, his little publication, was our version of Mao's *Little Red Book*." When Olin first considered the Bryant Park project he had a general sense of how he would open it up to the surrounding community. The details also had to respect the park's certified landmark status. To Olin's relief, Whyte's vision was similar to his own.[12] Whyte praised the work of Olin and his partner, Robert Hanna, as "a plan that looks very much like the old one but in function is the opposite of it."[13]

The chairs turned out to be not the first thing but close to the last thing determined. Movable chairs, Whyte knew from his Street Life Project, were the ultimate tool for engaging the public in urban spaces, allowing individuals to tailor a space to their individual need— or whim. Given that Bryant Park was about to deploy some two thousand chairs, the design team took its time selecting the model to buy. The chair that Whyte recommended was one with a wire mesh seat that was successfully in use at Paley and Greenacre Parks. But Andrew Manshel, hired as Biederman's assistant in 1991, anticipated heavy use of the Bryant Park chairs. Manshel lined up a dozen candidate chairs along a wall outside his office. Visitors were invited to sample each chair and pencil in a mark above their preferred model. The winner was a green French bistro chair, which became an icon of the very successful Bryant Park (and the cover image of Manshel's 2020 book, *Learning from Bryant Park*).[14]

*   *   *

Whyte also applied his "street life" smarts to the dreary downtown of Dallas, Texas. In 1974 Whyte spoke at the annual meeting of the Central Business District Association. He criticized his host city as an example of a "decentralized utopia," which had spread across twelve blocks when it could have been squeezed into three. He encouraged the city to allow street corner vendors and to put out some chairs. "Dallas is not a very sittable place," he said, using film clips from his Street Life Project to underscore his point. Whyte noted the uniformly well-behaved, smartly dressed people on the Dallas sidewalks and saw them not as pillars of the community but rather as signs of trouble. "If there are no characters in your city, there's something wrong," Whyte told the business crowd.[15]

It was not the kind of talk that would get a speaker invited back. But Whyte did get invited back—often. In 1977 some urban-minded citizens formed the Center for Civic Leadership, intended to address "the fantasy of growth" that seemed to have taken control of city planning. Such a fantasy of growth, the organization said in its mission statement, "has taken us farther and farther away from the center of the city." Gail Thomas, director of the civic leadership group, decided to invite a prominent urbanist to help Dallas recenter itself. Thomas first called Jane Jacobs, who was busy writing a book and watching after a granddaughter. Jacobs referred Thomas to Whyte.[16] Thomas invited Whyte back to Dallas in 1980 to join psychologist James Hillman and Canadian architect and urban planner Arthur Erickson to discuss the topic of "the city as dwelling."

In 1982 Whyte delivered what was essentially his stump speech on *The Social Life of Small Urban Spaces* to another nonprofit civic group. Some members of the city council were in the audience and later proposed to spend $10,000 to address a scar on the Dallas streetscape— the six-acre plaza in front of the gleaming new futuristic Dallas City Hall designed by world-famous architect I.M. Pei. The new city hall was supposed to be transformative, a landmark that would erase the memory of Dallas's other plaza, Dealey Plaza, site of the assassination of John F. Kennedy. Instead City Hall Plaza had become a wasteland. No one used it. When the time came for a vote, several council members said they would vote for the authorization, but only if Whyte did the study.[17]

Because one of the plaza's problems was its immense scale (it was twice as large as St. Mark's Square in Venice), and because it lacked enclosure and blended into the surrounding area, Whyte extended his study to the surrounding streets and downtown center a few blocks away. *The Social Life of Small Urban Spaces* formula was evident in Whyte's report: he called for providing movable chairs ("when you give them chairs you are enlisting the greatest experts in the world at gauging comfortable social distances and groupings"), a food kiosk, and events programming and making better use of the decorative pool in the plaza. Whyte's study had been complemented by a *Dallas Morning News* contest in which residents offered suggestions for improving the plaza. People had mentioned using the pool, 180 feet in diameter, for ducks, goldfish, porpoises, skating, mud wrestling, and water slides. Whyte passed no judgment but noted tactfully that since it had been "artfully designed" to be safe for wading, "why not have wading?"[18]

Whyte and Jenny Bell became good friends of Gail Thomas and her husband and often stayed at their house when in town. Whyte did not spare his hosts' city from criticism. He took Dallas to task for its attempts to seek relief from pedestrian congestion. The problem was just the opposite. "Dallas should have a lively street life. It has a compact core, high urban densities, and a vigorous and attractive work force." And he meant "attractive" literally. As he noted in the next sentence of the report: "For girl watching the city should be in a class by itself."

That lapse into midcentury male chauvinism notwithstanding, Whyte's report contained pragmatic, specific recommendations that a Dallas city planner could put to good use (if she wanted to). Monitor every aspect of construction closely, Whyte advised. The benches already installed on the plaza were aligned so that only four out of twenty were ever in the shade in the midday period. As for the trees, they were either dead or dying. The landscape plan had called for six inches of crushed stone at the bottom of each tree well, Whyte discovered. But the builders had omitted the stone.

Whyte called for stricter zoning that would reduce the "as of right" bulk of new buildings, set specific criteria for privately owned public spaces, require retailing on ground-floor frontage, and mandate sun and wind studies of proposed buildings. A favorite downtown Dallas space, Thanks-Giving Square, had already fallen into a shadow cast by a neighboring tower. "This need not have been," Whyte wrote. The tower was sited "broadside to the sun. Had it been canted to slice into the sun, the shadows would have been minimized."

Whyte's call for action got a cool reception. His city council support seemingly vanished. The only visible response to Whyte's plan was not quite mud wrestling, but close to it. One day in July of the next summer, and for several succeeding summers, sand was trucked to the plaza and the area around the pool was converted into a beach. Otherwise the space remained dead.

When he finally completed the book that had been under contract since the early 1970s, Whyte had plenty to say about Dallas. In *City: Rediscovering the Center,* Whyte called out Dallas as "the city that has done most to kill off its streets." Whyte found Dallas guilty of degrading its street system from below and above—a system of underground concourses and skyways that would effectively connect every downtown building. You could walk anywhere without ever venturing outside (today it connects three dozen downtown blocks). A Montreal-based city planner and associate of Mies van der Rohe, Vincent Ponte, directed this effort. "One of the chief contributing factors to traffic congestion is crowds of pedestrians interrupting the flow of traffic at intersections," Whyte quoted Ponte as saying. In other words, people on the streets get in the way of cars. Whyte argued that the walkways were killing the street life that sidewalks would normally encourage.

At the time Whyte studied Dallas the city had the highest ratio of parking spaces to office space in the country. But people in a survey created by Whyte in cooperation with some local newspapers insisted that there was not enough parking in the city. The survey asked those same people how far they had to walk from parking space to workplace. The average distance: about two and a half blocks. If parkers would just walk five more minutes to their parking spot, Whyte calculated, "the result could be an emancipation of downtown" from the tyranny of parking.[19]

Except for the West End Historic District and a few other neighborhoods, Whyte found Dallas a city of lost causes. He attended a hearing at the Dallas City Council when food vendors sought to operate on city sidewalks. Restaurateurs claimed it would kill free enterprise. The vendors won, street life improved, and restaurants still flourish. Years later David Dillon, the architecture critic for the *Dallas Morning News,* profiled Whyte. "The downtown of Dallas, hardly an urban oasis, is a more attractive and congenial place because of Whyte's work. The proliferation of sidewalk cafes and pocket parks there is a direct result of his hammering city officials about their antiurban, antipeople ordinances."[20]

*   *   *

In the 1980s, when he was in his sixties and early seventies, Whyte was a voice of reason whose opinion was sought on all manner of urban

Figure 14.1 In 1984 Whyte and Chattanooga civic leader Rick Montague, in sunglasses, looked for ways to revitalize the city, once called "America's dirtiest city." (Chattanooga Public Library / *Chattanooga Times Free Press.*)

issues. At a time when proponents of public space and environmentalists viewed developers as sworn enemies, and vice versa, Whyte moved gracefully back and forth across enemy lines. Thomas Balsley, a New York landscape architect and proponent of people-centered designs, worked with Whyte on several public space projects in Manhattan that required city planning approval. When hired by the developer, Whyte was essentially a "company man," Balsley says. Whyte would not fight the developer directly, but "he was very tactful in the way he tried to sell his ideas. He'd present it, back down, and then try to sell it again. He didn't steamroller anyone." When Whyte appeared before a review board, Balsley recalls, "he was very effective. He walked in with all those credentials" (not one of which, of course, was anything official).[21]

In 1984 a group of developers led by architect Philip Johnson proposed a $1.6 billion makeover for Times Square. The plan called for four office towers on the thirteen-acre site with a giant sculpture of an apple by Robert Venturi and Denise Scott Brown providing a ground-level visual pun on New York's nickname. If ever a development were controversial, this was it.

But as the *New York Times* discovered in its coverage, there was one thing everyone agreed on: Whyte's opinion on the subject was particularly important. Whyte's "language and many of his strategies have been adopted by almost everyone" weighing in on the project—pro and con, the *Times* reported. "He's bright and he's right," Johnson was quoted as saying of Whyte. "Every single project we talk to him." Whyte's protégé at the Project for Public Spaces, Fred Kent, invoked his mentor's thinking in opposing the office tower plan. "At a street level, those buildings lack a quality that makes people feel comfortable," Kent said. Whyte sagely did not offer the *Times* an opinion on the project, but he did tip his hand with this remark: "The social component of congestion is what most planners don't understand. They want to purify the street."[22] (The four towers were not built, but Times Square was revived, thanks in part to other, less grandiose projects and the conversion of some blocks into pedestrian plazas.)

When Doubleday finally published *City* in late 1988, the book's editor might have forgotten that it was delivered at least fourteen years late. In that time some of Whyte's original observations may have become dated. The problems of the homeless in New York, for example, had expanded greatly in that time frame. Not so many New Yorkers in the late 1980s would have agreed with Whyte's description of them as harmless eccentrics. The *New York Times* reviewer Edward A. Schwartz, director of housing and community development in Philadelphia, appreciated Whyte's interpretation of the city's messiness but objected to Whyte's generous allowance for it.

A city, Mr. Whyte concludes, rises and falls in proportion to the vitality of its points of assembly. Its housing, its companies, even its offices all can survive elsewhere. What cannot is its public life, the settings where people come together face to face. For citizens the warning is that there is a limit to how peaceful a city can get before it ceases to be one. For developers, his advice is to start with the plazas and the streets and the open spaces and commerce will take care of itself.

What is surprising here, however, is that Mr. Whyte ... doesn't acknowledge what most disgruntled city residents will say right away, namely, that there is a reason that they don't want to come "face to face" with many of their urban neighbors. He devotes a whole chapter to "undesirables," as they were traditionally under- stood in the pre-homeless era—winos, derelicts, delinquents—but he treats them as idiosyncratic types, almost amusing and pathetic intruders on the otherwise congenial urban crowd. It's not so simple, is it? Is it a dirty little secret that the flight from the marketplace, from the city itself, is a flight of whites from blacks and Hispanics, of the middle class from the poor, and this flight reflects no greater rationality than the contempt one class feels for the other? The tell- tale signs of this attitude pop up throughout "City," but this is one forest that Mr. Whyte misses for all his trees.[23]

The reviewer had a point. The forest was race and the underlying social and economic issues that racial discrimination has visited upon most American cities. Whyte, however, did not turn a totally blind eye to race in *City*. The skywalks and undergrounding intended to separate pedestrians from motorists also created a "social split." Referring to one such system in Charlotte, North Carolina, Whyte wrote that "the second level is used by middle-class whites; the street level by blacks and by people who have to use the bus."[24] He noted that when execu- tives announced they were moving their companies from the city to the suburbs they often cited the "environment" as the reason. "Shorn of euphemism," Whyte wrote, "here is what executives mean by it: 1.) The center city is a bad place: crime, dirt, noise, blacks, Puerto Ricans, and so on. 2.) Even if it isn't a bad place, middle Americans think it is and they don't want to be transferred here. 3.) To attract and hold good people we have to give them a better environment. 4.) We have to move to suburbia."[25]

In the new corporate corridors being formed in suburban areas, such as the Princeton–Route 1 corridor in New Jersey, Whyte noted, white-collar workers were in short supply. The nearby cities of Trenton and New Brunswick needed employment opportunities, but their workers were blue-collar. "For all the growth in the corridors the lower-income people are being more distanced from this white-collar world than ever."[26] New mass transit rail systems, Whyte argued, "disproportionately . . . serve the high-income people who least need mass transit, and they poorly serve the blacks and low-income people who need it the most."[27] In *City* Whyte reiterated his defense of gentrification made in the *Plan for New York City 1969*: "The poor are not being hurt by middle-class investment. They are being hurt by disinvestment—by landlords and owners who let buildings go to rot," extracting every last dime of rent until the place is uninhabitable, and then walking away.[28]

As he had in the 1950s, when he was writing and editing *The Exploding Metropolis*, Whyte perceived the racial divide as one caused by social and economic problems—problems that could be fixed "if the ancient rhythms of the city reassert themselves."[29] Many people today would view those social and economic problems as a part of systemic and institutionalized racial discrimination not likely to be moved by "ancient rhythms." But in the early 1980s that view was not so clear. Kenneth Jackson's 1985 book about the rise of the suburbs, *Crabgrass Frontier*, was one of the first accounts of the long-lasting (and still lasting) effects of redlining by the federal home loan program that underwrote much of the suburban expansion.

Those criticisms notwithstanding, *City* takes a broad view of the urban environment, devoting more than half the book to what makes a city work, or not work. The *New York Times* reviewer continued: "[Whyte's] main contribution in *City* is well worth the price of admission to his tour: to heighten our sensitivity to the design of our shared environment. There is genuine brilliance here, born of years of observation and research. Our collective understanding of cities has found a new point of departure."

Whyte's last book showed the city as an anatomical diagram, as shown by an X-ray view. He used the empirical measures from his *Social Life of Small Urban Spaces* to dissect the city as a whole in the expanded book in 1988. In characteristic fashion, Whyte considered metrics most people never would have noticed.

For example, in an early defense of pedestrians in their battles with motor vehicles, Whyte noted that even traffic lights can be stacked against them by being timed to favor motorists. On New York's Fifth Avenue, he determined, a pedestrian stopping for a light at a cross street and then setting out at normal speed would inevitably be stopped by another red light at the next cross street, 240 feet away. By increasing one's speed to what Whyte termed "flank speed," 310 feet per minute, one could beat the light. (Whyte defined normal walking speed for men as about 3.3 miles per hour, or 290 feet per minute; for women, slightly less.) Pedestrians demonstrated great bravado in "zigging and zagging," but it came at a price: New York's pedestrian fatality rate was the highest among major American cities.[30]

Residents of any city will tell you that parking is horrendous, and cars parking illegally and double-parking compound the problem. The real problem, Whyte believed, was mismanagement. Whyte enlisted the help of sixteen graduate students from Columbia University's architecture school to chart parking patterns in the entire Midtown Manhattan business district. The team counted 4,031 parked vehicles, of which 2,000 were parked illegally. But only 22 had tickets. "By giving away land to parkers, or renting it for a pittance," Whyte wrote, "cities are squandering some of the most valuable real estate that they have."[31]

Whyte devoted an entire section to steps. Most stairs in public places were too steep. To be comfortable they should have a pitch of less than 30 degrees. Most subway stairs had 7-inch risers and no more than 11-inch treads, producing a 35-degree pitch. But architects had a rationale: steeper stairs took up less floor space. By taking an inch away from the riser and adding an inch to the tread, the angle is reduced to 26 degrees. The steps leading up to the side entrance of the Seagram Building had 5-inch risers and 14-inch treads, resulting in a 20-degree pitch—"the best steps of any major office building," Whyte proclaimed. Architect Mies van der Rohe "was always meticulous about the design of steps."[32]

But many architects simply relied on meeting the requirement of the building code, commonly expressed that the sum of two risers plus the tread must be between 24 and 25.5 inches. A 5-inch riser with a 12-inch tread would make a comfortable staircase, but it would fall short of the code. The code, Whyte noted skeptically, had been formulated by the director of the Royal Academy of Architecture of France, François Blondel. That was an august title, but Whyte suggested Blondel's work might be a little out of date. The formula was derived in 1672. Since then people have grown taller and their strides have increased.[33]

* * *

In the 1970s and 1980s, as skyscrapers in Midtown Manhattan began to live up to their name, people took notice of the deepening shadows cast over the city. The Planning Commission undertook a study and hired Whyte as one of its consultants. In a 1981 cover story in *New York Magazine*, Whyte once again bit the hand that fed him: the entire concept of incentive zoning had been flawed; it should have been called "sweetheart" zoning. And it was the Planning Commission's fault. Whyte put forward thirteen recommendations that, he admitted, would "require a lot of courage and a lot of hard work" to effect.[34]

But by 1988, when he finally completed *City: Rediscovering the Center*, Whyte had discovered ways to look at the shadow problem in a new, more optimistic light. Whyte's chapters in *City* on sun and shadow, bounce light, and sun easements (that's correct, easements to prevent a building from casting a shadow on another) are, well, illuminating. Whyte pointed out that the street grid of Manhattan does not run due north and south but rather is angled twenty-nine degrees east of due north to fit the grid to the shape of the island. The fortuitous effect is that most side streets, running east and west (more or less), get some sun for a few hours a day.[35]

Whyte considered not only where a building would cast shadows but also where it would reflect light and whether that reflected light could be directed to a specific place. Of course, and only a zealous empiricist such as Whyte would consider this, some light is different from other light. Building materials are the key factor. Masonry that is painted white has a reflectivity factor of 0.85, Whyte reported. Dark glass has a reflectivity factor of only 0.12. Glass walls can reflect a harsh light. A dark wall could reflect a soft light. And all these considerations depend on two terms that a few readers might recall from a high school earth science course: the azimuth (the position along the horizon) and the altitude (the position above the horizon) of the sun.

In addition to considering the shadows on the ground, Whyte looked up and considered the sunlight above the shadow. A plaza at ground level might be in a shadow. But twenty feet above it, the sun might still be visible. Was there a way to capture that sun? One way would be to plant a tree in that plaza, with leaves that bask in the sun and cast some dappled light to the ground below. What if buildings were designed to capture the sun at higher levels and project it to darker spaces below? At the time of Whyte's *City*, the possibilities were being studied at Bell Labs and the University of Miami.

If sunlight—especially sunlight in a dense city—is so important, why couldn't you just buy it? Whyte asked that seemingly odd question in the 1980s as various public places fell not under the wrecking ball but under the shadow of neighboring developments. The key to purchasing sun was the same legal device that Whyte championed in preserving first open space and then historic landmarks: easements. To preserve sunlight, Whyte envisioned property owners selling "scenic easements"—or donating them in exchange for tax deductions—that would prohibit them or any future owners from increasing the height of a building past a set point. The adjoining space would be guaranteed its place in the sun forever.

Whyte's theory got challenged, however, by a 1980 congressional act limiting the tax treatment of easements and limiting the easement protection to buildings of "architectural and historic significance." The act still allowed conservation and scenic easements, but the wording of the Internal Revenue Service guidelines presumed that such easements would be created in rural and suburban open spaces. Whyte went to Washington, DC, to lobby the IRS official who was writing the regulations that would accompany the new act. Whyte argued that scenic easements should be included in the category of conservation easement. Such easements would promote the conservation of the urban landscape. The IRS bought it. The final regulations included the following criteria in considering whether a view is scenic:

Relief from urban closeness. . . .

The degree to which the land use maintains the scale and character of the urban landscape to preserve open space, visual enjoyment, and sunlight for the surrounding area.[36]

In the early 1980s Greenacre Park, the vest-pocket park on East 51st Street between Second and Third Avenues in Manhattan, was threatened by a skyscraper planned a block and a half away at 505 Third Avenue. The architects and planners won approval for the plan after telling the Planning Commission that the shadow cast on the park would be "redundant," falling only on another shadow already cast on the park. Whyte worked with the Pratt Institute's Environics Design Studio to convince the review board that the building would cast an additional shadow on the park. The Planning Commission was overruled, and the height of the proposed building was reduced by three stories—a financial hit for the developer.[37]

But looking ahead, and also up, Whyte and other defenders of Greenacre Park recognized more overshadowing projects waiting in the wings. A four-story building across the street looked like a prime target for development. The owner, developer Seymour Durst, agreed to donate a scenic easement to the New York Landmarks Conservancy. Then the Greenacre defenders faced the prospect of another ominous shadow. A bar and grill called Real McCoy's was only three stories high, and the park advocates wanted to keep it that way. A person described by Whyte as a "friend of the park" purchased the building for $1 million, assigned an easement to forestall any further vertical development, and then put it back on the market. It soon sold at the same price but with the easement permanently attached.

The "friend" working quietly behind the scenes was Abby M. O'Neill, daughter of Abby Mauzé, the former Abigail Rockefeller, eldest of the six children of John D. Rockefeller Jr. The big sister of the five Rockefeller brothers had originally funded the Hideo Sasaki–designed park with its twenty-five-foot waterfall. Mauzé, who died in 1976, also funded the Greenacre Foundation, which continues to maintain the park. In 2017 a city rezoning plan allowed development of even taller buildings near the park. The Greenacre Foundation commissioned a sun study, which claimed that higher buildings on six specific sites would put the park in complete shadows. The foundation launched a Fight for Light campaign to oppose the zoning. The campaign did not stop the development, but it did gain some concessions. The Fight for Light continues.[38]

For Whyte warding off shadows and chasing sunlight was another blend of art and science in the urban laboratory. "If only we think of them, there are all sorts of things we can do to bend light and reflect it to felicitous effect," he wrote in *City*. There were already inspiring examples in the built environment, such as the Chrysler Building, "which glints at you wherever you are and makes you feel better for it. We need more follies like this."[39]

Chapter 15

Revisiting the Organization Man— and Woman

In the 1980s William H. Whyte was a public intellectual with an impressive and diverse portfolio. While Whyte was defending Abby Rockefeller Mauzé's Greenacre Park on Manhattan's posh East Side, he was also testifying—literally—in defense of several street musicians trying to eke out livelihoods on the downtown streets of American cities. Whyte also participated in two fiftieth anniversary celebrations in 1980—one for *Fortune* magazine and another for St. Andrew's School. He continued to speak out on open space preservation. At the same time he was asked to reconsider *The Organization Man* and its import, at a time when people were viewing it as irrelevant, merely a reminder of how different the world was in the 1950s. Even for a public intellectual, or for a "connected critic," as he was described in the history of Time Inc. intellectuals, Whyte's breadth of expertise and the depth of his engagement were extraordinary.

In 1983 Whyte helped defend a bagpiper, Lee Davenport, who had been banned from playing on the sidewalks of Alexandria, Virginia. The city, alleging that pedestrians sometimes had to walk into the street to get around the bagpiper's audiences, had passed an ordinance restricting such performances to designated parks and plazas. Whyte testified that his studies, as well as the city's own counts, showed the sidewalks to be "very roomy" and capable of supporting a "comfortable pedestrian environment."

In striking down the Alexandria ordinance, the federal judge's ruling sounded like a page from the Whyte hymnal. "Persuasive testimony satisfies the court that, overall, pedestrian traffic is not congested—no more than 2.8 persons per foot per minute of passing pedestrians, a pedestrian 'ease' level well below the standard for pedestrian comfort." Moreover, Judge Albert V. Bryan continued, playing in a designated park or plaza was not the same as playing on the sidewalk: "The exponent of the First Amendment expression is entitled to be 'encountered' by those he wishes to receive his or her message. The sidewalk is a traditional place for such expression. Pedestrian flow and turnover is the 'lifeblood' of the street performer."[1]

In 1985 guitarist Wally Friedrich and a group of buskers in Chicago filed a class action suit against the city for an ordinance banning their performances on the sidewalks of Michigan Avenue and other downtown streets. As Whyte wrote later, "of all the avenues in the United States, they could not have picked one with broader sidewalks than upper Michigan Avenue." Whyte presented pedestrian counts—closely matching the city's own counts—that showed a generous amount of space. There was so much space, in fact, that the city had converted some of the sidewalk to planting beds. The court ruled that the ban was justified on some Chicago streets but not on Michigan Avenue.

Audiences of street performers also caught Whyte's eye. "It is interesting to watch people as they chance upon a street entertainer," he wrote.[2] "For a few moments, they seem utterly at ease, their shoulders relaxed, temporarily forgetting the realities of daily life. People enjoy programmed entertainment, too, but not the same way. It is the unexpected that seems to delight them most. . . . There is a communal sense to these gatherings and though it may be fleeting, it is the city at its best."

Fortune magazine commemorated its fiftieth anniversary in 1980 with the publication of *Writing for Fortune*. Among the magazine's alumni commissioned to write reminiscences were Archibald Mac-Leish, John McDonald, Daniel Bell, John Kenneth Galbraith, and, of course, Whyte. In an essay called "How to Back Into a Fortune Story,"

Whyte drew on insights from his study of urban design. In journalism as in urban development, too much planning could lead to cookie-cutter results. Editors like to convene a schedule committee to plan a single-subject issue or a multi-issue series. It was all very logical, and "very logical for other magazines, too, and that is why so many cover stories are so alike." Whyte advised that journalists "do the legwork before the scheduling." The trails could lead to ideas that the committee might never have anticipated.[3]

During this period Whyte remained an authority on open space preservation. In a letter to the *New York Times* in 1983, he supported a bill to authorize conservation easements. A recent *Times* editorial on the issue, Whyte charged, was "about 20 years out of date," in part because it had referred to the easement bill as a "wilderness bill." In fact, its "greatest usefulness" would be in a metropolitan area, where development is most intense. And the bill could greatly benefit the city itself. "The New York Landmarks Conservancy has been stimulating gifts to preserve old buildings of architectural and historic value. Thanks to the new regulations drafted by the IRS for easement donations [the ones that Whyte himself had lobbied for], the public benefits have just been broadened to include preservation of the 'urban landscape.' The conservancy hopes to broaden its program similarly, and secure easements that will conserve such neighborhood amenities as sun, light, and scale."[4]

And on two notable occasions in the 1980s, Whyte was challenged to defend the relevance of *The Organization Man*. The challenge was not unreasonable. The world that gave Whyte most of the fodder for his 1956 best seller was built on three pillars, each one at or near its peak in the 1950s and 1960s: large organizations that offered the prospects of job security and sometimes even lifelong benefits; the suburbs, which provided the comfortable setting for those men and their families; and nuclear families, with their stay-at-home mothers providing unpaid support for the organization men.

By the 1980s each of those pillars was crumbling. The organizations and institutions that provided the grist for Whyte's analysis were undergoing their own vast transformation. Corporations no longer promised the long-term security to the men—or the women—who

Figure 15.1 At the school's fiftieth anniversary in 1980 Whyte praised St. Andrew's for being "somewhat out of step" and worried only that it wasn't "out of step enough." (St. Andrew's School.)

pledged their allegiance. Defined benefit retirement plans were being replaced by 401(k) accounts and individual retirement accounts—portable funds that could be moved with the worker from company to company. During the late 1970s and 1980s big corporations shriveled up. AT&T went from 850,000 workers to around 50,000, to cite an extreme example. "By 1990 no one was talking about the Organization Man," Nicholas Lemann wrote in his 2019 book, *Transaction Man*.[5]

The second pillar, the suburbs, remained in the 1980s, but they were no longer an idyllic retreat far removed from the urban centers. The suburbs were facing increased costs of services and of land for new housing.[6] The most affordable housing was that located farthest from the urban employment centers and mass transit hubs.

The third pillar, the classic nuclear family of the 1950s and 1960s, with mom as the bulwark of the organization man's support system, was soon split by various forces. Betty Friedan's *The Feminine Mystique*, published in 1963, illuminated the growing women's liberation movement. Women saw an alternative to the stay-at-home choice offered to them by their organization men. In the expensive suburbs, housewives became working women and began the fight—still ongoing—for equal pay for equal work. That midcentury dominance of the nuclear family turned out to be, according to cultural critic David Brooks, a "freakish historical moment."[7]

If anyone did talk about the organization man, what was there to say? The person to ask was Whyte.

The WNET–Channel 13 public television show *The Open Mind* had debuted in 1956 with an interview of Whyte, whose *Organization Man* had just been published. A little more than a quarter century later the host, Rutgers University professor Richard D. Heffner, invited Whyte back. Citing Whyte's contention that the Protestant ethic had given way to a social ethic, embodied by corporations and other institutions, Heffner wondered if the pendulum had not swung back to the rugged individualism of the Protestant ethic. Whyte stuck to his thesis. The protest movement of the 1960s "didn't really go very deep," Whyte said. Companies continued to use personality tests in their hiring efforts. People have become "more sophisticated" in talking about organizations and would now proclaim that "we want individuals here." But in reality gregarious people were still in high demand.

Corporate executives, Whyte continued, still gave their moral proxy to the corporation. "There's been one shocking incident after another," said Whyte, referring to recent discoveries of illegal pollution by various companies. "Wouldn't it be nice if four or five executives came forward as whistleblowers?" But thanks to the organization and its social ethic, "they spread the culpability so that no one is culpable." Whyte was not optimistic that this would change anytime soon.[8] (The parade of corporate and institutional scandals has continued since then, of course, and whistleblowers are rarely heard.)

A few years after the WNET interview Whyte got a letter from Paul Leinberger, son of the minister in Park Forest, Illinois, who had welcomed Whyte, then reporting for *Fortune*, into the family home in the early 1950s. As a little boy Paul Leinberger had accompanied Whyte on some of his walks through the suburban enclave. Whyte's attention to the physical layout of Park Forest had impressed the young Leinberger. At the University of Illinois he studied urban and regional planning, and he then took a job with the Chicago-based Urban Investment and Development Company. Headed by Philip Klutznick, the developer of Park Forest and an important source for Whyte during his *Organization Man* research, the company pursued a vision of "vertical" developments of offices, housing, and retail in urban settings, including Water Tower Place in Chicago, which opened in 1975. Klutznick turned to Whyte for consulting advice on several occasions, giving Leinberger the opportunity to reconnect with Whyte.[9]

In the mid-1980s, Leinberger (not related to the land use strategist Christopher Leinberger) envisioned a book on the sons and daughters of the organization men—in some cases literally kids he had grown up with in Park Forest—to determine whether they had carried on with the social ethic embraced by their parents or had forged something new. Leinberger asked Whyte if he would open his files so he could follow up with those original sources. Whyte cheerfully answered yes.

That led to Leinberger paying a half dozen visits to Whyte in Manhattan in the mid- to late 1980s. Most visits would include an extended lunch at the Century Association club in Midtown Manhattan. For Leinberger it was an adventure, starting with the walk from the maître d' station to Whyte's table. There was always someone who needed to have a special word with Whyte as he walked by. One time it was John Updike. Once Whyte and his guest were seated, the waiters were solicitous. "They already knew what he liked and what he didn't like," Leinberger recalls. "And there were certain things he loved. He would always order for me as well as for himself."

On one occasion the visit included a long walk—more than three miles—from the club, at 7 West 43rd Street, to the Whyte brownstone, on East 94th Street. Even though the purpose of Leinberger's visit was to continue the examination of the generation that followed the organization men, he found himself fascinated by Whyte's lessons in urbanism. "For him walking the New York streets was super fascinating," Leinberger recalls. "He would point out which sidewalks were wider than others and explain how just a few extra feet would make such a big difference. He couldn't understand why others didn't do it."

The talk also turned to *The Organization Man*. Leinberger says that Whyte viewed Michael Maccoby's 1977 book, *The Gamesman: The New Corporate Leaders*, as a piece of "corporate pop psychology" that borrowed from Whyte's book to create one of the four leadership models profiled in the book, the "company man." That Maccoby's book became a best seller irritated Whyte as well. Whyte was more generous in his view of Leinberger's effort, possibly because of their personal connection and possibly also because he thought Leinberger was "looking for corroboration" of his ideas. Whyte shipped (at his own expense) a dozen metal boxes filled with thirty-year-old notes, most handwritten jottings on three-by-five-inch index cards. These original notes from interviews with more than 175 people ended up being "not all that useful" to Leinberger (in part because he had a difficult time deciphering Whyte's scrawl). But they added potential contacts to be interviewed. Leinberger would eventually travel some hundred thousand miles and interview more than three hundred people for his 1992 book, *The New Individualists: The Generation after* The Organization Man. In that book Leinberger would conclude that the social ethic had largely been transformed into a self ethic, which was "based on a genuine moral imperative—the *duty* to express the authentic self."[10]

In 1986, on the thirtieth anniversary of *The Organization Man*'s publication, the *New York Times* heard about Leinberger's project. It commissioned him to write an op-ed for a business supplement to the *New York Times Magazine*. Leinberger's piece would be followed by a rejoinder from Whyte. The following is an excerpt from Leinberger's argument:

> The younger corporate men and women I have interviewed [the children of Whyte's organization men] were born not in the throes of depression and war, but in the flush of prosperity and relative peace. They value caution less than risk, security less than autonomy. For them, the organization-man contract has lapsed. To be sure, the giant corporation seems destined to survive. Indeed, in a world

marketplace filled with mammoth, government-backed business empires, the corporation is likely to grow even larger. But if American companies are going to compete, as [economist John Kenneth] Galbraith says, "we had better find a way of rejuvenating them."

Some signs of this rejuvenation are already visible. Companies are increasingly offering employees more flexible hours that permit them better integration of their work and family lives. On-site day-care facilities are appearing and, with the personal computer linking home to workplace, the living room may increasingly serve as just another branch office. . . .

The organization man, as Whyte portrayed him, seems to be a vanishing breed. His sons and daughters endure, but unlike their fathers, they endure on their own terms.[11]

Three decades after publication of his landmark book, Whyte still felt the need to set the record straight concerning organization men and their presence on the social and cultural landscape. An excerpt from Whyte's rejoinder:

Some years ago I wrote a book about the people who work for large organizations. I called them organization men. Some people got mad at me for this. They said I was calling them dirty conformists. But I wasn't. I was an organization man myself (Vicks, *Fortune* magazine, the Marine Corps), and I meant no slight. Quite the contrary. My point was that these were the people who were running the country, not the rugged individualists of American folklore. And that they had better beware of the bureaucratic ethic. . . .

Leinberger says that a new generation, disillusioned by the corporation, less willing to extend loyalty, more venturesome, is taking over. It is an attractive argument, and it is based on a lot of research. But I do not agree with the conclusion. I think the organization man is still very much alive. He may talk differently than he once did, but he does not act so very differently; indeed, today's MBAs and young urban professionals exhibit a faith in the system every bit as staunch as that of the junior executives of former years. It is this faith, not disillusionment, that is unsettling. . . .

Paul Leinberger sees some hopeful signs of rejuvenation: more flexible human relations; the spinning off of small, entrepreneurial operations. He sees a younger generation more inclined to risk and innovation than the previous.

Fine. Fine. I hope this optimism proves warranted. But I am not persuaded that this means the death of the organization man. It is true that he may be less inclined to give his loyalty to one organization. His allegiance now is to organizations. When he speaks of being free to go where his self-interest leads, he is citing the interchangeability of organization life. To use a vogue term, if he "networks," it is not just within one organization, but across a complex of them.[12]

As Whyte wrote in *The Organization Man*, the corporation was not the only bastion of organization men and women. The ivory tower of academe was equally well organized. And at this point in his life, Whyte was strongly engaged with his own alma mater, Princeton University, in concert with his friend and patron Laurance Rockefeller, also a Princeton alumnus and an organization man in his own right. They didn't need to resist the university, but they did feel compelled to shape it, particularly its physical campus and the way students used that campus.

Whyte, the defender of the urban streetscape, was also asked to apply his expertise to some other high-profile suburban settings in central New Jersey: the quiet and relatively quaint Princeton downtown and the sprawling new office developments of the Princeton–Route 1 corridor. If the principles of urbanism could be applied in places like Princeton and its environs, Whyte suggested, maybe they could be applied anywhere.

Chapter 16

Applying Urban Principles in Suburban Places

From his own point of view, William H. Whyte must have relished his assignments in suburban New Jersey, virtually in the backyard of his longtime friends Peter and Joan Cook. Holly and Jenny Bell had spent many summer months with the Cooks through the 1970s and 1980s. Jenny Bell found Princeton to be a hospitable setting for her various artistic pursuits. She sold some of her heirloom clothing at a benefit for the Princeton Medical Center. After publishing a children's book, *Adelaide Stories*, based on her mother's childhood in a small town in central Pennsylvania,[1] Jenny Bell hosted an autograph and lemonade party at a downtown shop. At a gala for the private Princeton Day School, she sold African fashions and acted as a fashion consultant.

Holly, meanwhile, enjoyed socializing with the Cooks' circle of friends, including Hugh Hardy, the architect and theater designer who also worked on Bryant Park; Hardy's wife, the architect Tiziana Spadea; and the artist Andrew Wyeth. "Holly and Jenny Bell set up camp around the house," recalls Steve Cook, one of the kids to whom Jenny Bell dedicated her *Jingle Book* in 1954. Holly created a makeshift working space in the living room and fussed over making the proper martini in the evening. "My father didn't have any record player around, but Holly brought a hi-fi system into the house."[2]

Holly, a fastidious dresser in the city, maintained his coat-and-tie uniform in the country. For the most part. Once in a while, several of the Cook children now recall, the scene was "pretty bohemian." Probably at the instigation of Jenny Bell, there was some occasional midnight skinny-dipping in the pool. "Jenny was a lot of fun," John Cook recalls. "Holly got a kick out of that."[3]

Whyte's Princeton work began at his alma mater. Compared with his fellow alumnus Laurance Rockefeller, Whyte maintained a relatively low profile on the Princeton University scene. He had been suggested (but passed over) for an alumni trustee position in 1970. He served a term on the School of Architecture's advisory board and was on the graduate board of the *Nassau Literary Review*. He raised his head, however, in 1975 when his cousin Alec Hemphill's daughter, a St. Andrew's School alumna, was waitlisted for the Class of 1979. "Holly was furious," Alec's widow, Jean Hemphill, recalls. "He intervened with some of his Princeton friends." The daughter was admitted and graduated summa cum laude.[4]

In the late 1970s Princeton University renovated the open space between the library, chapel, and student center. As a centerpiece of this plaza, the university installed a seventy-foot granite ledge, which, students complained, was uncomfortable to sit on for any length of time. The university also paved over a grassy area where students used to sit. Laurance Rockefeller, a Princeton trustee and head of the board's grounds and buildings committee, was spearheading the $250,000 renovation. Rockefeller invited Whyte to join him in trying to ameliorate some of the plaza's faults and to assist in other campus projects.

Given his connection to Rockefeller, Whyte publicly came to the plaza's defense. "The essence of the plan is to make it sittable. There will be lots of places to sit—on benches, on the steps around the statue, best of all, chairs and tables for outdoor eating," he wrote to the student newspaper. "But there is no need to theorize. Within a month the facilities will be put to the test of the market."[5]

Possibly inspired by Whyte's Street Life Project, Rockefeller took an interest in creating outdoor "tarrying places" on the campus, where social interaction could occur outside the classroom. Over the next half dozen years (even after Rockefeller became a trustee emeritus in 1980), Rockefeller supported efforts to "humanize" various campus spaces. More seating, especially in the form of movable chairs, was high on the Whyte–Rockefeller wish list. Obviously mindful of Rockefeller's involvement, administrators consulted with Robert Zion, the landscape architect who had designed Paley Park in Manhattan. Robert Venturi, the celebrated Philadelphia architect and also a Princeton alumnus, Class of 1947, weighed in with Whyte on the placement and design of benches. Whyte encouraged Venturi to consider a "concave-in-plan teak-wood" bench. Venturi shared with Whyte the specifications for an "English Lister" bench.[6]

Various benches were indeed installed, but in most cases they were anchored to the ground. Rockefeller's financial underwriting notwithstanding, administrators resisted the call for movable chairs—they kept getting stolen. Whyte persisted. The university was as much an organization as any large corporation, and Whyte had some ideas about what buttons to push. In a memo to Rockefeller in March 1978, Whyte astutely identified the potential pushback from university administrators.

> It will probably be helpful to press the administration officials to be more venturesome. Bridle as they may at critiques, articles in the *Princetonian* and the like, these help keep the focus on the great human benefits involved rather than on ease of maintenance and housekeeping details that can preoccupy administrators. They dragged their feet on the movable chairs and they still fret over the possible loss of some. They should be bragging about the obvious success of the chairs and the lack of vandalism. Similarly, they should be encouraged over the lively interest people are taking in the plaza—even the griping, which amounts to fine-but-why-not-more. But there is an educational process going on.[7]

Knowing Whyte's belief in the value of movable chairs over fixed benches, the university's director of physical planning in 1982 apprised Whyte of the challenges faced by his department. Of twenty chairs put out in the spacious plaza of what was then known as the Woodrow

Wilson School, eight had been stolen. Two of the five tables put out
with the chairs had been vandalized. The student center was a "special
problem" possibly caused by the "carefree attitude" of students leaving
the pub after midnight.[8] As we will see in the afterword, Princeton
University continues to be cautious about deploying movable chairs.

*   *   *

While Whyte and Rockefeller prowled the campus looking for "tarrying" places, Princeton University put one of its major real estate
holdings up for sale: Palmer Square, the mixed-use retail, office, and
residential complex built during Whyte's undergraduate years directly
across the street from the main campus. Palmer Square affected a Colonial Revival architecture style. Its mixed-use configuration was reminiscent of old-fashioned downtowns. Several dozen retail shops lined
the streets, with more than one hundred apartments above them. The
119-room Nassau Inn and the post office framed a village green. A
movie theater and commercial office space were on the outer edge of
the project. By the 1970s the downtown square faced growing competition from suburban malls and freestanding office buildings on the edge
of town. Realizing its limitations in the fields of retail and commercial
real estate, the university sold Palmer Square in 1981 to a Connecticut-
based developer, Arthur Collins Jr., a member of Princeton's Class of
1952 who had earned a master's degree in architecture from Princeton
in 1956.

The Collins Development Corporation became a name that some
Princeton residents loved to hate. They protested the addition of a news
kiosk in a public plaza on Nassau Street. They lamented the loss of a
movie theater and the large surface parking lot surrounding it, which
were removed to make room for more retail, office, and residential
space. They objected to an expansion of the Nassau Inn that required
the town to sell air rights over an existing street. The "bridge" leading
to the hotel's new wing, residents feared, would cast the street below
into dark shadows, possibly creating a haven for criminals. The head of
the Environmental Design Review Committee proclaimed that "there
is no socially redeeming value to hotel rooms going across a street.
If this were literature, with no redeeming social features, it would be

pornography."[9] Mindful of the opposition, Collins sought a way to integrate the expanded Palmer Square into the existing community. Jim Harvie of Collins Development met Whyte in 1982 following his presentation at an Urban Land Institute gathering in Houston and invited him to review the project: "We are very anxious to make sure that our plan works as efficiently as possible, vis-à-vis retail shopping and people gathering."[10]

Whyte offered some constructive criticism. "I hope you will continue to develop alternative plans for the specific open spaces of the condominium development," he wrote to Harvie. "I felt some of the spaces in the previous plan were neither fish nor fowl—ambiguous spaces that would not be really public space, but not very private either." But Whyte also praised the plan partly for what it did not do. "The mistake many communities make is to strive for one monumental, imposing central space. They usually don't get used very much, for they are out of scale with the individual. A series of smaller spaces usually works out much better." In addition, the storefronts were highly visible and "not arcaded way back out of sight."[11]

The expanded Palmer Square did not attempt to emulate the growing number of shopping malls and big-box retail centers being built just a few miles away on Route 1. *Progressive Architecture* magazine in 1983 praised the Collins plan for concealing the edges of the parking garage facing the street, for maintaining the mixed-use approach of the original square, and for "[addressing] the classic problem of American towns—reinforcing the center with added commercial and parking facilities as a defense against peripheral shopping sprawl—without turning the town center itself into an introverted, single use shopping center."[12]

Whyte believed the Palmer Square approach would work in Princeton and in similar communities with traditional downtowns fighting for survival in the face of the suburban shopping mall. Small cities "are the ones most immediately hurt by suburban shopping malls and most tempted to fight their tormentors by copying them," Whyte wrote. "Like its suburban model, the city mall will be car-oriented and will require vast amounts of parking." To gain that parking for the downtown, the suburb would often demolish more of the downtown—a vicious

circle. Whyte argued that "a first step to liberation" would be reducing
the knee-jerk zoning requirements for a certain number of parking
spaces to accompany every new development.[13] That battle continues
in the twenty-first century, waged against a generation of planners and
consultants that Whyte envisioned in the 1980s. "Now coming of age,"
Whyte wrote then, "is a whole generation of planners and architects
for whom the formative experience of a center was the atrium of a
suburban shopping mall."[14]

Happily, from Whyte's point of view, Princeton had chosen to be a
small city, rather than a large suburb. Small cities, Whyte argued, had
qualities similar to large ones. In smaller cities the density may not be
high enough to support mass transit, street life might be a little less
intense, and pedestrians might walk a little slower, but "the basic patterns are there. People are not all that different. Given the elements
of a center—high pedestrian volumes, concentration, and mixture of
activities—people in one city tend to respond like people in another."[15]

Whyte saw similarities between Princeton and his hometown of
West Chester, Pennsylvania, where he had family connections until
1985, when his mother died at the age of ninety-two. West Chester, another college town, though slightly smaller in population than Princeton, had also successfully fended off the suburban competition. It had
(and still has) the advantage of having been laid out in a classic urban
grid by surveyor Thomas Holme, who also established Philadelphia's
street layout. Thanks to the grid, all houses were within walking distance of downtown. Then, in the 1950s, the city fathers turned down an
offer for urban renewal funds. In 1973, when James Rouse, a developer
whom Whyte respected, opened up the Exton Square Mall five miles
outside West Chester, the downtown's department store closed, along
with several other smaller stores. But West Chester kept its downtown
intact, resisting mall-style "improvements," and it survived.[16] (More
recently, but well before the 2020 pandemic, the town took back some
on-street parking spaces to create outdoor dining areas.)

A larger city, Bellevue, Washington, was at a similar crossroads. Located just across Lake Washington from Seattle, Bellevue was turning
into a classic car suburb of its larger neighbor. But in the late 1970s,
Whyte reported, "the leaders were jolted into taking stock, one reason

being the threat of a huge shopping mall beyond the city limits. Quite literally, Bellevue was at a fork in the road. They had to decide, and sooner [rather] than later, what kind of place they wanted it to be. They decided that Bellevue should be a city." The town fathers used zoning to reinforce the value of their walkable downtown. A developer in the heart of the city could build within a high floor area ratio (FAR), eight to ten times the area of the building lot. Beyond the central business district, however, the FAR was reduced to a "meager" 0.5.

"It is a city and wants to be a city," Whyte wrote in *City*. On the basis of reports from Bellevue's principal urban designer at the time, Whyte reported that Bellevue's downtown was "shaping up as intense and urban. Even discordant."[17]

*   *   *

As the town of Princeton expanded and revitalized its Palmer Square, it faced more competition than just the nearby regional shopping mall. Out on Route 1, the four-lane highway less than a mile east of Princeton, the landscape largely resembled what it had looked like for decades—acres of open land including agricultural lands as well as dense forests. But midcentury American sprawl—in the form of fast-food franchises, motels, retail strip centers, gas stations, and auto repair shops—was spreading south from New Brunswick, about fifteen miles away, and north from Trenton, about ten miles away. In the 1970s and 1980s, investors and developers were snapping up underutilized land outside Princeton. Officials fretted about the sprawl, but acting regionally was difficult. The "Princeton–Route 1 corridor," as it was called, traversed seven municipalities and two counties between New Brunswick and Trenton, but it did not go through Princeton itself.

When Whyte worked on the *Plan for New York City 1969* and the Street Life Project, the principal threat to the city was seen as people and companies fleeing the cities for existing suburbs or—occasionally—rural locations. By the time Whyte was wrapping up his work on small urban spaces in the 1980s, urban-based businesses and city dwellers had other possible havens to which they could escape: enclaves of offices, retail malls, and housing developments, usually organized around a major highway network, and often transcending various municipal boundaries. Unlike the tacky developments that dotted ex-urban highways in the early days of urban sprawl, these developments were dressed up by architects, planners, and landscape architects. Think of a new town but without the town (and pesky problems such as maintaining a school system and a public works department). You could call it an "edge city," the title of a 1991 book by Joel Garreau.[18] Whyte referred to such entities as "semi-cities."

Technology, including advanced high-speed communication networks, allowed companies to communicate internally among multiple geographic locations, making these new clusters more valuable. This technology, wrote Robert Fishman in his 1987 book, *Bourgeois Utopias*, had "superseded the face-to-face contact of the traditional city." Fishman believed that "the most important feature of post war American development" was "the almost simultaneous decentralization of housing, industry, specialized services, and office jobs; the consequent breakaway of the urban periphery from a central city that it no longer needs; and the creation of a decentralized environment that nevertheless possesses all the economic and technological dynamism we associate with the city." Fishman called these places "technoburbs."[19]

Whyte was not impressed. There might be some economic and technological dynamism, but not much more than that. These techno-burbs, Whyte believed, tried to retain all the advantages of the center without having a center—it would be "the city without tears."[20]

In the early 1980s two new office centers that fit Fishman's description loomed on large, undeveloped tracts in the Princeton–Route 1 corridor. One development, the Princeton Forrestal Center, was started by the deep-pocketed Princeton University, which wanted to protect its nearly one thousand acres of landholdings from urban sprawl. The university foresaw a large corporate center that would eventually attract large-scale users such as Merrill Lynch, Siemens, and the headquarters of the Robert Wood Johnson Foundation. At Forrestal the main development was linked to the outside highways by just three entrances. Several high-capacity interior roads connected the clusters of buildings. A hotel and conference center, suited for corporate events, occupied an isolated site, providing guests with the feel of a rural environment.

The other, the Carnegie Center, on nearly five hundred acres about four miles south of Forrestal on Route 1, was developed by a for-profit group. The Carnegie investors imagined that an urbanist, people-centered development could gain a competitive advantage, especially against the stand-alone office buildings popping up along the highway. Alan Landis, an accountant by training who became a developer early in his career, assembled a group of commercial real estate investors who envisioned clusters of offices arranged around open greens. The interior roads were narrower than those at Princeton Forrestal Center, and the road network included seven connections to existing streets and Route 1, more than double the connectivity at Forrestal. Mindful of short- and long-term costs, the private developers of the Carnegie Center realized that roads, sewers, and utilities would cost less if the buildings were closer together.

To tie it all together Landis hired the prominent Boston-based architect Hugh Stubbins, who had designed the Citicorp Center in Manhattan, among other projects. As the first phase of the center was underway, the Carnegie developers realized they "needed a team to complement Hugh," recalls Bill King, then the center's director of design and construction. "Alan said he knew Amanda Burden, who was working on Battery Park City at the time." Burden, a onetime Manhattan socialite who had taken a serious interest in urban planning thanks to Whyte, recommended Robert Hanna, also working on the Battery Park City project in New York, as the landscape architect. Hanna in turn said that hiring an anthropologist or sociologist would also be helpful. At that point King recalled reading *The Organization Man*. The Carnegie Center soon added Holly Whyte to the list of architects and planners mentioned in the center's promotional materials.[21]

The first Carnegie Center cluster was anchored by a Hyatt Hotel, not of the commuter style located along highways but rather a "regency" model designed for urban downtowns. Whyte first visited the project when it was barely underway in the early 1980s, with the first cluster of buildings just being completed. He asked the developers to take him outside so he could walk around. It was midmorning and the central plaza was empty. Whyte pointed to the various landscaping elements. By lunchtime, he predicted, someone would be sitting on a planter eating a bag lunch. There would be two people sitting on a retaining wall, and another person would be standing facing the two, chatting with them. And on the interior roadway there would be two groups of people walking side by side. Bill King recalls exchanging skeptical glances with his partners. When lunchtime came they returned to the same spot. Almost everything Whyte had predicted was happening. "This guy is a character," the developers concluded. "But he knows what he's talking about."

Whyte's immediate reaction to the first cluster of buildings was that the central court was too big, about the same size as Copley Square in Boston, he said, and never likely to have as much pedestrian traffic. The center included not only a circle of open space in the middle but also a circular driveway around the green and the individual buildings beyond that. Too big. "Some heroic measures are going to have to be taken to bring it down to pedestrian scale," Whyte wrote.[22] The design of the proposed second cluster was much better, with no interior driveway. Subsequent clusters also eschewed the interior drives. The centers were linked with walking paths, forming a greenway.

Whyte's views reinforced those of others working on the project. "I was opposed to suburban offices—we were trying not to do them," says Laurie Olin of the Hanna/Olin firm. To Olin the suburbs were neither rural nor urban. The "in-between" didn't appeal to him. But in the case of Stubbins's request to work on the Carnegie Center, Olin recalls, "we thought it was a good job and a good architect. Bob [Hanna, Olin's business partner] said 'Why don't we come up with a plan that devolves into a town. It could have a central park, with a parking garage and secondary streets.' But then we wondered if we knew what we were doing." The landscape architects were reassured by the involvement of Whyte, whom they knew from the Bryant Park work. "Why don't we ask Holly what things we could include for employees, not just the executives? The environment matters," Olin recalls.[23]

The Carnegie Center advertising agency eventually boiled the concept down to a catchphrase: "Urban convenience meets with suburban comfort." Landis explained to a local reporter: "We wanted Carnegie Center to be unique. It's neither urban nor suburban, but combines the best of both worlds. It's planned meticulously, both in its land use and in its architecture. . . . We have worked closely with 'Holly' Whyte to help us create public areas, gardens, and greenways that our tenants can really use."[24]

The best of both worlds? Not surprisingly, Whyte recommended that the urban world be given more weight than the suburban. Whyte praised Landis's concept as "splendid," especially for putting "cars in their places, quite literally," and for making the spaces between the buildings "pedestrian spaces, in scale and feel and function." To emphasize the pedestrian scale, the center added gazebos and pavilions at strategic points.

But Whyte still worried about the size of the open spaces and felt that the design leaned too much to the suburban. "Where there is much more open space to work with, it would seem in order to be more generous in sizing the space. This would further such competitive advantages as relief from urban congestion." But do not be too generous, Whyte warned.

Whyte was optimistic about the possibilities for the successive clusters. The second series of buildings would "enclose some of the most interesting topography of the site" and would include a small lake, an amphitheater, and a greenway that would link it to the other clusters." To "seed the place with activity," Whyte suggested that Landis borrow from the practices of the best European squares and create "generators" of activity on the periphery of the buildings and let them push the activity outward into the open space. The first-floor cafeteria should provide outdoor dining, with lots of tables and—of course—movable chairs.

The Carnegie Center management, Whyte advised, "should play it loose" as to where people place the chairs. "Nobody is better at judging where they like to sit best than people." And the outdoor spaces intended for people should whenever possible be at the same grade as the adjoining land. "A park with a wall around it goes unnoticed," said Whyte, reflecting one of the lessons learned from Bryant Park in Manhattan.

Whyte suggested an additional amenity: "recreational activity *within* the central spaces. Few things could so liven up the scene as some people having a good time doing something within these key spaces." It would not take many, as just a handful of ice skaters ani-mating Rockefeller Plaza in New York proved. Whyte suggested one possibility: a croquet court, which has a standard size of 84 by 105 feet but can be scaled to a smaller space. He believed there were "quite a few addicts" in the Princeton area. He added in a parenthetical aside, "This non-addict has never figured out what the players are up to but they do make a good scene."[25]

Not wanting to be the last word on recreational opportunities, Whyte recommended Setha Low, then teaching at the landscape ar-chitecture school at the University of Pennsylvania. Low had studied similar office parks and concluded that the "sport" most favored by of-fice workers was walking. Moreover, they had few places to walk safely. In the Carnegie Center planning, croquet was soon out, and pedestrian paths and jogging trails were in. In acknowledgment of the competi-tive nature of some office workers, the paths were marked with indica-tors every eighth mile so that walkers could record their distances.[26] (Bocce courts were added later.)

On November 24, 1985, Whyte spent an evening at the Institute for Advanced Study in Princeton, appearing at a fundraiser for Channel 13, the New York station of the Public Broadcasting Service. On that visit Whyte might have noticed the most recent edition of what he would later describe as a "sprightly" newspaper serving the new of-fice corridor. The paper was *U.S. 1*, which I founded in 1984 to serve the new business community in the Princeton–Route 1 corridor. The paper marked its first anniversary by printing an editorial on the ten "essential truths" about the corridor. The very first "truth," I realized much later, was undoubtedly inspired by a book that had impressed me in the early 1970s, *The Last Landscape*. The truth, I wrote, was that "the biggest problem with Route 1 is not that there are too many people out there, but rather that there are too few." The paper went on to bemoan the lack of housing to complement the new developments and the high vacancy rates of the newly built office space. "People can be expected to humanize even the largest of the office behemoths on the highway. They also can be expected to give the entire corridor a sense of com-munity." But for that to happen, the editorial concluded, "Route 1 still needs a critical mass, and a critical mix."[27]

Whyte cited the newspaper and quoted the first truth in *City: Rediscovering the Center*. He added a corollary: the Route 1 developments also suffered because of too much space rather than too little. "Open space, like development, needs the discipline of function. Use it or lose it," he wrote in *City*.[28] In an interview with a real estate trade magazine in 1989, Whyte admitted his continued preference for urban offices over suburban office parks. But overall, he felt, the Carnegie Center had realized most of its goals: "The cafes, lakes, ponds, ducks, and setting look rather jolly. There is reason to be there and to stay there."[29]

Both office centers, Princeton Forrestal Center and the Carnegie Center, stopped most of the ticky-tacky development that was sprouting up along the Route 1 highway to the north and south of them. But despite the pleasing aesthetics, the centers still suffered from underlying sprawl. Whyte saw it instantly. "The open space is inefficiently used. Too much of it is institutional: vast lawns setting off the corporation's logo [a feature of Princeton Forrestal Center more than of the Carnegie Center]; interminable stretches of unrelieved greenery."

For an example of how to do it better, Whyte believed, one needed only to look across the highway. "There is one development in the corridor that is an exemplar in this respect. It has a wealth of open spaces; they connect with one another; they are enjoyed day in and day out by a great many people, and on foot. Yet the development density is much greater than in the Route 1 developments. I refer to the campus of Princeton University." Whyte noted that the density of development on the campus was about three times greater than that of the Route 1 office parks. "Yet for all the infilling that has taken place, the open spaces do not feel cramped. The very enclosure the buildings afford makes the spaces congenial in scale. Pathways provide fine linkages. And people walk."[30]

The competition between Princeton Forrestal Center and the Carnegie Center was fierce. Eventually the market spoke. The Carnegie Center outperformed Princeton Forrestal Center in terms of rental levels and vacancy rates. The Urban Land Institute, an independent real estate and land use association, produced a 160-page study on the value of landscape, site planning, and amenities in 1994. One of its case studies was the Carnegie Center, which "generally led Forrestal

Center in rental rates by about $1 a square foot, or five percent of the going rate."

It was a victory for the urbanist approach. "Amenities at Carnegie Center are generally closer to the office buildings and more easily reached," the Urban Land Institute reported. "The notable difference between amenities at the two projects is that Carnegie Center features the greenway, with all of the amenities located along it. Tenants at Carnegie Center can walk to all of the amenities and activities, while tenants at Forrestal are more likely to need to drive to them."[31]

Whyte's influence certainly contributed to the Carnegie Center's competitive edge. But did the Carnegie Center and all the other new office complexes in this "edge city" achieve the status that Fishman had envisioned in his *Bourgeois Utopias*? Did the Princeton–Route 1 corridor become a place that possessed "all the economic and technological dynamism we associate with the city?" If so, then it would have been an appreciable threat to the original "center" in the region, downtown Princeton and Palmer Square.

As it turned out, the town fared very well compared with the new highway development. A few of the leading law firms in town expanded into larger quarters in the Route 1 corridor. The Merrill Lynch brokerage office expanded by moving from Nassau Street to an office near the Carnegie Center. Nevertheless, the expanded Palmer Square was completed much in line with Whyte's initial recommendations. Downtown vacancies were quickly filled. Commercial rental rates in the new offices in the traditional center of Princeton consistently exceeded those in either Princeton Forrestal Center or the Carnegie Center. *U.S. 1*, my "sprightly" newspaper serving the new corporate corridor, grew into a sustainable small business. But *Town Topics*, the staid old community weekly that served the residents, retailers, and businesses in the heart of Princeton, always had more advertising and made more money. As Whyte had predicted in *City*, the center prevailed.

Downtown Princeton was walkable. The developments out on the highway were not. Whyte proved his point about the lack of walkability by, yes, walking it. On a beautiful day when he had plenty of time, he decided to walk from downtown Princeton to a meeting at the Carnegie Center, about two and a half miles away. The following is his account of that trek:

> Along the still bucolic Washington Road the path was soggy but challenging, and I managed. When I came up to Route 1, however, the path vanished. There was no way across—no legal one anyway. I finally made a dash for it, cars honking at me. On the other side was a brief sidewalk. It vanished as Route 1 went through an underpass. I squeezed along one side, inches from a roaring mass of cars and truck-trailers.
>
> When I arrived at the meeting I was greeted with incredulity. *Walked?* From *Princeton?* People came up to ask me about it. They thought I was some kind of nut.[32]

Any pedestrian then (or now, for that matter, despite a new overpass spanning Route 1) would have to be a nut to make that walk. But Whyte was not so much a nut. He was a researcher, doing what needed to be done to study his subject. As he had first pointed out in 1958, in the introduction to *The Exploding Metropolis*, plot plans, models, and bird's-eye renderings are not sufficient when you are examining the urban landscape. "You have to get out and walk."[33]

Chapter 17

The Final Years

For anyone who loved cities, and who walked them block by block to determine what made them work and not work, the conference "Sustainable Cities: Preserving and Restoring Urban Biodiversity" in October 1990 must have been an alluring event. The Chicago Historical Society and the Chicago Academy of Sciences, the cosponsors, hoped that their keynote speaker on a Saturday morning, William H. Whyte, would attract as many conference participants as possible from both organizations.

The night before the keynote Whyte went to dinner with two of the conference organizers. Rutherford H. Platt had read *The Last Landscape* when he was an attorney working on open space issues in Chicago in the late 1960s. In the 1970s, after earning his PhD in geography, Platt taught at the University of Massachusetts Amherst and maintained his interest in urban ecology. The high point of one visit to New York was a meeting with Whyte in Room 5600—as Platt says now, "a pilgrimage to the oracle of Manhattan."[1] The other organizer, Ann Louise Strong, a professor of city and regional planning at the University of Pennsylvania, had worked with Whyte decades before in the land preservation effort in the Brandywine Valley. After dinner at a noisy restaurant, they headed back to the hotel. Whyte wobbled a little, dropping the slides that he would use to illustrate his lecture. He scooped them up from the sidewalk and managed to get them re-sorted.

The next morning Strong met Whyte at breakfast. Whyte seemed to be suffering from a bad cold, Strong recalled later, but otherwise was, "as ever, full of tales of achievements in preservation from around the country, many of which he had fostered."[2]

The lecture, before a crowd of several hundred, was a great success. Afterward, however, Whyte struggled to reach a room offstage, where he collapsed on a sofa. At first it seemed like a simple case of exhaustion. But Platt, Paul Heltne, president of the Chicago Academy of Sciences, and others were sufficiently alarmed that they called for an ambulance. Whyte pleaded with the group not to notify Jenny Bell. He didn't want her to rush to Chicago from New York. "It will be too expensive," Platt recalls Whyte saying. But Jenny Bell was called and did rush to Whyte's side at the hospital. For both Platt and Strong, Chicago was the last stop on their respective rides with Holly Whyte.

Whatever the cause of Whyte's collapse, it was just one of many medical episodes in the final decades of his life. In 1984 Whyte checked into Memorial Sloan Kettering Cancer Center in New York for the successful removal of a squamous cell carcinoma. He sent a handwritten note to Laurance Rockefeller (a major donor to the center) expressing his admiration for the treatment. "What has most struck me is how non-institutional it is. . . . In so many ways it is a cheerful and reassuring place. To cite the chairs again, someone has taken care to provide for the fact that most people come to institutions in groups and made the waiting be more congenial for them. The same kind of thoughtfulness is apparent everywhere, even to the cheerful yellow of the walls of the below grade corridors."[3]

In late 1988 Whyte took a writer for *Smithsonian* magazine on a tour of Manhattan public spaces. But they were forced to travel by car—Whyte, "spry of tongue at age 71," had been "temporarily slowed down by recent heart surgery."[4] A profile of Whyte in the winter 1990 issue of the St. Andrew's School alumni magazine reported that he was "temporarily kept from the streets that he loved by a bone infection." Later, even as he was laid up in a hospital for unspecified heart problems, Whyte was still the careful observation man, taking notes for what he hoped would be a book about the design of hospitals. Elevators, for example, were "grossly inefficient," Whyte asserted. "They are responsible for a large share of the minutes wasted by people waiting. There is no triage."[5] Whyte imagined a book written "from the patient's point of view" and addressing what Whyte called the patient's "radius of accessibility."[6]

Another book was not beyond the realm of possibility. *City: Rediscovering the Center*, once it was finally published, had more than repaid its $30,000 advance. The royalty report at year end 1989 showed sales of more than thirteen thousand books in its first year, with Whyte owed an additional $3,388 in royalties.[7] Whyte also had dreams of producing another film, a sequel to *The Social Life of Small Urban Spaces*. This film, he hoped, would be "on the life of the street. I'll focus on U.S. cities mostly, but my subject will be street people and they are not very different from one place to another. Their behavior is always fascinating. (I have become an expert on the rituals of prolonged goodbyes.)"[8]

Whyte still had his moments in the public spotlight. In May 1992 Whyte attended the dedication marking the reopening of Bryant Park, a physical embodiment of Whyte's urban thinking. The dais was packed with Whyte's friends and admirers, including the Bryant Park Restoration Corporation's Dan Biederman; Lynden Miller, the landscape designer; and the architect Hugh Hardy. The stage was also filled with politicians, commissioners, and bureaucrats eager to be part of such a successful project.

But Whyte was missing. He was sitting in the audience with Jenny Bell and Laurie Olin, the landscape architect. Olin recalled the moment in an oral history recorded in 2012: "I was kind of surprised. There was a stage . . . with a lot of people sitting on it, there were park commissioners, there were city councilmen, there was the mayor, there were various other people . . . but I wasn't invited. I was sitting in the audience with Holly Whyte and his wife. We were really pleased and proud of the project, but we were also kind of surprised."[9]

Whyte, the man who would announce "happy hour" when he came home after receiving a standing ovation for his narration of the *Social Life of Small Urban Spaces* film, could not have been pleased. The oversight must have been somewhat assuaged by the *New York Times*

architecture critic Paul Goldberger. His column in the *Times* shared
the names of all the prominent players in the Bryant Park effort. Then
Goldberger added this:

> For all that the architects, landscape architects and the restora-
> tion corporation have achieved here, the true guiding light of this
> park was William H. Whyte Jr., the distinguished observer of pub-
> lic space. Mr. Whyte's theories about how people use urban space
> formed the philosophical basis for the redesign and guided all the
> decisions the designers made. He understood that the problem of
> Bryant Park was its perception as an enclosure cut off from the city;
> he knew that, paradoxically, people feel safer when not cut off from
> the city, and that they feel safer in the kind of public space they
> think they have some control over. . . .
> Bryant Park is a triumph for many—but most of all, it stands as a
> reminder that William H. Whyte Jr. is our prophet of urban space.[10]

Whyte, sometimes needing a cane, was well enough in June 1992
to travel to Philadelphia to testify at a congressional subcommittee
hearing conducted by Peter H. Kostmayer. His congressional district
included the Brandywine Valley of eastern Pennsylvania, the landscape
that Whyte had fallen in love with as a child and the original impetus
for his work in open space preservation. More than thirty years after he
wrote his initial article on urban sprawl for *Fortune* magazine, Whyte
the urbanist continued to be the go-to source for people trying to save
the farms, forests, and meadows of rural landscapes.

Land preservationists, Whyte told the subcommittee, sometimes
took an altruistic view that would not withstand economic pressures.
"People say, 'Well, you don't need to go through all this rigamarole.
Our people would never sell out to developers.' . . . As is so often the
case, they are surprised when their neighbors develop a shopping center." Whyte noted that he spoke with some resignation on this subject.
"Half my relatives are interested in making money."[11]

Whyte's pro bono support of street musicians continued in 1994,
when he filed an affidavit on behalf of a Manhattan street musician,
bass player Robert Turley. After the city required Turley and other

buskers to buy permits before performing in public (and on at least one occasion had Turley jailed and his equipment confiscated), Turley sued the city. "New York City has the greatest street life in the world, due in no small part to its street entertainers," Whyte wrote in Turley's defense. Such entertainers create "a sense of community through spontaneous entertainment. Their solicitations are entirely appropriate, non-coercive requests to be paid for their entertainment. They rarely obstruct pedestrian traffic and generally accommodate competing uses of public spaces, including other street entertainment."[12]

In October 1994 Turley's lawyer, Robert T. Perry (no relation to Whyte's step-relatives), visited Whyte at his home on East 94th Street to get the affidavit notarized. At the time Whyte was in a wheelchair. The case went back and forth with appeals. The ultimate outcome was in favor of Turley and his fellow buskers. The permitting process was ruled too complex and unreasonably costly. Turley ultimately got a six-figure award. Whyte provided his 1,800-word affidavit for no remuneration.[13]

Whyte's pro bono altruism notwithstanding, money was by then a growing concern. If Whyte had swallowed his pride in the 1950s when he was not promoted to managing editor of *Fortune* magazine, at this point in his life he might have been supported by a Time Inc. retirement plan. Fortunately for Whyte, however, he had chosen another deep—and caring—organization as his principal freelance client. By the late 1990s, Room 5600—the Rockefellers—had become concerned about Whyte's physical and financial well-being. An internal Rockefeller memo from 1997 showed that the Whytes' annual expenses of $93,240 exceeded their income of $86,730 by about $6,500. The single greatest expense item was home health aides: $65,000. Whyte's income already had been buttressed by Rockefeller largesse. The income, according to the ledger, was as follows:[14]

Reverse mortgage	$1,800
Social Security	24,000
Trust (per Caroline Hartshorne)	7,200
JHPI	20,730

| LSR | 13,000 |
| Estimated year-end bonus | 20,000 |

"JHPI" stands for Jackson Hole Preservation Inc., a Rockefeller-supported foundation. "LSR" is Laurance S. Rockefeller. The trust was from Whyte's paternal grandmother, established in the 1930s and directed to flow to Whyte's father. A handwritten note stated that the Hartshorne distribution varied from year to year, from about $7,200 to as much as $9,600.

But the memo also referred to more bad news. Holly and Jenny Bell owed about $20,000 to the Internal Revenue Service and $9,000 in back real estate taxes. Some utility bills were also in arrears. A nonprofit that assists people overwhelmed with medical bills was negotiating with an insurance company over $15,000 in unpaid bills. The reverse mortgage on the brownstone on East 94th Street that generated $150 per month for the rest of the Whytes' lives also had been used to pay some of Holly's outstanding bills. "It seems that at the end the bank will have the right to sell the apartment.... The balance, if any, would be paid to Alexandra." Jenny Bell's annual income, ranging from $10,000 to $20,000 per year, had been curtailed by a recent accident and hip surgery. She was in discussion with Christie's to dissolve her inventory of museum fabrics.

On one occasion, a friend and colleague at Room 5600, Ellen Fister Oxman, urged Laurance to make another gift to the Whytes. Oxman, who had become friendly with Holly, Jenny Bell, and Alexandra (and who danced with Holly at her wedding in 1985), later asked Jenny Bell if the Rockefeller money had allayed some of the Whytes' financial concerns. It had, Jenny Bell allowed. In fact, she had gone to Bergdorf Goodman and bought a new purse for herself and a pair of silk pajamas for Holly. "They were both brilliant and impractical," says Oxman of the Whytes.[15]

After Dan Biederman worked with Whyte on Bryant Park, he stayed in touch with the Whytes. Alexandra occasionally babysat the two Biederman children. In a 1996 interview for a profile of Whyte, Biederman noted that, by the standards of Manhattan consultants,

Whyte had charged very little for his work on Bryant Park. "Holly could have made a lot of money, but his attitude seemed to be 'I have no overhead. How can I charge so much?' The answer, of course, is that he's the master. But he doesn't think that way. He's always been more interested in doing the work than making a killing."[16] In a *New York Times* feature story a few years later on Jenny Bell's fashion career, she revealed a similarly ambivalent attitude toward the bottom line: "Holly always said: 'When are you going to cut the melon? When are you going to make some money?'" Jenny Bell created more than she sold. When her handcrafted apparel began to consume the remaining open space in their cluttered home, Holly threatened to give the dresses away to Jenny Bell's homeless friends.[17]

The Whyte family suffered more trauma in 1995 when a fire caused smoke and water damage to their brownstone, forcing them to relocate temporarily to a hotel. The Rockefellers once again offered assistance. Hands-on help came in 1996, when Whyte was hopelessly behind on the deadline for his memoir with Henry Holt and Company. A young editor, Albert LaFarge, was assigned to ride herd on Whyte's output. But the pace did not pick up, given Whyte's various medical challenges and his failing eyesight. At that point LaFarge volunteered to serve as Whyte's amanuensis. For several months LaFarge visited twice a week, taking dictation on his laptop, prodding Whyte's memory, culling notes from various files.

"Holly was cheerful, buoyed by our progress," LaFarge recalls.[18] But LaFarge was frustrated. The conversation kept reverting to Whyte's childhood, his military service at Guadalcanal, and the blueberry patches near his grandmother's summer home on Cape Cod. LaFarge turned over the notes for the memoir to Whyte's stepbrother, Jim Perry. The result, *A Time of War*, a "partial memoir," was published posthumously in 2000. LaFarge, meanwhile, began assembling the articles and excerpts that would become *The Essential William H. Whyte*. (LaFarge later started his own literary agency, which now includes Whyte's literary estate among its clients.)

Whyte faced more mobility issues. Herndon Werth, another St. Andrew's alumnus who served on the school's board of trustees with

Whyte, had dinner with Holly and Jenny Bell in Manhattan. "He was so weak he couldn't walk a block to get a taxi," Werth wrote in a remembrance of Whyte.[19]

David Dillon, the influential architecture critic for the *Dallas Morning News* from 1983 to 2006, interviewed Whyte for a 1996 feature profile in *Preservation* magazine. The photographer wanted to shoot Whyte at the site of his great urban design success, Bryant Park. It was a huge undertaking to transport Whyte from his house to the park, recalls one of the organizers of that photo session. In the article, published in the magazine's September/October 1996 issue, Whyte looked distinguished in gray dress slacks, dark blazer, white shirt, and tie. But another photo from that shoot showed a full-length view. Along with the organization man suit, Whyte was wearing ankle-high white shoes. They were probably orthotic shoes, but with the appearance of sneakers—the last item of clothing that Whyte would ever be caught in, according to Paco Underhill, the former Street Life Project intern.[20] "In the last stages of his life, he was a pretty troubled guy," says Underhill, recalling his final visit with Whyte a year before he died.[21]

Among the troubling aspects of Whyte's life may have been a wistful feeling that his legacy would be short-lived. Lynden Miller designed the gardens at Bryant Park and got to know Holly and Jenny Bell even better when they assisted her fundraising efforts for restoration of the Conservatory Garden in Central Park. "He was my hero," Miller says. And she recalls him confiding in her, "No one will ever remember what I've done."[22]

Jane Jacobs, of course, continued to reign as the preeminent urbanist around the world. LaFarge sensed Whyte's wistfulness about the fact that his onetime protégée had eclipsed him in the pantheon of urban thinkers. "He felt she really took it to the bank."[23] When LaFarge came across the first edition of *The Death and Life of Great American Cities* on Whyte's bookshelf, he saw the inscription and felt compelled to show it to Whyte, to remind him of his role as expressed in Jacobs's hand: "To Holly Whyte, who had more to do with this book at a crucial stage than he probably realizes, but which I, at least, will always remember with gratitude."

David Dillon, in a 1996 article in *Preservation* magazine, pointed out that "there is no school of Whyte, no army of Whyte disciples to carry his message, no Whyte chair or Whyte prize. Too modest to franchise himself, he is also too uncalculating, or unselfish, to try to cash in on his discoveries." Dillon sensed that Whyte was disappointed "that his ideas haven't been more enthusiastically received in architecture and planning schools. He's still something of a pariah among professionals, who suspect something wrong with proposals that are so practical and comprehensible." In his interview, Dillon raised the issue with Whyte. "I can't say there has been any kind of revolution," Whyte responded, "but I'm hopeful that as time goes by some of these ideas will be institutionalized in the general courses. It isn't that the professions aren't interested, it's that there's no follow-through because it involves a hell of a lot of hard work."[24]

But by that time, probably unknown to Whyte, an army of disciples was forming—an army that would advance many of the values held by Whyte. Peter Katz, an urbanist with unconventional credentials in graphic design and real estate marketing, had worked early in his career with Underhill, who by then had become an expert in retail design. Underhill had alerted Katz to Whyte's *Social Life of Small Urban Spaces*. On one occasion Underhill brought Whyte to Katz's office at 1466 Broadway in Manhattan for an informal meeting. Later Katz read *City: Rediscovering the Center*. "I understood Whyte's significance," Katz says. As Whyte had called out suburban retail centers that were called "villages" but in fact had no houses, so Katz questioned projects that were called "town centers" when they were really nothing more than shopping centers. He was living in Greenwich Village at the time. "Why can't we build charming neighborhoods like this anymore?" he wondered.[25]

Katz soon connected with architects who had similar values. They included husband-and-wife team Andrés Duany and Elizabeth Plater-Zyberk, whose firm is based in Miami; Stefanos Polyzoides and Elizabeth Moule, another couple, who practice in Pasadena, California; and Peter Calthorpe, based in San Francisco. In the spring of 1992, Katz invited them to a dinner meeting at the Lotos Club, a private dining club on East 66th Street, just off Fifth Avenue and not far from Whyte's home.

The new urbanists would infuse urban planning and architectural design with principles that Whyte had long practiced, among them the value of density and the virtue of considering the space between buildings as important as the buildings themselves. Places and place-making would become an enduring theme of urban planners in the twenty-first century.

* * *

A few days after William H. Whyte died, on January 12, 1999, Paul Goldberger, by then architecture critic for the *New Yorker*, ran into Dan Biederman of Bryant Park at the corner of Sixth Avenue and 46th Street. It was exactly the kind of chance "human congress" that Whyte believed was the "genius" of the city.[26] "We stopped, and stood on the corner and talked about Holly, and what he had done, and what he had meant for the city, and for planning, and for the way we see the world. Dan reminded me that Holly was in every way the guiding philosopher behind the resurgence of Bryant Park, and how critical his thinking, his advice, his wisdom had been to what was done there, and his words made clear how everyone who has struggled with how to make civilized public space in New York is in his debt."

Goldberger told the story of that meeting with Biederman at Whyte's memorial service on January 19, 1999. The architectural critic concluded his remembrance by sharing the essence of what he had learned from Whyte: "He taught all of us, more than anything, to look, to look hard, with a clean, clear mind, . . . and then to look again—and to believe in what you see. . . . Believe in the fact that the people who use cities are often way ahead of the people who design them."[27]

The setting for the memorial service, the Episcopal Church of the Epiphany on York Avenue at East 74th Street, was where Whyte had delivered his laymen's sermon in 1953. His daughter, Alexandra, his stepbrother, Jim Perry, and Donald Elliott, the former planning commissioner, also offered remembrances.

Ellen Oxman, the colleague from Room 5600, who was also an aspiring opera singer and a graduate of Columbia University and the Juilliard School, sang a song selected by Jenny Bell, reflecting her Quaker heritage and Holly's love of pastoral settings: "Simple Gifts," with its classic refrain, "'Tis the gift to be simple, 'tis the gift to be free." Oxman also sang a Samuel Barber arrangement of "Sure on This Shining Night," a poem by James Agee, one of the "connected critics" in the early years of *Fortune* magazine. Oxman knew that Whyte had appreciated Agee's poetry.[28]

There was one more Whyte–Barber connection. The composer, like Whyte, was born in West Chester, Pennsylvania, seven years before Whyte. And Barber was buried there, in Oaklands Cemetery, in what is still a rural setting but just a short bicycle ride from town. Whyte, whose three most favored cities were New York, New York, and New York, would nevertheless soon be buried in that same wooded cemetery, not far from Barber's grave.

Chapter 18

Whyte in the Twenty-First Century— the Urban Imperative

After Rutherford Platt left Chicago at the conclusion of the "Sustainable Cities" conference in 1990, he never saw William H. Whyte again. He also never forgot him. Three years after Whyte's death in 1999, Platt, director of the Ecological Cities Project at the University of Massachusetts Amherst, organized another conference, this one honoring Whyte and building on the book he wrote and edited in 1958, *The Exploding Metropolis*. "The Humane Metropolis: People and Nature in the 21st Century—a Symposium to Celebrate and Continue the Work of William H. Whyte" attracted about three hundred participants over two days in June 2002 at New York University.

Whyte's daughter, Alexandra, reminisced about her father at the opening and at the closing of the symposium. Though visibly frail, Jenny Bell, who would die just three months later at the age of seventy-five, asked several questions from the floor.[1] Albert LaFarge, by then the literary agent for Whyte's estate, hosted a reception for the new trade paperback edition of *The Organization Man*. It would be followed by reprints of *The Last Landscape* and *City: Rediscovering the Center*, with eventual publication of all three books in China, as well, in 2018. LaFarge also sold the Chinese rights to *The Social Life of Small Urban Spaces* in 2020.[2]

Architecture critic David Dillon's 1996 profile of Whyte noted that there was "no school of Whyte, no army of Whyte disciples to carry his message."[3] But an army, or at least a battalion, of disciples has assembled. You can encounter them in the halls of academe, or in a real estate developer's office, or—as I recounted in the preface—in a back alley in your hometown. Where to begin tracking them down? I started with the roster of participants at the 2002 symposium. The "army" there included some names that have already appeared in this biography: Donald Elliott, the former planning commissioner of New York; Paul Goldberger, the architecture critic; Lynden B. Miller, who designed the gardens at Bryant Park; Dan Biederman of Bryant Park; Charles E. Little, whose reading of *The Organization Man* prompted him to leave his Madison Avenue job to work in open space preservation; and Tony Hiss and Adam Rome, who contributed perspective to Whyte's role in the open space preservation movement.

There were plenty of other Whyte disciples at the 2002 gathering, including three—Amanda Burden, Jerold S. Kayden, and Thomas Balsley—whose work continues to be inspired by Whyte.

Amanda Burden at one point in her life would have been the last person to attend a symposium on the "humane metropolis." In the early 1960s, Burden headlined gossip columns as a Manhattan socialite and partygoer. But then came reality, and a return to college for a degree in animal behavior in 1976. When Burden ran into an old friend from high school, Fred Kent, he asked what she was planning to do next. "I don't know," she replied. "I do know that I can take quantitative analysis of behavior. That's my only skill." Kent promptly walked Burden down to Rockefeller Center to meet Whyte, who had just launched the Project for Public Spaces (PPS), the successor organization to the Street Life Project. Upon meeting Burden, Whyte immediately took her down to the street level. "Let me show you the sidewalks," Burden recalls him saying. She soon realized that "cities would be my way to live a life of public service."[4]

Burden was appointed to the New York City Planning Commission in 1990 and served as chair from 2002 to 2013. In that position, she supported the development of New York's celebrated High Line, built out of an abandoned elevated rail track. A year or so after Whyte's death, Burden introduced his film *The Social Life of Small Urban Spaces* at a Municipal Art Society benefit. On the way to the lectern, Burden walked past Jenny Bell, squeezed her hand, and said (in earshot of a reporter), "Your husband changed my life."[5] Burden now works for Bloomberg Associates, a philanthropy dedicated to improving cities around the world.

Jerold Kayden, who had provided Whyte with data showing the value of plaza incentives to developers (chapter 13), reported to the "Humane Metropolis" audience on his efforts to ensure that privately owned public spaces (POPS) were maintained in the manner that developers promised when they first received the bonuses. In the late 1990s Kayden, by then a professor of planning law at the Harvard Graduate School of Design, spent three years taking an inventory of more than five hundred POPS. In conjunction with the New York City Department of City Planning and the Municipal Art Society, Kayden published his findings in 2000 in *Privately Owned Public Space: The New York City Experience*, partly "a paean to William H. Whyte" but more importantly a wake-up call for public space advocates.[6]

While Kayden reported some improvement in spaces created after the 1975 zoning code revisions, enforcement remained spotty and there was widespread neglect. In 2000 the Municipal Art Society created a volunteer effort to monitor the plazas. They called it "the Holly Watch." Kayden continued that effort in 2005 by forming Advocates for Privately Owned Public Space (APOPS), which in 2012 joined with the Municipal Art Society to collect citizen complaints about noncompliant POPS and forward them to the city. Kayden's initiatives became headline news in 2015 and 2016, when he alerted officials of the removal of a frequently used bench in the lobby of a Fifth Avenue office and residential tower. That building, Trump Tower, had gained twenty extra stories as an incentive bonus. The bench, a resting spot for many weary tourists, had been replaced—in violation of the POPS agreement—by two counters filled with Trump merchandise for sale. Kayden sat through six meetings with city officials and Trump representatives (the final ones with then Trump attorney Michael Cohen)

Figure 18.1 Amanda Burden, pictured here with Whyte late in his life, found her calling in urban planning after a chance meeting with him in the 1970s. (David Dillon Papers / University of Texas at Arlington.)

before the city finally levied a $14,000 fine and the Trump Organization reinstalled the public seating.[7]

In 2011 two Midtown Manhattan architects—Brian Nesin, who had studied the POPS concept with Kayden at Harvard, and David Grider—realized that a series of POPS could be used to walk from 51st to 57th Streets between Sixth and Seventh Avenues. Nesin and Grider created an ad hoc group called Friends of Privately Owned Public Space (F-POPS) to celebrate that walk, known formally as 6½ Avenue but which they dubbed "Holly Whyte Way." Working with a public artist, Graham Coreil-Allen, F-POPS organized an "arcade parade" that marched with a band from one end to the other, at one point passing through Le Parker Meridien Hotel between 56th and 57th Streets. The POPS literally passes through the lobby of the hotel (now the Parker) as a result of a deal that gave the developer eight extra floors in 1979. "I do not believe Le Parker Meridien had ever had the spectacle of a marching band blow through it," recalls Grider.[8]

Thomas Balsley, the landscape architect who worked with Whyte in the 1980s (chapter 14), appeared with Kayden at the 2002 symposium. Since working with Whyte, Balsley says, he has been guided by Whyte's "gentle whispers from just over my shoulder." In 2018 Balsley's firm, SWA/Balsley, tested how Whyte's "observations, recommendations, and scientific methods would adapt themselves" to present-day circumstances. Many of the spaces now being turned into gathering spots, Balsley says, are "leftovers of streets," such as traffic islands and other "weird spaces"—spaces Whyte had called "tremendous trifles." Using some twenty-first-century tools, such as machine learning algorithms, as well as some of the same observational techniques employed by the Street Life Project in the 1970s, the Balsley study showed that the use of these newer public spaces has changed along with the nature of the daytime workforce utilizing the spaces. "We're a much more collaborative society," says Balsley. "We now work together." Some of Balsley's designs for public spaces feature swivel stools with bar tables and attract younger professionals. "People are no longer going to the park to escape the city; they're going to connect with the city."[9]

But some usage patterns were remarkably similar to what Whyte had observed more than forty years earlier. The SWA/Balsley observers

watched people making furniture out of anything—peaked curbs, security bollards, Jersey barriers, and electrical boxes. Whyte showed
people using trash bins as temporary desktops and resting a foot on
a standpipe to tighten up a shoelace. Times change; public spaces
endure.[10]

*   *   *

Throughout his career Whyte played whack-a-mole, deflecting one
report after another of the death of the city, especially big cities and
older cities. Despite all the bad news, Whyte believed, the city center
would hold. He based his faith on two premises, both of which have
been borne out by events in the first quarter of the twenty-first century.
The first was that the exodus of established firms from a city center
was not a death knell but rather an opportunity for growth. The second
was that public spaces were as critical as gleaming new buildings to a
city's health.

Whyte believed that new vacancies made the commercial real estate
market more affordable for smaller companies and start-ups—types
of companies that typically grew more quickly and created more jobs
than mature corporations. The start-ups (and this would prove true
also of dot-com start-ups), Whyte wrote, "need older, somewhat beat-
up quarters off to the side but not too far from the center." The new
office towers were usually too expensive for small start-up companies.
"The belief that major office projects are the prime source of new jobs
dies hard," Whyte wrote in *City*.[11]

In the urban renaissance of the early twenty-first century, some of
the companies that had left in the "great exodus" studied by Whyte
came back. General Electric, for example, had vacated Manhattan for a
suburban location in Fairfield, Connecticut. But in 2016 GE abandoned
that location for a new headquarters in Boston. The Connecticut office,
one of the departing executives noted, was "a morgue."[12] The city was
seen, as Whyte had predicted, as "the place for news and gossip, for the
creation of ideas."[13] McDonald's, not specifically referenced by Whyte
but nevertheless a symbol of the suburbs' allure, with its golden arches
dotting the sprawling landscape, left its seventy-four-acre campus in

Oak Brook, Illinois, in 2018 and retrenched in Chicago, in what is said to be an excellent restaurant district.

Suburbs, which had appeared to be a perpetual engine of growth in the second half of the twentieth century, faced challenges of their own in the 2000s, most visibly the rapid decline of their once dominant shopping malls. In response some mall owners are turning to urban models for salvation. Robert J. Gibbs, a Michigan-based landscape architect, redesigns and repurposes failed shopping malls around the country. Drawing on what he calls Whyte's "mythologies and research," Gibbs helps mall owners convert their properties into mixed-use centers with residential, office, and civic spaces.[14] As e-commerce grows, one can envision malls turned into Amazon warehouses.

Kids who grew up in the suburbs have not always been eager to live there as adults. In studying the influx of bright young people into hip urban centers, economist Richard Florida gave these new city dwellers a name and used it in the title of his 2002 book, *The Rise of the Creative Class and How It's Transforming Work, Leisure, Community, and Everyday Life*. "Places have replaced companies as the key organizing units in our economy," Florida wrote.[15] The coolest places boasted dynamic, walkable, livable mixed-use neighborhoods, usually created with little or no help from city hall. There are now many such places across the country, and new ones keep getting added to the mix. But they all serve as comfortable cocoons for on-the-move and affluent millennials, much as the suburbs did for the corporate families studied by Whyte in the 1950s.

The coolest places might also be the greenest places. In the 1980s Whyte mused that if his hometown of West Chester, Pennsylvania, had expanded its street grid by just two blocks on each side the town could have accommodated about three decades' worth of sprawl in the adjoining countryside.[16] Today towns across America are revisiting their twentieth-century zoning ordinances, which by default favored single-family houses on spacious lots, and considering denser housing and mixed uses in walkable neighborhoods. Minimum parking requirements are being replaced with regulations limiting the maximum number. To address the missing middle of housing and make housing more energy efficient, urbanists advocate auxiliary dwelling units. Whyte's *Cluster Development*, published in 1964, made the same point: clustered housing leaves room for a network of open spaces "that will weave the outdoors into the very heart of the metropolitan areas."[17] Within cities, building up will be critical. Whyte's discussion of capturing light off neighboring tall buildings in *City* in 1988 may become an even more important consideration in city planning.[18]

A substantial portion of the 2002 Whyte symposium considered the promise of a "green" metropolis. Even then the presenters considered the city, with its denser footprint and more efficient transportation systems, to be the key to decreasing the world's energy consumption. Today climate change activists point out, for example, that converting to electric vehicles is not enough. People need to drive less to reduce their carbon footprint. The "fifteen-minute city," with all essential goods and services within a short walk, is seen as one step toward a net-zero carbon footprint. Healthy cities are also a critical component of another environmental goal aimed at combating climate change: The "30 by 30" plan—protecting 30 percent of open space by 2030. That is now a goal in California, and it is also under consideration by the Joe Biden administration and the European Union.[19]

Harvard University economist Edward Glaeser's critically acclaimed 2011 book built on Florida's work and confirmed all of Whyte's highest hopes in its title: *Triumph of the City: How Our Greatest Invention Makes Us Richer, Smarter, Greener, Healthier, and Happier.*[20]

In 2017, when Amazon announced its competition to determine the location of its proposed second headquarters, HQ2, its request for proposals read as if it been lifted from the pages of Whyte, Florida, or Glaeser. The company made clear that it had no interest in escaping from the urban environment, as other corporate behemoths did in the 1970s and 1980s. Amazon said it had "a preference" for metropolitan areas with more than a million people and that the new location could be "an urban or downtown campus." It wanted the location to be within forty-five minutes or less of an international airport, and it wanted "at site" access to mass transit. Rather than build from scratch on empty land, Amazon sought sites with existing buildings of at least five hundred thousand square feet. Opportunities for "renovation/re-development" were encouraged. More than 220 cities submitted pro-posals, and many of them touted long-abandoned industrial sites as assets.

Whyte would have smiled at Amazon's final choice for HQ2: the Crystal City complex in suburban Arlington, Virginia. Whyte had described Crystal City in 1988 as an example of a mixed-use develop-ment that sprang up around a freeway interchange and didn't work very well. "As in most such complexes, there is an enormous amount of superstructure used by not very many people. The problem is not that it kills off the street. There is no street to kill off."[21] For Amazon that underused space turned into an opportunity. And the grand plan for the area might bring another smile to Whyte's legion of followers. Amazon proposes a pedestrian link between the office complex and Reagan National Airport. The developer of the Amazon project, JBG Smith, proclaims on its website that "placemaking is a core part of our DNA." Many people at the firm are said to be familiar with Whyte's work. Their goal is to make the new Amazon neighborhood a lively place at night as well as during office hours. If they succeed, Crystal City may soon resemble an actual city.[22]

The second premise of Whyte's faith in cities was that the spaces between buildings were as important as the buildings themselves. This counterintuitive view was not immediately clear to many cities. Time and again, public officials and civic boosters have tried to cure their cit-ies' problems with a gleaming new conference center, stadium, or office tower designed by a "star-chitect." Glaeser made the same point in *Tri-umph of the City*, referring to declining cities that thought they "could build their way back to success" with various grandiose projects. These cities made "the all-too-common error of confusing a city, which is re-ally a mass of connected humanity, with its structures."[23]

Whyte was skeptical of megastructures. He championed instead the public realm's streets, sidewalks, and public and private open spaces, as well as "abandoned rights of way of railroads, unused aqueducts, the wastelands underneath the high tension lines, . . . empty lots, leftovers from public works projects, dumps, sand and gravel pits, and sanitary land fills."[24] As he noted, "where there is waste there is opportunity."[25] By the late 1980s Whyte marveled at the proliferation of outdoor cafés on urban sidewalks and at the increased usage of many public spaces.

> Cities should take a closer look at what they already have. Most of them are sitting on a huge reservoir of space yet untapped by imagination. They do not need to spend millions creating space. In their inefficiently used rights-of-way, their vast acreage of parking lots, there is more than enough space for broad walkways and small parks and pedestrian spaces—and at premium locations, at ground level.[26]

Whyte's advice fell on deaf ears at plenty of city halls. But ordinary citizens sometimes had their own imaginative ideas. In 2005 in San Francisco, some employees of an art and design firm took over a vacant parking space on the street and set up a seating area, complete with turf on the pavement and a potted tree. They invited visitors to feed a few coins into the meter and enjoy themselves. People did just that. When the architects got a call from city hall, they braced themselves for a scolding. Instead the city asked how more of these parklets could be created.[27]

In 2010 Jason Roberts, a musician and information technology consultant living in Dallas, took a four-lane street and turned it into a two-day "living block" art project, with outdoor café seating and other amenities. The city picked up on the idea, and "Better Blocks" were eventually implemented in more than a hundred cities worldwide. In 2011 Roberts and some allies recalled Whyte's 1983 proposal for City Hall Plaza. Though very little of the Whyte plan was implemented, the Roberts group brought several elements to life in 2012 and even produced a video of their efforts, interspersed with clips of Whyte speaking in Dallas and narration from *The Social Life of Small Urban Spaces*.[28]

These efforts soon had a name, "tactical urbanism." A guidebook published in 2015, *Tactical Urbanism: Short-Term Action for Long-Term Change*, explained that the movement drew on that "huge reservoir" of spaces that Whyte had described. The authors, tactical urbanists Mike Lydon and Anthony Garcia, praised the design suggestions in Whyte's

Social Life of Small Urban Spaces book and film. They only wished that Whyte had extended his research to the "auto-centric" streets that continue to make up such a large portion of the public realm.[29]

In 2020 even public officials suddenly began looking at tactical urbanism in a much different light. When the coronavirus pandemic, which would last through 2020 and well into 2021 (as this book was being published), ripped through the major urban centers, some observers immediately raised the old bogeyman: density. Could so many people, so close together, be a fatal combination in the face of this disease? But the coronavirus ultimately hit rural areas just as hard as it hit cities. Overall density appeared to be not so much the problem. Rather it was densely packed places, such as nursing homes, crowded bars and restaurants, raucous political rallies, and celebratory receptions.

Even assuming that vaccines will bring COVID-19 under control, the pandemic experience—and the fear that another one could be on the horizon—will have lingering effects on society as a whole. Whether the residual harm will be greater in cities than in suburbs or rural areas may take years to ascertain. What seems clear, however, is that all the changes that made communities safer and more livable during the pandemic have been the same things that Whyte and other urbanists have advocated for decades: better public spaces, more room on the streets for pedestrians and bicyclists, more outdoor dining and open-air markets. For years cities have considered plans for converting a downtown block or two into a car-free public open space with room for dining and entertainment. The pandemic suddenly turned plans into action in many places.

In 2021 people around the world wished for a return to normal. Some worried that the new normal would leave urban centers with acres of vacant office space, devastated mass transit systems, and bankrupted public works departments. But there is another scenario, a "snap back" to the old ways of doing business. In this scenario young "creative class" workers flock to the city to take advantage of temporarily cheaper rental housing. Work-from-home employees resume some or all of their commuting to escape the grind of domestic partners, children, and household chores and rediscover the "third places" such as coffee shops, bars, and bookstores. Cities thrive, as economist Paul Krugman has written, in part because of "information-sharing and brainstorming ... over coffee breaks and after-hours beers; Zoom calls aren't an adequate substitute."[30]

Urbanists might hope for a return to something close to normal, but not the same old normal. Some of the lingering effects of the pandemic could become enduring positive changes for urban centers—more people-centered streets, more public spaces that are accessible year-round, and a greater appreciation for the public realm.

* * *

In his 1996 interview with David Dillon, Whyte hoped that some of his methodology would be incorporated into academic curricula. But, as Dillon pointed out, Whyte could be viewed as a "pariah among professionals." He had not always treated the profession kindly, and architects do not always take kindly to criticism. Whyte also might have been discounted by architects who, Dillon wrote, "suspect something wrong with proposals that are so practical and comprehensible." Some architects and academicians are drawn to the politically and culturally framed theories of philosophers such as Henri Lefebvre and his analyses of "everyday life." As several of Whyte's disciples have noted, the scholars might view Whyte's declarative sentences and straightforward explanations as simplistic, rather than a "gift to be simple" celebrated by the Quaker hymn at Whyte's memorial service.[31]

But architecture is changing—in the direction of Whyte-style placemaking. The Congress for the New Urbanism (CNU), which came to life at the Lotos Club in 1992, advanced an urban vision in its 1994 charter that sounded more like Whyte's own thinking than that of the "star-chitects" and designers of megastructures: "We stand for the restoration of existing urban centers and towns within coherent metropolitan regions, the reconfiguration of sprawling suburbs into communities of real neighborhoods and diverse districts, the conservation of natural environments, and the preservation of our built legacy."[32]

From its headquarters in Washington, DC, CNU works with nineteen state and local chapters to champion "walkable urbanism," diverse neighborhoods, and environmentally sustainable design. CNU's annual congress, approaching its thirtieth anniversary and hosted by a different city each year, regularly attracts more than a thousand urban-minded participants. In 2016 the United Nations Conference on Housing and Sustainable Urban Development (Habitat III) adopted its own New Urban Agenda, with goals similar to those of CNU, especially an emphasis on the role of public space and culture in the urban setting and the integration of diverse uses.

Architects in the new urbanism movement seem less concerned with the grand buildings they create and more concerned with the spaces between the buildings—Whyte's focal point. Stefanos Polyzoides, a cofounder of CNU (now dean of architecture at the University of Notre Dame and coincidentally a roommate of mine at Princeton University in the late 1960s), made this point in an interview for the CNU journal *Public Square*.

> One of the things we've learned as new urbanists is that the prime ingredient of urbanism is really public space and the public realm. So the urban plan comes first and the building second. It becomes an issue of whether the building is a monument or a piece of fabric. Then does this building dominate what's in place or does this building add to it or transform it? New urbanists essentially believe in compatibility between building and place.[33]

Whyte's work is well known to the founders of the new urbanism movement. In their book *Suburban Nation: The Rise of Sprawl and the Decline of the American Dream*, Andrés Duany, Elizabeth Plater-Zyberk, and Jeff Speck call for a new design of the old suburbia. The suburbs could profit from the hard-earned lessons of cities. Published in 2000, the book is to the suburbs as Whyte's *City* is to the urban core. In their acknowledgments, the authors credit writers who influenced their work, "most notably William Whyte" and a handful of others, including Jane Jacobs.[34]

The suburbs are by no means the sole focus of Duany, Plater-Zyberk, Speck, and the new urbanists. Duany recalls reading *City* from beginning to end. Whyte's analysis of the Seagram plaza, Duany says, taught him how to design plazas. But more important, he says, he "learned how to see, not just how to look." Whyte and Jacobs, among a few others in the late 1950s and 1960s, says Duany, brought a socio-logical view to the relatively new profession of urban planning. The fact that these outsiders had no formal training in architecture was an advantage. "If Whyte had been trained in architecture, he wouldn't have been able to see—he would have been trained not to notice. He would have had blinders."[35]

Whyte's methodology for studying the urban landscape was prag-matic, rather than theoretical, and Whyte shared it readily with others. Whyte "didn't lock the door," says Duany. "He didn't say this is all you need to know so now you should just go do it. He left the door open for other people to follow. He allowed a lot of people to follow him."

That has happened. At University College Dublin, Ireland, Miriam Fitzpatrick, who has intensively studied Whyte's Street Life Project (chapter 13), teaches Introduction to Urban Design. First item on the reading list: *The Social Life of Small Urban Spaces*—the book and the accompanying film. Fitzpatrick says she brings her research on Whyte "into all my teaching—whether it is design studio, history of cities, methods for observing public space, or seminars on writing."[36]

Kim Rollings, until recently a professor at Notre Dame's School of Architecture, presented Whyte's observation techniques from *The Social Life of Small Urban Spaces* as a model for students to use when evaluating public spaces as part of the "Healthy Places ND" research group. Rollings's students read some of Whyte's work, watched *The Social Life of Small Urban Spaces* film, and completed observational and mapping exercises to help them understand the elements of successful public spaces. "Many of my environmental psychology colleagues af-filiated with the Environmental Design Research Association [formed in the 1960s to improve relationships among people, their built envi-ronments, and natural ecosystems] also teach Whyte's work," Rollings says.[37] (She moved in July 2021 to the University of Michigan.)

Ron Henderson refers his students at the Illinois Institute of Tech-nology to Whyte's *Social Life of Small Urban Spaces* film. "I tell them to watch people in the everyday situations that enrich the city that are just as powerful as the walking axes at the Palace of Versailles." To ap-preciate the Whyte approach, Henderson notes, he also has to instill in the students some "modesty of ambition."[38] Not everyone can practice in Paris.

Setha Low, the cultural anthropologist who worked with Whyte at the Carnegie Center in central New Jersey in the early 1980s, founded the Public Space Research Group at the City University of New York in 1995. Building on "Holly's work on small spaces," Low has developed guidelines for making large parks work well for their various constituencies. Low presents "Holly-type" observational techniques that "anyone can use" to evaluate a public space. The challenge in the twenty-first century, Low says, is not just one of unused spaces. It's also "patterns of design and management that exclude some people and reduce social and cultural diversity." There may be no formal School of Whyte, but, Low says, "there is no place that doesn't read about Whyte. All of the work cites him over and over."[39]

Students in the Department of Information Science at the University of Colorado Boulder need to master the skill of observing digital spaces. Professor Leysia Palen uses Whyte's film *The Social Life of Small Urban Spaces* as an analog tool for teaching ethnographic skills that can be applied to digital spaces as well as physical places. The film, she says, shows "the power we have when we really notice" the world around us, especially "things that appear to be on the margin but that are really important." The Whyte film has served one other purpose for Palen. Her three children used to clamor to watch the film before bedtime. "Children are the best ethnographers in the world—their business is to notice," she says, echoing Whyte's observations in *The Last Landscape*.[40]

In a world that increasingly turns to visual rather than textual representations, Whyte's *Social Life of Small Urban Spaces* film has become a long-lasting teaching tool—an important part of the Whyte legacy. The Municipal Art Society (MAS) was the principal underwriter of the film as Whyte honed its contents in the 1970s. MAS initially handled its distribution—not an easy task in the predigital age. In 1988 MAS connected with Mitchell Block, who operates a California-based independent film distributor, Direct Cinema Ltd. Block acquired the rights to the movie, digitized it, and now sells it on DVD for $95 or rents it to universities as a teaching aid, with royalties going to MAS. The film is "very much an academic film," says Block, one that goes from generation to generation as students who saw the film become teachers themselves. It's also frequently posted to YouTube without permission. Interviewed for a story on video piracy, Block cited an upload by the University of South Carolina's history department in February 2018. By August of that year, *The Social Life of Small Urban Spaces* already had registered 21,369 views.[41]

* * *

As an open space preservationist who forged common ground between conservation groups and developers, and as an urban visionary who worked with municipal planning commissions to effect changes in the zoning code, Whyte created a broad legacy. It includes not one but two active organizations—expanding and advancing his ideas in the United States and abroad. It should not be a surprise. He was an organization man himself, after all.

The Project for Public Spaces (PPS), the successor organization to Whyte's Street Life Project, is now approaching its fiftieth anniversary. Formed in 1975 with Whyte's organizational support (and with $40,000 in support from the Rockefeller Family Foundation), PPS was directed from its founding until 2018 by Fred Kent. After Whyte and Kent connected during planning sessions for the first Earth Day in 1970, Kent volunteered to work for Whyte's Street Life Project, which eventually hired him to work full-time.

The Project for Public Spaces grew quickly into a nationally recognized placemaking organization. PPS helped increase the public's use of Rockefeller Center; Chapel Street in New Haven, Connecticut; Harvard Plaza in Cambridge, Massachusetts; and a plaza in Detroit known as Campus Martius Park, a two-and-a-half-acre island in the center of a busy downtown intersection that had become almost inaccessible to pedestrians as adjoining streets were widened and lights timed to maximize traffic flow. Over the course of years, PPS worked with Quicken Loans and other sponsors to transform this intersection into Detroit's "gathering place" with year-round programming. Many more PPS initiatives made discrete spaces incrementally more useful to immediate neighbors. Look for "lighter, quicker, cheaper" solutions, PPS advised its clients, and don't always defer to architects, planners, and other experts.[42]

Kent challenged the experts just as much as Whyte did, but not always as diplomatically. In one infamous encounter in 2009, Kent challenged the architect Frank Gehry, who was appearing at the Aspen Ideas Festival, to explain how his iconic buildings could fail as public places. Gehry rejected Kent's charge, but Kent persisted. In an exchange captured by James Fallows of the *Atlantic*, Gehry eventually told Kent bluntly, "You are a pompous man," and then "waved his hand in a dismissive gesture, much as Louis XIV might have used to wave away some offending underling." Kent later told the *Atlantic* that he hoped the design establishment "will begin to recognize the emergence of interest among young designers and the public as a whole in making great places rather than 'branded,' 'iconic,' stand-alone buildings that never give a thought to the broader context of their surroundings."[43]

At a 2015 New York City Planning Commission hearing, Kent objected to a plan for high-rise apartment buildings in Brooklyn Bridge Park. The commission cut him off before his allotted speaking time had expired. Kent refused to give up the microphone. With the crowd chanting "Let him speak," security officers forcibly removed him from the room. His style, Kent readily concedes, "is more confrontational than Holly's." Kent also concedes that his management approach reflected that of a business start-up more than that of an established institution. "We recreated Project for Public Spaces every year," Kent says, "because we had no idea one year to the next what was in store for us." As for planning, Kent sounds like his mentor, Whyte, when addressing the subject: "Any time people tried a master plan, it's been a failure," says Kent.[44]

Given these institutional realities, no one should have been surprised when, early in 2018, Fred Kent briefly disappeared. E-mails to him were returned as undeliverable. PPS eventually explained that Kent's e-mail account had been suspended while he was "on sabbatical."[45] The organization finally hired a new chief executive officer, Philip Myrick, also a Whyte acolyte. Myrick had begun his career as a sculptor living in small towns in Africa and Portugal. When he returned to the United

States he wondered why cities in America couldn't have the same sense of place and community as the villages he had just left. He wandered into a Manhattan bookstore started by the Municipal Art Society. A clerk directed him to *The Social Life of Small Urban Spaces*. "I soaked up that book, called PPS, and landed myself an unpaid internship." When he returned in 2018 the entire world had taken notice of the placemaking movement—"it almost exceeded what PPS could hold in one organization," Myrick says.[46]

By 2020, PPS had announced a new focus: "to develop corporate social responsibility partnerships that offer more communities the chance to create, transform, and sustain their public spaces." The goal is to help corporate clients "who are looking for more ways to have impact" in the communities they serve. PPS emphasizes underserved communities, places that often lack the resources to create a new public place and then develop programming that will ensure its success.[47]

Like other organizations buffeted by the pandemic, the Project for Public Spaces gave up its central office in 2020–2021 and adopted, temporarily at least, a virtual office model. At least one in the new senior leadership carries with him an appreciation for Whyte and his influence. Nathan Storring is coeditor of *Vital Little Plans: The Short Works of Jane Jacobs*. Through that project, and his ongoing involvement with PPS, Storring appreciates the complementary relationship of Jacobs and Whyte.[48]

As the Project for Public Spaces was refocusing its mission, Fred Kent also reappeared on the urban planning horizon with a start-up called PlacemakingX, a nonprofit that launched itself at the World Urban Forum in Abu Dhabi, United Arab Emirates, in February 2020. Led by Fred's son Ethan Kent, PlacemakingX also operates as a virtual organization, connecting a network of more than one hundred "placemaking thought leaders, public space activists, regional network leaders, and professionals from all over the world."[49]

The websites of the forty-five-year-old Project for Public Spaces and the one-year-old PlacemakingX and its sister organization, the Social Life Project, eventually all contained appropriate salutations to each other, along with promises to work together as opportunities arose. The saga of how Whyte's Project for Public Spaces evolved into two separate and complementary organizations might be simply a watercooler drama. But regardless of who played what role in that drama, it does offer two lessons pertinent to Whyte.

The first is that the placemaking movement started by Whyte was substantial enough to have—a half century later—two viable organizations advancing its goals.

The second lesson is that Whyte's organizational insights from the 1950s remain relevant today. "Group harmony is not an unmixed blessing. . . . Progress is often dependent on producing rather than mitigating" frustrations and tensions.[50] And the denial of conflict between the individual and organization "is bad for the organization. It is worse for the individual."[51]

Chapter 19

Whyte in the Twenty-First Century—
Battling the Status Quo

The 2002 "Humane Metropolis" symposium celebrating William H. Whyte attracted a nice bustle (a word he liked) of urbanists, planners, landscape architects, and placemakers. The husband-and-wife team of Frank J. Popper, an urban studies professor at Rutgers University, and Deborah E. Popper, a geographer at City University of New York, showed up at the symposium, appearing to fit nicely into that urbanist-environmentalist mold. In the 1980s the Poppers had advanced the idea of a "Buffalo Commons," in which a sparsely populated swath of the Great Plains could be returned to grazing land and removed from large-scale and environmentally unsustainable agricultural use.[1] That topic would be a logical extension of Whyte's *The Last Landscape.*

But the Poppers had another subject in mind. With a master's degree and a PhD in public administration and government, Frank Popper had worked early in his career for the American Society of Planning Officials. In the 1970s he published an article in *Planning* magazine on the relevance of *The Organization Man.* The theme stuck with him, and the Poppers decided to address that subject at the 2002 symposium. Whyte's 1956 book "formed our ideas about conformity, resistance to it, and the meaning of being part of an organization,"

the Poppers wrote in *The Humane Metropolis*, the book commemo-
rating the Whyte symposium. The Poppers admitted that the 1956
Whyte at first seemed like a different person from the Whyte who
later wrote about open space preservation, small urban spaces, and revitalizing downtowns. But they eventually realized that the two phases
of Whyte's career, "seemingly so different," in fact revealed "two sides
of the Whyte coin, namely the focus on the individual in relation to
surrounding context: social, organizational, and physical."[2]

As the Poppers viewed contemporary society, the organization still
wielded its powers, positive and negative, throughout society: "Today
we are all organization people because organizations dominate our
world more extensively and intensively than ever." In the 2000s organization men and women move from one organization to another as
easily as the organization men and their families moved between suburbs in the 1950s and 1960s. "Interchangeable organizational spaces,"
the Poppers wrote, now included gated communities, industrial parks,
megaplex movie theaters, gyms that differ by acceptable body type
more than anything else, and even nursing homes run by national organizations and situated in "over-scaled Victorian or Georgian buildings from which their aged residents rarely venture."

Frank and Deborah Popper, armed with PhDs from Harvard and
Rutgers Universities, respectively, said they had fooled themselves
when they thought they were "avoiding or outsmarting the organization man by going into academia." They were very familiar with organizational pressures in higher education, they wrote, where "output is
measured in pages produced and grants obtained."

* * *

The organization man is very much alive in the twenty-first century.
Whyte would not have been surprised at the Poppers' assertion in 2002.
Nor would he be surprised if he considered the same statement in 2021.
As he wrote in 1986, in the time since his *Fortune* magazine report-
ing, corporations had experienced a "massive comeuppance.... The
American corporation has gone awry, with some of the biggest of
them stumbling from debacle to debacle. Beneficence has gone out the

window. In the wake of mergers, buyouts and failures, there have been wholesale firings, sometimes of whole divisions, and executed with unwonted cruelty." But through all that upheaval, large organizations continued to dominate the American way of life. "The bureaucratic ethic," Whyte wrote in 1986, was very much in force.[3]

Personality tests were an index of that power, Whyte wrote. "These odious intrusions may caricature the scientific method, but they are highly accurate in defining" the type of person the institution still highly valued—the good team player, the person who values harmony, who can disagree without being disagreeable.[4] No element of scientism bothered Whyte more than personality tests—so much so that he included an appendix suggesting ways in which people could cheat on them. Despite the passage of more than sixty years, psychological or personality tests continue to be utilized by companies in search of new employees who will fit in with their particular company culture. One leading personality testing firm, Caliper, noted in a 2018 press release that the company's "robust solutions and analytics platform enable customers to make data-driven talent decisions. Caliper's science helps organizations create an intentional culture."[5]

For some companies, creating an "intentional culture" may be no more than continuing the current culture. To ensure they get the right people, companies may use applicant tracking software (ATS) to search for keywords in résumés. Tests now purport to measure EQ (an emotional quotient) or XQ (a factor of some trait, possibly unrelated to the job at hand, that is shared by others who have been successful at the job in the past). Some personnel managers use software to screen short video clips submitted by applicants and then employ an algorithm to score candidates on the basis of facial and vocal cues and word choices.[6]

But there was one big difference between the world described by Whyte in 1956 and that which he reexamined in the 1980s. In the era of organization men, he urged people to resist the tempting allures of the organization. The consequence of not resisting was at worst a lost opportunity for the individual and a blissful status quo for society at large. By the 1980s, however, Whyte saw a different kind of organization at work—the quest for harmony enabling corporate polluters, for example, to operate without being called to account by anyone within the ranks. The consequences of that inaction were more pernicious.

In the 1950s Whyte and his colleagues writing in *The Exploding Metropolis* took note of graft at municipal building departments and contractors duping the Federal Housing Administration into larger than necessary mortgages. By the 1980s Whyte observed a world in which review boards and building officials often were inattentive or did nothing when more rigorous action was warranted. Whyte told the story of a "puckish" designer in Louisville, Kentucky, who inserted into a rendering of a proposed pedestrian mall a very visible light hovering about twelve feet aboveground with no visible means of support. Elsewhere in the rendering the designer placed a woman leading a lion by a leash. During many hearings addressing the plans, Whyte reported, no one ever raised an eyebrow at the floating light or the lion on the leash.[7]

When Donald Trump planned his glitzy tower to replace the elegant eleven-story Bonwit Teller building on Fifth Avenue in the early 1980s, he qualified for an atrium bonus that enabled a fifty-eight-story building on the site. The application for that bonus required answers to several pertinent questions: Will the project change "in scale or character" the surrounding area? Will the project change the demand for municipal services such as police, fire, sewage, schools, and so forth? Trump's architect checked the "No" box on those questions and provided similarly favorable answers on all other questions. Whyte reported:

> There is no evidence that any independent investigation was made of these matters—such as a study of the shadows that might be cast. In due course, the environmental review process produced its determination: the project would "have no significant effect on the environment."
>
> No significant effect. No change in scale. Wow. . . . The [City Environmental Quality Review] board might well have . . . said that yes, indeed, the building will affect its surroundings, but on balance the good will outweigh the bad. It might also have raised a question

about the additional municipal services needed and the palpably silly statement that the building would require none. But the board said "no significant effect."[8]

After Whyte completed *City: Rediscovering the Center*, his attention was diverted to medical issues. The next big book he had in mind was about the design of medical facilities, with which he had more experience than he would have preferred. If he had remained healthy and had lived a few more years, he might have taken notice of the continuing presence of institutional failings he had first observed in the 1950s. Among them: groupthink, credentialing, and scientism.

But at least one other social critic did look at those issues and did so in distinctive Whytean terms. That was Jane Jacobs. While some of her acolytes might still object to Whyte's seemingly cavalier dismissal of her early career in the 1993 foreword to *The Exploding Metropolis*, Jacobs in her final years appeared to harbor no ill will toward her mentor. Urban economist and author Richard Florida, who visited with Jacobs in Toronto in the early 2000s, recalls Jacobs speaking highly of Whyte. In a 2001 interview, James Howard Kunstler asked Jacobs if there were any writers on urbanism whom she admired. "Holly Whyte, William H. Whyte," she replied. "He was an important person to me. . . . We were on the same wavelength."[9]

That wavelength at the end of Jacobs's career included some of the same themes raised by Whyte at the beginning of his career, including the perils of groupthink and the tension between individuals and institutions. In Jacobs's 1992 book, *Systems of Survival: A Dialogue on the Moral Foundations of Commerce and Politics*, one of her characters (the book is an essay presented in fictional form) warns that "seeking harmony is a false lead" and that procedures may "help substitute for individual conscience."[10]

In her final book, *Dark Age Ahead*, published in 2004, Jacobs asserted that what should have been the "stabilizing forces" of a culture had "become ruined and irrelevant."[11] This pessimistic view at first seemed out of touch with a world that, surely, would never reach such a "dark age." A dozen years later, however, with once esteemed government and academic institutions under attack from prominent politicians, and with climate change and medical science dismissed as fake news by a significant portion of the population, Jacobs's warning deserves a second look. Florida has called *Dark Age Ahead* "eerily prescient," a work that could serve as "a survivors' guide to the Age of Trump."[12] It was certainly a dark age, one that could return.

The bureaucratic ethic, with its premium on groupthink and organizational harmony, is not just a relic of the 1950s. It remains a reality in twenty-first-century social consciousness. In *Dark Age Ahead* Jacobs looked closely at a killer heat wave in Chicago in the summer of 1995. A team of some eighty researchers from the Centers for Disease Control and Prevention (CDC) concluded that the victims had been—by and large—the ones who failed to heed the authorities' advice to use air conditioning, drink plenty of water, and seek cool places to escape the heat. The victims essentially just failed to take care of themselves, the CDC researchers concluded.

But then, Jacobs reported, a relatively unknown sociology graduate student, Eric Klinenberg (who would become widely known later for his writing about social infrastructure), looked more carefully at the same data.[13] Klinenberg discovered that residents in one neighborhood had a death rate ten times higher than those in an adjoining neighborhood, even though both neighborhoods had similar socioeconomic characteristics. What was the difference? The neighborhood that fared better was denser, with retail stores and service businesses that the residents visited often. In the other neighborhood people rarely went outside and distrusted strangers, including the people knocking on their door during the heat wave to check up on their health.

As author of *The Death and Life of Great American Cities*, Jacobs could have used Klinenberg's research to underscore the argument she made in 1961 about the importance of mixed-use neighborhoods and "eyes on the street." But in her 2004 book, Jacobs derived a different lesson from this tragedy, one that could have been cited by Whyte in either of his first two books: "Were any of [the eighty CDC researchers] potential Klinenbergs so to speak? If so, why didn't they object to the inappropriate investigative strategy? . . . Would they have been regarded as pariahs and troublemakers?"[14]

In *Dark Age Ahead* Jacobs addressed several other themes that aligned with concerns Whyte identified in his earlier work. Whyte, nearly a half century earlier, devoted a chapter of *The Organization Man* to the influence of business on education. While some chief executive officers kept imploring the academic community to produce "well-rounded" graduates and leave the specialization to company training programs, the personnel managers were hiring more and more graduates with vocational degrees. "Relatively speaking, the liberal arts man remains in the cellar. About the only kind of a job he is seriously considered for at the outset is sales work." Whyte also feared that education was being diluted by moving from the liberal arts and sciences to technical and vocational applications.[15]

In *Dark Age Ahead* Jacobs traced the rise of credentialing to the 1960s, when courses of study began to grow in relation to the employment prospects in a particular field. But, as Jacobs wrote, "a degree and an education are not necessarily synonymous." And on that scale, higher education has declined. "A vigorous culture capable of making corrective, stabilizing changes depends heavily on its educated people, and especially upon their critical capacities and depth of understanding."[16]

In the 1950s Whyte had pointed to the potential dangers of "social scientists" turning into "social engineers," hoping to integrate the individual into the group. As Whyte explained it in *Is Anybody Listening?*, the social engineer believed he could use "measurement and codification" (rather than old-fashioned intuition and hunch) to find out how everyone is "thinking and unthinking" and then react as necessary.[17] In the world of advertising and marketing, another form of scientism was beginning to rely on "closer collaboration between the agency and the social psychologist's laboratory, increased study of the regularities in man's behavior that admit of 'actuarial prediction,' more refinements in statistical analysis and probability sampling."[18] Whyte was essentially describing the potential of a tool now used every day—for better or for worse—by Facebook, Google, Amazon, and others: the algorithm. (The word did not appear in the dictionary until 1957, five years after Whyte described the phenomenon.)

Jacobs, like Whyte, sensed that science was an important discipline, but one that could be exploited to further a particular agenda. In *Dark Age Ahead* she cited the unflagging belief among traffic engineers that traffic is like water, and that if you impede its flow at any one point, the excess will be felt at some other point. The traffic engineers were "another generation of nice, miseducated young men, about to waste their careers in a fake science that cares nothing about evidence; that doesn't ask a fruitful question in the first place and that, when unexpected evidence turns up anyhow, doesn't pursue it."[19]

Holly and Jane's common wavelength encompassed more than traffic studies, environmental impact statements, and opposition to unwise development. In 2004, writing *Dark Age Ahead*, Jacobs saw the same power in the status quo that Whyte did in his early writing. "Most people do not enjoy having their entire worldview discredited," Jacobs wrote. "It sets them uncomfortably adrift. Scientists are no exception." So how does one break down a paradigm that has become obsolete? Jacobs described the challenge:

> If a paradigm is truly obsolete, it must finally give way, discredited by the testing of the real world. But outworn paradigms ordinarily stand staunchly until somebody within the field makes a leap of insight, imagination, and courage sufficient to dislodge the obsolete paradigm and replace it.[20]

Jacobs's call in 2004 was in full accord with—and remarkably similar in tenor and tone to—Whyte's message more than a half century earlier in his laymen's sermon at the Episcopal Church of the Epiphany:

> Every great advance has come about, and always will, because someone was frustrated by the status quo; because someone exercised the skepticism, the questioning, and the kind of curiosity which, to borrow a phrase, blows the lid off everything.[21]

*   *   *

William H. Whyte's legacy, like his life, is a two-sided coin. The army of Whyte continues to develop and nurture the common spaces where we all come together at one point or another, often as friends and sometimes as complete strangers. By rediscovering Whyte's life, we can better appreciate the elements that make those spaces work for all of us: an inviting entrance; steps that are not trip hazards; trees, sun, food, seating (please include movable chairs!); and density. Bring us together; don't force us apart.

Operating in the public realm also means working with others. Working with others often means working with organizations. To create the kind of public realm that we all desire, Whyte might recommend that we charge ahead with our empirical minds open, with disciplined observation procedures, and with camera and tape measure ready. But, he would add, we should also pack our skepticism, questioning, and curiosity. Up ahead, the status quo awaits.

Taking Cues from Whyte's Way

S pend a few hours with William H. Whyte and you may never look in the same way at the place where you live or the company where you work. You may look more closely at things you once took for granted; you may measure more things. Recently, when some business owners in my hometown complained about traffic flow in the central business district, I suggested that a one-way street be made two-way. Impossible, I was told: the street is too narrow. I should have known, I thought. Then I thought again and measured the width of the street. It was the same width as a two-way street a half block away. And that street functions fine with traffic in both directions. And I really should have known: I have lived on that two-way street for nearly forty years.

The seed for this biography, as explained in the preface, was planted when I met some craftspeople transforming a small alley in the heart of my hometown into an art and performance space. The only reason I saw this piece of "tactical urbanism" was that I walked by it. If I had been driving to my destination, I would have missed it.

A few months after that encounter, on the other side of town, Princeton University opened a new $330 million arts and transit center. To develop the center the university exercised its considerable clout in the community to move the train station 460 feet farther away from the center of town. Some townspeople objected, but the university argued that the new arts neighborhood would be more than worth the inconvenience.

Once the station was moved and the arts center opened, some of us wondered: Was it worth it or not? While many townspeople found the new center off-putting, there seemed to be no objective way to assess the project. But by then I had been immersed in Whyte's work. I used some of his benchmarks to evaluate this new public space.[1]

The university had promised to create lively and attractive public spaces at the new center. But the blank walls bordering the spaces deliver just the message that Whyte said they would when he wrote that blank walls "proclaim the power of the institution." The space offered a few ledges for seating but no movable chairs. The grand stairway leading from the relocated train station to the central court of the center has 5.5-inch risers and 60-inch treads. The architect, Steven Holl, boasted that it replicated the steps at the Piazza del Campidoglio in Rome, designed by Michelangelo in 1536. But did Michelangelo ever have to run for a train? Some people identified the stepped ramp, or "stramp," as the architect called it, as a tripping hazard. In low light it certainly is. Hold that handrail.

My overall mark was C+, not the kind of grade Princeton receives in the national rankings of colleges and universities. I published the review in the weekly newspaper that I edited. No one disputed my grade, but almost everyone lowered their voice when they discussed the new arts center and my review. Never underestimate the power of a star architect nor the architect's well-endowed client.

*   *   *

As a recent visitor to my house got up to leave, I reminded him, "Hold that handrail." People have come close to tripping, for some unknown reason, I explained. He acknowledged the warning, went out, and tripped nevertheless—landing, happily, without injury. Later I measured the steps: six-inch risers (that's okay, by Whyte's standard), but only ten-inch treads (that's the problem!). The steps were installed pre-Whyte. Next time they will be at least twelve-inch treads. Even better,

Whyte would suggest: five by fourteen.[2] I deserve no better than a C for my step design.

* * *

Trenton, the capital of New Jersey, lies about a dozen miles south of Princeton. It is a beleaguered city, riddled by poverty, abandoned houses, and a commensurate amount of crime. Yet when Amazon issued its request for proposals for the site of its second headquarters, HQ2, Trenton filed one. It made sense. Trenton was within range of a major metropolitan area and within forty-five minutes of both the Philadelphia and Newark airports; it was accessible to major highways; and it was directly served by mass transit, including Amtrak and NJ Transit. Even better, the city had hundreds of thousands of square feet of once flourishing factory buildings, ready to be repurposed.

When Trenton failed to make the first cut, the result seemed to be one more negative outcome for New Jersey's capital city. Nothing, it seemed, was going to change the script for Trenton. I wondered about that. One of the city's strongest attributes is walkability—the entire city is compressed into just over eight square miles—there's little sprawl. But most visitors to the city have no idea. On many days several hundred jurors drive into the city for various state and county proceedings. The jurors are directed to a parking lot near a sports arena. Then they wait for a bus to the courthouse. On busy days jurors sometimes wait for a second bus after the first one is filled up. In fact, the parking lot is a fifteen-minute walk to the courthouse.

The train station, another major league asset for the downtrodden state capital, also turns out to be a fifteen-minute walk to the heart of downtown. But a visitor arriving by train would never know how close downtown is or the best route to get there.

In an op-ed piece I urged city officials to mark the routes so that pedestrians could make their way easily around town.[3] Start with simple signs to point the way, I wrote. But the city had bigger plans, including a complete sidewalk redesign between the town and that parking lot, and an even more ambitious plan to create a walkway between the train station and downtown. That plan was presented in July 2018 in a glossy booklet produced by two nonprofits concerned with Trenton's future, and enhanced by an architecture and planning firm. The cost of that plan alone would have paid for all the improvements I had recommended for both walking routes. As of early 2021 nothing yet had come of the plan. The community arts group ready and eager to do the work was awaiting approval from the state department of transportation. As noted in chapter 11, Whyte knew that action could drive out planning. And he also was aware of the converse.

* * *

If there is a heaven for pedestrians it could be a mile-long stretch of boardwalk on the southern coast of the island of Barbados. For a midwinter refugee from the north, Barbados offers consistently warm and sunny weather, good food, drinkable water, and welcoming hosts. The boardwalk is a carefully maintained promenade that is perfect for walking or jogging, with a sandy beach and the Atlantic Ocean on one side and cottages, small hotels, beach bars, and cafés on the other side.

But at either end of the boardwalk, the spell is broken. If you want to continue your walk without going through ankle-deep sand, you have to venture onto the street. Sidewalks in Barbados are often merely scraps of land left after construction crews got done with their business. At one point a two-foot-wide strip between the street and a retaining wall functions as a sidewalk. Pedestrians walk single file as cars and buses and jitneys whiz by. In some places a halfway decent sidewalk enables pedestrians to move easily for a block or two. But then it ends, at a point where a building or wall butts up to the road. The choice is to walk into the busy roadway or dash to the other side to pick up another section of sidewalk.

During the first four years that I vacationed in Barbados I was resigned to the fact that no place is perfect. On the fifth visit, however, inspired by Whyte, I looked at those streets and their makeshift sidewalks again. I soon realized that by crossing the road at some strategic places I could follow fairly safe sidewalks to my destinations. As few as three new crosswalks would create a path from the west end of the boardwalk to the horse racing park and the George Washington House, where our first president as a young man made his first and only temporary home outside the American mainland.

Instead of spending millions of dollars to extend the boardwalk (an option requiring long-term and expensive planning), the government could spend a few thousand dollars painting some new crosswalks and installing some signs—extending heaven in both directions. I have presented this plan to a Barbadian government official.[4] Nothing has been done yet, but a seed may have been planted.

*   *   *

When I began reporting on Whyte's life, I assumed I could dispatch the discussion of his early work in a chapter or so and move on to his important contributions in urban planning and placemaking. In the course of reporting for this biography, I heard the refrain "Holly is my hero" from at least a half dozen sources. But I soon realized there was more to Whyte's early work than I had initially realized. The study of the organization and its practices, including groupthink, while not well known to many of Whyte's urbanist admirers, was important in its time, and it continues to be relevant today.

I wish I had known more about Whyte's *Organization Man* much earlier in my career. After nearly thirty years as sole proprietor of my weekly newspaper, I decided to switch to a more sustainable business model. I merged with a group of community newspapers. A few years into that new partnership I finally read Whyte's 1950s treatises on business communications and organizations. I realized then that, well into the twenty-first century, much of what Whyte wrote about in the 1950s still rang true. What Whyte called "the little manipulations for morale, team spirit, and such" are part of the twenty-first-century workplace. Meetings and "forced fun" events may seem harmless and on occasion even productive. But if you want to really stimulate an individual's creativity, Whyte wrote, cut down on the amount of time he (or she) spends in conferences, meetings, and "team play."[5] That is still good advice, I came to realize.

Also, as in Whyte's time, personality tests still help screen job candidates and help determine promotions and staff assignments. Smaller companies that cannot afford costly personality tests sometimes instead use informal panels, consisting of two or three current employees, to evaluate job seekers for a particular position. Each candidate moves from one panel to another. Candidates are often asked the same question by the different panels—the extent to which they change their answer might be revelatory, at least in theory. The group discussion afterward often dwells on which individual would best fit into the group. The panels might identify the "best fit" for the group. But—I came to believe—they may not always identify the best person for the job.

The goal of these "human relations" initiatives, I concluded, was to achieve the unstated company goal of harmony in the workplace. When faced with a team interview, a candidate who is a team player tends to shine. True in the 1950s, true today. As Whyte wrote in 1956, "the supervisor who concentrates on making the group happy may produce belongingness but not very much else."[6]

So what is the answer? I gained some insight from an unlikely source, the internet entrepreneur Eli Pariser. In his 2011 book, *The Filter Bubble*, Pariser described the self-reinforcing effect of the digital world. More recently Pariser has spoken about his new effort to reconstruct online platforms to be less polarized and more tolerant of different points of view. As a model of what he would like to see, Pariser holds up Whyte's vision of a good physical public space. While the digital world steers people into contact with like-minded people, Pariser says, Whyte's ideal physical space promotes "triangulation," where some external stimulus prompts two strangers to exchange ideas as if they were old friends. A social trust develops, says Pariser, that doesn't happen when people are engaging in "big political arguments."[7]

Pariser cites one online forum that operates in a way a physical space might—even its name is derived from an architectural element that has enlivened and civilized many a community. The Front Porch Forum started in 2006 in Burlington, Vermont, and today hosts forums in every community in the state. The heavily moderated site is open to community members only. Users sign their comments with their real names. "It's like wearing a name tag and showing up at a block party with your neighbors," says the cofounder of the site.[8]

My vision of the ideal workplace also draws on some of Whyte's vision of a successful urban space. A good urban space stimulates unexpected conversations and interactions. Good public places allow people to express their views without fear of being ridiculed or criticized. But many of us are more guarded at work, where colleagues tend to have predetermined expectations of how you should think. Some companies now realize that these expectations may cause their staff to hold back work before sharing it with colleagues. Google, for example, now encourages the sharing of early drafts, labeled as such, with the hope of receiving informal feedback.[9] At the ideal workplace business dreams could be shared as easily as personal dreams are at the corner bar or neighborhood coffee shop.

Some of the best public spaces are created out of leftovers on the urban landscape. An effective business enterprise might similarly draw on resources others have passed over—a crazy dame, for example, who rides a bicycle to work and smokes a pipe in the office (as Jane Jacobs did in the 1950s).

An effective business can learn from good public places. They can sometimes be messy. People interacting with people can lead to a spilled drink here or there, a chair left out of position, some litter. Like any other asset, a public space requires some maintenance and—every so often—some capital investment. Over time the space may even be redesigned. Good companies also know that their best workers will make mistakes, create waste, and hit Send when they mean to press Delete. Some desks may be extremely messy. (As Albert Einstein said, "If a cluttered desk is a sign of a cluttered mind, then what are we to think of an empty desk?") Projects may be started, and then stopped, as new information becomes available. It's part of the process.

From all this reporting, Holly has become my hero as well, not just for his urbanism but also for his insights as an organization man. As Andrés Duany notes in his appraisal of Whyte's approach to urban issues, he didn't pretend to have a secret recipe for how people would interact with their physical environment. The same is true in Whyte's study of individuals operating within their institutional realms. Whyte leaves the door open for us to enter both arenas. Like a marine at Guadalcanal, we should be ready for action, based not on "slipshod thinking" but rather on "a sound estimate."

Acknowledgments

My thanks go first and foremost to each of the many people interviewed for this biography. Their names appear in the index. Trust me that the word "thanks" is printed in invisible ink in front of each of those names.

More thanks are due to those who read some or all of my work in progress. Readers of my early, flailing drafts had to grasp—sometimes divine—my intention and then add comments and corrections to help me achieve that intention. Architectural historian Clifford Zink wielded his pencil on many of my chapters, making me feel the pain Whyte felt when his prep school English teacher, "Bull" Cameron, took him to task for muddled writing. Gary Diedrichs, one of my college roommates who has since forged a distinguished career as an editor and writer, counseled me to be direct and assertive. Roger O'Neil, a former oil industry executive, provided insights into the world of the organization man, as well as tips for a terse writing style. Richard Reid, a Princeton neighbor with a lawyer's keen eye for the written word, brought some military precision to my chapter on Whyte's Marine Corps service. Mary Lovell, the esteemed British biographer, directed me to keep calm and carry on. My younger brother, David Rein, graded each chapter in the first assembled draft in terms of what worked and what didn't. Sara Hastings, my former colleague at *U.S. 1* newspaper, pored over the next version of the manuscript, turning up errors that editing software—and many humans—never would have caught.

Author and social critic Edward Tenner, a longtime friend, encouraged me to consider Whyte as an organization man in his own right. Scott Sipprelle, a loyal alumnus of St. Andrew's School, introduced me to Chesa Profaci, director of alumni engagement. She led me to the school's wonderful archives, begun by Edith Pell, the wife of the school's first headmaster.

The Chester County Historical Society provided excellent information on the Whyte family in West Chester, Pennsylvania. I am also indebted to organization men and women who had the foresight to preserve records from Princeton University, especially the Larry DuPraz Digital Archive of the *Daily Princetonian* in the Papers of Princeton database and the alumni records at the Seeley G. Mudd Manuscript Library; Richardson-Vick Inc., with archives in the Southern Historical Collection at the University of North Carolina–Chapel Hill; the United States Marine Corps and its digitized records of the *Marine Corps Gazette*; Time Inc., with its famous morgue now secure at the New-York Historical Society; and the Rockefeller Archive Center, where most of Whyte's papers are held. When I completed my fruitful first day at the Rockefeller archives, I left knowing that I would have to return, possibly several times. When the coronavirus pandemic thwarted that plan, archivist Mary Ann Quinn made individual forays into the center to dig up items that I had identified as possibly valuable, as well as other items that she thought I would value. Her finds were more useful than mine—thank you, Mary Ann.

Lanny Jones, one of my first editors as a freelance writer, alerted me to the friction between Whyte and Hedley Donovan and also to the power of Whyte's opening line in *The Organization Man*. Another college roommate, Stefanos Polyzoides, much more famous as a new urbanist architect, and his partner, Liz Moule, assured me in the very beginning that Whyte was a worthy subject. Peter Dougherty, editor at large at Princeton University Press, helped me turn my idea into a book proposal.

Many others provided inspiration and insight: Dan Aubrey, Kent Barwick, Rob Boynton, Jim Britt, Rita Chu, Jim Constantine, Nick Corcodilos, Tom Dellessio, Bill Earle, Jim Floyd, Sam Hamill, Alison Isenberg, Bruce Katz, Mark Lamster, Nancy Linday, Douglas Luke, Tony Nelessen, John Reading, Joe Reilly, Carlos Rodriguez, Bill Sanservino, Maryel and Dick Schneider, Joel Schwartz, Richard D. Smith, Nikki Stern, Paige Thompson, Bruce Tucker, Jayson White, Nick and Ruth Wilson, Tom Wright, and Greg Zieman and Ardith Black. I had hoped that Alexandra Whyte's name would be on this list. Alas,

Holly and Jenny Bell's daughter did not respond to several invitations to participate.

The spark for this biography occurred in an alley in my hometown, a space being enlivened by a nonprofit organization formed by three people who all had met Holly Whyte on various occasions: the late Princeton University president Robert F. Goheen; the former Princeton architecture dean Robert Geddes; and a forward-thinking resident, Sheldon Sturges, who continues to direct Princeton Future, which now includes me as a board member.

Another chance encounter led me, a writer with no agent, to my editor. During a casual conversation following a presentation by Richard Florida in Philadelphia, Katrina Johnston-Zimmerman, an urban anthropologist, suggested that I pitch the Whyte idea to Island Press. My thanks go to Heather Boyer, the executive editor, for her initial enthusiasm, and to editor Courtney Lix, who challenged me to make numerous improvements to the text. As the work progressed, Annie Byrnes, Rachel Miller, Sharis Simonian, Jaime Jennings, and others at Island Press, along with copy editor extraordinaire Pat Harris, provided timely support. And in one more small-world moment, I discovered that Courtney is the daughter of two friends from college days, Vernon and Monica Lix.

Bibliographic Notes

At various points in this biography, the text may resemble an exegesis of William H. Whyte's writings. I fought the idea at first but then relented. In explaining Whyte's vision of successful public spaces and urban centers to interested friends, I found them eager to discover ways to turn theories into action. Moreover, when I read *The Exploding Metropolis*, I discovered that virtually all the urban challenges identified by Whyte, Jane Jacobs, and the other contributors in 1958 remain in place today, more than six decades later. The title of Whyte's first book, in 1952, was *Is Anybody Listening?* Not enough have listened, apparently—more reason to share Whyte's wisdom today.

The following, listed in order of publication date, are the specific editions of Whyte's own books that I relied on. Page number references in the endnotes refer to these specific editions:

Is Anybody Listening? How and Why U.S. Business Fumbles When It Talks with Human Beings. Whyte, William H. Jr., and the editors of *Fortune*. New York: Simon and Schuster, 1952.

The Organization Man. Whyte, William H. New York: Anchor Books, 1957. First published 1956 by Simon and Schuster (New York).

The Exploding Metropolis. Whyte, William H. Jr., ed. Foreword by Sam Bass Warner Jr. Berkeley: University of California Press, 1993. First published 1958 by Doubleday (Garden City, NY).

Cluster Development. Whyte, William H. Foreword by Laurance S. Rockefeller. New York: American Conservation Association, 1964.

The Last Landscape. Whyte, William H. New York: Anchor Books, 1970. First published 1968 by Doubleday (Garden City, NY).

Critical Issues. Whyte, William H. Vol. 1 of *Plan for New York City 1969: A Proposal*, by New York City Planning Commission. City of New York, NY: Department of City Planning, 1969. Whyte also narrated the accompanying film, *What Is the City but the People?*, included on DVD in the book *Imaginary Apparatus: New York City and Its Mediated Representation*, by McLain Clutter (Zürich: Park Books, 2015).

The Social Life of Small Urban Spaces. Whyte, William H. New York: Project for Public Spaces, 13th printing, 2016. First published 1980 by the Conservation Foundation (Washington, DC). Whyte also edited and narrated the accompanying film by the same name, now distributed on DVD through Direct Cinema Limited.

The WPA Guide to New York City: The Federal Writers Project Guide to 1930s New York. Federal Writers' Project of the Works Progress Administration in New York City. New York: New Press, 1990. First published 1939 by the Guilds Committee for Federal Writers' Publications Inc. (New York). Reissued 1982, with a new introduction by William H. Whyte, by Random House (New York).

City: Rediscovering the Center. Whyte, William H. Foreword by Paco Underhill. Philadelphia: University of Pennsylvania Press, 2009. First published 1988 by Doubleday (New York).

A Time of War: Remembering Guadalcanal, a Battle without Maps. Whyte, William H. Introduction by James C. Bradford. New York: Fordham University Press, 2000.

Two books published after Whyte's death are particularly valuable to anyone seeking a greater appreciation of the man.

The Essential William H. Whyte. LaFarge, Albert, ed. Foreword by Paul Goldberger. New York: Fordham University Press, 2000. Whyte's editor and amanuensis in the last years of his life, and still a dedicated guardian of Whyte's literary estate, LaFarge collected excerpts from Whyte's books and also some of his best articles from *Fortune* magazine, as well as sample easement deeds and his affidavit in the case of street musician Robert Turley.

The Humane Metropolis: People and Nature in the 21st-Century City. Platt, Rutherford H., ed. Amherst: University of Massachusetts Press, in association with the Lincoln Institute of Land Policy, 2006. "Rud" Platt not only organized the two-day conference in 2002 that expanded on Whyte's work; he also collected two dozen relevant essays for this volume.

Of special interest to me was Albert LaFarge's entry, "The Wit and Wisdom of Holly Whyte." My favorites (pp. 38–39):

"What attracts people most, it would seem, is other people";

"Food attracts people who attract more people";

"It is difficult to design a space that will not attract people. What is remarkable is how often this has been accomplished."

Endnotes

Ten of Whyte's works are cited here in abbreviated form: *City, Cluster Development, Critical Issues, Exploding Metropolis, Is Anybody Listening?, Last Landscape, Organization Man, Small Urban Spaces, Time of War,* and *WPA Guide.* Full references are given in the bibliographic notes.

Preface

1. John Reading, "President Conducts Opening Ceremony," *Daily Princetonian,* September 20, 1965.
2. *Organization Man,* 152.
3. Iver Peterson, "Ballad of Route 1: Everyone Wants to Be Princeton," *New York Times,* October 30, 1987.
4. *City,* 304.

Introduction: A Man of Many Missions

1. C. Wright Mills, "Crawling to the Top," *New York Times,* December 9, 1956.
2. W. H. Ferry, letter to Whyte, December 2, 1959, Fund for the Republic Records, Seeley G. Mudd Manuscript Library, Princeton University.
3. *Organization Man,* 14.
4. Edward Tenner, "The 737 MAX and the Perils of the Flexible Corporation," *Milken Institute Review,* October 28, 2019.
5. Whyte, "The Organization Man: A Rejoinder," *New York Times,* December 7, 1986.
6. *Is Anybody Listening?,* 210–211.
7. Whyte, "Groupthink," *Fortune,* March 1952.
8. *Organization Man,* 8.
9. *City,* 293.
10. Nathan Glazer, "The Man Who Loved Cities," *Wilson Quarterly,* Spring 1999.
11. *New York Times Magazine,* January 2, 2000.
12. Richard Florida, discussion at post-lecture reception, Thomas Jefferson University, Philadelphia, March 26, 2019.
13. *Exploding Metropolis,* 8.
14. *City,* 4–5.
15. *WPA Guide,* xxviii.
16. *Small Urban Spaces,* 48.
17. *St. Andrew's Magazine,* Fall 1980.
18. *Last Landscape,* 387.
19. Whyte, *The Social Life of Small Urban Spaces* film (New York: Municipal Art

Society of New York, 1970), distributed by Direct Cinema Ltd., Santa Monica, CA. Comment at the thirty-minute mark.

20. *Organization Man*, 44.
21. *Small Urban Spaces*, 28.
22. *Exploding Metropolis*, xvi.
23. *Time of War*, 27–28.

Chapter 1: The Cast of Characters, from White to Whyte

1. Brendan Gill, "Holding the Center," *New Yorker*, March 6, 1989.
2. Whyte, "The Country Gentleman," *Nassau Literary Review*, October 1938.
3. Frank E. White Jr., *The Governors of Maryland, 1777–1970* (Annapolis, MD: Hall of Records Commission 1970), 179–183.
4. Scope and Contents note for papers of Campbell P. White and Harriet (Banyar) White, New-York Historical Society Library, New York.
5. "Whyte-Hartshorne—Hymen's Silken Knot 'Mid Banks of Roses and Well-Wishing Friends," *Daily Local News* (West Chester, PA), June 16, 1887, archived at the Chester County Historical Society, West Chester, PA.
6. *Daily Local News*, June 22, 1901.
7. A. P. Butt, MD, reading before the surgical section of the West Virginia Medical Association, May 1919, later printed in the *West Virginia Medical Journal*.
8. Butt, reading before West Virginia Medical Association.
9. *Time of War*, 2.
10. *City*, 103.
11. *Time of War*, 7.
12. Chester County Historical Society, West Chester, PA.
13. *Daily Local News*, June 19, 1936.
14. Louise Whyte, letter to the editor, *Daily Local News*, May 24, 1969.
15. The details of Whyte's time at St. Andrew's are drawn largely from the St. Andrew's School Archive collection, which was begun during the school's very first years by the first headmaster's farsighted wife, Edith Pell.
16. Whyte, "The Pleasure of Anarchy," in *A History of Saint Andrew's School at Middletown, Delaware: The First Thirty Years, 1928/1958*, compiled by the Reverend Walden Pell II (New York: C. N. Potter, 1973), 66–70.
17. Whyte, "Pleasure of Anarchy," 68.
18. Whyte, anniversary luncheon address, *St. Andrew's Magazine*, Fall 1980.
19. Alumni files, Seeley G. Mudd Manuscript Library, Princeton University.
20. Alumni files, Mudd Library.
21. Alumni files, Mudd Library.

Chapter 2: Princeton—from Rower to Writer

1. Alumni files, Seeley G. Mudd Manuscript Library, Princeton University.
2. "Yearling Brush on Lake Concludes Fall Season," *Daily Princetonian*, November 27, 1935.
3. Whyte, "Hienie," *Nassau Literary Review*, June 1938.
4. Whyte, "The Country Gentleman," *Nassau Literary Review*, October 1938.
5. W. B. C. Watkins, *Daily Princetonian*, February 16, 1939.

6. Whyte, "Driftwood," *Nassau Literary Review*, December 1938.

7. Sanders Maxwell, *Daily Princetonian*, March 14, 1939.

8. *St. Andrew's Magazine*, Spring 2005.

9. John T. Osander, Princeton Class of 1957, asked to write a thesis on F. Scott Fitzgerald, Princeton Class of 1917. The English department denied the request, stating that Fitzgerald's reputation was not yet established.

10. Jack Washington, *The Long Journey Home: A Bicentennial History of the Black Community of Princeton, New Jersey, 1776–1976* (Trenton, NJ: Africa World Press, 2005), 136–139. Washington was quoting from Paul Robeson's *Here I Stand*.

11. Fred Jerome and Rodger Taylor, *Einstein on Race and Racism* (New Brunswick, NJ: Rutgers University Press, 2006).

12. Lawrence Heyl Jr., "Bad Housing Bad Business," *Nassau Literary Review*, October 1938.

13. *Time of War*, 8.

Chapter 3: Vicks and the Marines—Information to Intelligence

1. *Organization Man*, 124–132.

2. *Time of War*, 8–9.

3. Richard Lee, "Shepard Recalls His Days of Making the Sale," *Greenwich Time*, August 10, 2014.

4. Richardson-Vicks, Inc., Records, Louis Round Wilson Library Special Collections, University of North Carolina at Chapel Hill.

5. *Time of War*, 11.

6. World War II Stories and Recollections, St. Andrew's School Archive, 1995.

7. *Time of War*, 17.

8. *Time of War*, 19.

9. *Time of War*, 19–20.

10. World War II Stories and Recollections, July 1942.

11. *Time of War*, 25–26.

12. *Time of War*, 50.

13. Whyte, "Hyakutake Meets the Marines," *Marine Corps Gazette*, August 1945.

14. "3,500 Workers Needed by Dravo," *Morning News* (Wilmington, DE), July 31, 1943.

15. Whyte, "Information into Intelligence," *Marine Corps Gazette*, April 1946.

16. *Time of War*, 13–14.

17. "Advanced Base Operations in Micronesia & Tentative Landing Operations Manual: The Words That Won WWII," Story by James Andrews, Marine Corps Base Quantico, posted May 11, 2017, Defense Visual Information Distribution Service.

18. *Time of War*, 14.

19. Whyte, "Throw Away the Book?," *Marine Corps Gazette*, March 1944.

20. *Time of War*, 58.

21. Whyte, "Observation vs. the Jap," *Marine Corps Gazette*, April 1944.

22. Whyte, "Information into Intelligence," April and May 1946.

23. *Organization Man*, first edition, Simon & Schuster, 1956.

24. Whyte, "Outguessing the Enemy," *Marine Corps Gazette*, November 1945.

25. Whyte, "Observation vs. the Jap."

26. Whyte, "Information into Intelligence," April 1946.

27. *Time of War*, 104.

28. Whyte, commencement address, St. Andrew's School, June 1, 1946.

Chapter 4: *Fortune* Magazine—the Foundation for a Career

1. Whyte, commencement address, St. Andrew's School, June 1, 1946.

2. Time Inc. Records, Patricia D. Klingenstein Library, New-York Historical Society Library, New York.

3. Class of 1939 Archives, Seeley G. Mudd Manuscript Library, Princeton University.

4. Robert E. Herzstein, *Henry R. Luce: A Political Portrait of the Man Who Created the American Century* (New York: Charles Scribner's Sons, 1994), 49.

5. Robert Vanderlan, *Intellectuals Incorporated: Politics, Art, and Ideas inside Henry Luce's Media Empire* (Philadelphia: University of Pennsylvania Press, 2010), 262–271.

6. "Current Magazines," *New York Times*, February 2, 1930.

7. Francis Brennan, "Welcome to Parnassus," in *Writing for* Fortune: *Nineteen Authors Remember Life on the Staff of a Remarkable Magazine*, edited by Gilbert Burck (New York: Time Inc., 1980), 55.

8. Robert Coughlan, "A Collection of Characters," in Burck, *Writing for* Fortune, 74–75.

9. John Kenneth Galbraith, *A Life in Our Times* (New York: Ballantine Books, 1982), 267.

10. Joseph Nocera, foreword to *Organization Man*, xii.

11. Whyte, "How to Back into a *Fortune* Story," in Burck, *Writing for* Fortune, 187–194.

12. James M. Perry, "An Amazing Eye for Detail," *St. Andrew's Magazine*, Spring 1999.

13. Plot synopsis for *The Silver Box*, described as "somewhat uncompleted," Rockefeller Archive Center, Tarrytown, NY.

14. *Harper's* editor Russell Lynes, letter to Whyte, September 18, 1950; Eric Hodgins, memo to Whyte, n.d., Time Inc. Records, Patricia D. Klingenstein Library, New-York Historical Society Library, New York.

15. The *Fortune–New Yorker* feud is reported by Michael Augspurger in *An Economy of Abundant Beauty:* Fortune *Magazine and Depression America* (Ithaca, NY: Cornell University Press, 2004), 55–57.

16. Whyte, "You, Too, Can Write the Casual Style," *Harper's*, October 1953.

17. Augspurger, *Economy of Abundant Beauty*, 162–163, 248–249.

18. Whyte, "Is Anybody Listening?," *Fortune*, September 1950.

19. F.Y.I. newsletter, September 22, 1950, Time Inc. Records, Patricia D. Klingenstein Library, New-York Historical Society Library, New York.

20. Jack Goodman, letter to Whyte, October 13, 1950, Rockefeller Archive Center, Tarrytown, NY.

21. Whyte, *Fortune*, October and November 1951.

22. Whyte, "Groupthink," *Fortune*, March 1952.

23. "Group 'Orthodoxy' Held Harmful to U.S.," *New York Times*, October 19, 1953.

24. Whyte, "How to Back into a *Fortune* Story."

25. Augspurger, *Economy of Abundant Beauty*, 251.

26. Carnegie Institute of Technology, Graduate School of Industrial Administration, *Fundamental Research in Administration* (Pittsburgh: Carnegie Press, 1953). Another excerpt of Whyte's remarks appeared in the *Harvard Business Review*, March 1954.

27. Class of 1939 notes, *Princeton Alumni Weekly*, May 16, 1952.

28. Whyte, memo to Ralph D. Paine Jr., March 12, 1952, Rockefeller Archive Center, Tarrytown, NY.

29. Hedley Donovan, memo, November 10, 1953, Rockefeller Archive Center, Tarrytown, NY.

30. Vanderlan, *Intellectuals Incorporated*, 184, 339.

31. Reference to memo of September 6, 1955, regarding Whyte's interview of John D. Rockefeller III, Rockefeller Archive Center, Tarrytown, NY.

32. *F.Y.I.* newsletter, April 5, 1957, Time Inc. Records, Patricia D. Klingenstein Library, New-York Historical Society Library, New York.

33. Eric Hodgins, note to Henry R. Luce, December 21, 1956; Luce, letter to the Century Association, December 28, 1956, Time Inc. Records, Patricia D. Klingenstein Library, New-York Historical Society Library, New York.

34. Robert Kanigel, *Eyes on the Street: The Life of Jane Jacobs* (New York: Alfred A. Knopf, 2016), 162.

35. Whyte, memo to R. D. Paine Jr. and Hedley Donovan, November 12, 1952, Time Inc. Records, Patricia D. Klingenstein Library, New-York Historical Society Library, New York.

36. Whyte, memo to R. D. Paine Jr., November 10, 1953, Time Inc. Records, Patricia D. Klingenstein Library, New-York Historical Society Library, New York.

37. Hedley Donovan, memo, July 30, 1956, Time Inc. Records, Patricia D. Klingenstein Library, New-York Historical Society Library, New York.

38. Whyte, memo to Hedley Donovan, December 13, 1956, Time Inc. Records, Patricia D. Klingenstein Library, New-York Historical Society Library, New York.

39. Hedley Donovan, *Right Places, Right Times: Forty Years in Journalism, Not Counting My Paper Route* (New York: Henry Holt, 1989), 129.

40. Hedley Donovan, memo to "Mr. Luce," June 30, 1958, Time Inc. Records, Patricia D. Klingenstein Library, New-York Historical Society Library, New York.

41. Whyte, "How to Back into a *Fortune* Story."

42. Whyte, letter from Finland to Del Paine, October 3, 1958, Time Inc. Records, Patricia D. Klingenstein Library, New-York Historical Society Library, New York.

43. Vanderlan, *Intellectuals Incorporated*, 21.

44. Vanderlan, *Intellectuals Incorporated*. Vanderlan refers to Michael Walzer's *The Company of Critics: Social Criticism in the Twentieth Century* (New York: Basic Books, 1988).

Chapter 5: Is Anybody Listening?—the High Cost of Harmony and Groupthink

1. C. F. Rockey, "Opinion Meter," *Radio-TV Experimenter*, Spring 1961.

2. *Organization Man*, 63.

3. William Safire, "On Language: Groupthink," *New York Times*, August 8, 2004.

4. Jay Dixit, "Groupthink: Origins of a Word," NeuroLeadership Institute, January 19, 2021, https://neuroleadership.com.

5. Books of The Times, *New York Times*, April 6 and 7, 1952.

6. Whyte, "Groupthink," *Fortune*, March 1952.

7. Whyte, "Observation vs. the Jap," *Marine Corps Gazette*, April 1944.

8. James C. Bradford, introduction to *Time of War*, xxii–xxiv.

9. Robert Vanderlan, *Intellectuals Incorporated: Politics, Art, and Ideas inside Henry Luce's Media Empire* (Philadelphia: University of Pennsylvania Press, 2010), 265.

10. *Organization Man*, 57.

11. Whyte, "Groupthink."

12. Whyte, "Groupthink."

13. *Organization Man*, 62–63.

14. *Organization Man*, 61.

15. Cliff Kuang and Robert Fabricant, *User Friendly: How the Hidden Rules of Design Are Changing the Way We Live, Work, and Play* (New York: Farrar, Straus and Giroux, 2019), 167.

16. See https://mikeclayton.wordpress.com/2010/08/19/groupthink-abilene-and -risky-shift/.

17. Whyte, "Is Anybody Listening?," *Fortune*, September 1950.

Chapter 6: The Organization Man—More than an Epithet

1. *Organization Man*, 152.

2. Grinnell College convocation, October 26, 1957, Time Inc. Records, Patricia D. Klingenstein Library, New-York Historical Society Library, New York.

3. *Organization Man*, 434.

4. Grinnell College convocation.

5. Grinnell College convocation.

6. *Organization Man*, 3–4.

7. *Organization Man*, 11.

8. *Organization Man*, 15.

9. *Organization Man*, 235.

10. *Organization Man*, 230–238; Jon Gertner, *The Idea Factory: Bell Labs and the Great Age of American Innovation* (New York: Penguin Press, 2012).

11. *Organization Man*, 124–132.

12. The account of Adolf Berle's influential views of the fast-growing corporate world was drawn largely from Nicholas Lemann, *Transaction Man: The Rise of the Deal and the Decline of the American Dream* (New York: Farrar, Straus and Giroux, 2019), 60.

13. David Brooks, "The Nuclear Family Was a Mistake," *Atlantic*, March 2020.

14. Paul Leinberger, telephone interview, July 7, 2020.

15. *Organization Man*, 315–316.

16. *Organization Man*, 118.

17. *Organization Man*, 366–382.

18. *Organization Man*, 175.

19. *Organization Man*, 14.

20. *Organization Man*, 440.

21. *Organization Man*, 26.

22. *Organization Man*, 54.

23. *Organization Man*, 440.

24. *Organization Man*, 209–210.

25. *Organization Man*, 449–456.

26. C. Wright Mills, "Crawling to the Top," *New York Times*, December 9, 1956; Orville Prescott, Books of The Times, *New York Times*, December 14, 1956.

27. Albert LaFarge, ed., *The Essential William H. Whyte* (New York: Fordham University Press, 2000), xiii.

28. Sloan Wilson, *The Man in the Gray Flannel Suit* (New York: Four Walls Eight Windows, 1983), published originally in 1955.

29. Alan Harrington, *Life in the Crystal Palace* (New York: Alfred A. Knopf, 1959).

30. The Advertising Council, "Moral Attitudes and the Will to Achievement of Americans," American Round Table conference, Princeton, NJ, April 10–11, 1961.

31. Charles E. Little, "Holly Whyte's Journalism of Place," in *The Humane Metropolis: People and Nature in the 21st-Century City*, edited by Rutherford H. Platt (Amherst: University of Massachusetts Press, in association with the Lincoln Institute of Land Policy, 2006), 32–34.

32. J. Donald Kingsley, "The Productive Individualist and the Organization," presentation to the annual meeting of the American Public Health Association, October 29, 1958, Seeley G. Mudd Manuscript Library, Princeton University.

33. Mason is quoted by Nicholas Lemann, *Transaction Man: The Rise of the Deal and the Decline of the American Dream* (New York: Farrar, Straus and Giroux, 2019), 68–69.

34. Lyman W. Porter, "Where Is the Organization Man?" *Harvard Business Review*, November/December 1963.

35. Earl B. French, "The Organization Scientist: Myth or Reality," *Academy of Management Journal*, September 1967.

36. *Daily Princetonian*, November 3, 1966. The series of ads featuring Robert W. Galvin of Motorola ran concurrently in student newspapers at Ivy League and other highly selective colleges.

37. *Organization Man*, 182.

Chapter 7: The Exploding Metropolis—Discovering Jane Jacobs

1. "The Origins and Evolution of 'Urban Design,' 1956–2006," *Harvard Design Magazine*, Spring/Summer 2006.

2. Robert Kanigel, *Eyes on the Street: The Life of Jane Jacobs* (New York: Alfred A. Knopf, 2016), 144.

3. Kanigel, *Eyes on the Street*, 131–132.

4. Kanigel, *Eyes on the Street*, 153.

5. *Ideas that Matter*, edited by Max Allen (Ginger Press, 1997), 16.

6. "Syracuse Tackles Its Future," *Fortune*, May 1943.

7. *Exploding Metropolis*, xv.

8. "The Businessman's City," *Fortune*, February 1958.

9. Jane Jacobs, "Downtown Is for People," *Fortune*, April 1958.

10. Harrison E. Salisbury, "Cities in the Grip of Revolution," *New York Times*, October 5, 1958.

11. Charles Poore, *New York Times*, October 9, 1958.

12. Ian Nairn, draft submitted to *Architectural Review*, Summer 1958.

13. *Exploding Metropolis*, 16.

14. *Exploding Metropolis*, 19. Whyte alludes to Jacobs's words on page 159.

15. Seymour Freedgood, "New Strength in City Hall," in *Exploding Metropolis*, 81–109.

16. *Exploding Metropolis*, 145.

17. *Exploding Metropolis*, 23.

18. *Exploding Metropolis*, 51.

19. *Exploding Metropolis*, 65.

20. *Exploding Metropolis*, 25.

21. *Exploding Metropolis*, 104–105.

22. Kanigel, *Eyes on the Street*, 162.

23. Peter L. Laurence, *Becoming Jane Jacobs* (Philadelphia: University of Pennsylvania Press, 2016), 257.

24. Laurence, *Becoming Jane Jacobs*, 275.

25. Kanigel, *Eyes on the Street*, 209–210.

26. Kanigel, *Eyes on the Street*, 176–177.

27. *Exploding Metropolis*, xv.

28. Laurence, *Becoming Jane Jacobs*, 3–4.

29. Kanigel, *Eyes on the Street*, 158.

30. Roberta Brandes Gratz, CityLab, November 16, 2011.

31. *Exploding Metropolis*, 52.

Chapter 8: With Laurance Rockefeller, Conservationist Turned Environmentalist

1. W. H. Ferry, letter to Whyte, December 2, 1959, Fund for the Republic Records, Seeley G. Mudd Manuscript Library, Princeton University.

2. Whyte, handwritten note to "Ping" Ferry, December 12, 1959, Fund for the Republic Records, Seeley G. Mudd Manuscript Library, Princeton University.

3. Lester E. Munson Jr., "Coming Years Difficult Ones, Claims Whyte," *Daily Princetonian*, May 10, 1960.

4. Class of 1939 twenty-fifth reunion yearbook, 1964, Seeley G. Mudd Manuscript Library, Princeton University.

5. Whyte, *Fortune*, October and November 1955.

6. Reference to "Mr. R 3rd thanking [Whyte] for sending copy of his article" on urban sprawl, January 20, 1958, Rockefeller Archive Center, Tarrytown, NY.

7. Daniel Seligman, "The Enduring Slums," in *Exploding Metropolis*, 123.

8. Julia L. Foulkes, "Lincoln Center, the Rockefellers, and New York City," Fall 2005, Rockefeller Archive Center, Tarrytown, New York.

9. Whyte, *Securing Open Space for Urban America: Conservation Easements* (Washington, DC: Urban Land Institute, 1959).

10. Robin W. Winks, *Laurance S. Rockefeller: Catalyst for Conservation* (Washington, DC: Island Press, 1997), 128.

11. Winks, *Laurance S. Rockefeller*, 156.

12. Winks, *Laurance S. Rockefeller*, 49–50.

13. Laurance Rockefeller, "Dear Holly" letter, July 26, 1966, Rockefeller Archive Center, Tarrytown, NY.

14. Letters to Carl Buchheister of the National Audubon Society, May 21, 1965;

Ralph V. Chamblin, March 15, 1966; and Gordon Harrison of the Ford Foundation, May 24, 1968; Rockefeller Archive Center, Tarrytown, NY.

15. Laurance S. Rockefeller, foreword to *Cluster Development*, 7.

16. Whyte, letter to New Jersey agriculture secretary Phillip Alampi, January 13, 1969, Rockefeller Archive Center, Tarrytown, NY.

17. Frances F. Dunwell, *The Hudson: America's River* (New York: Columbia University Press, 2008), 219.

18. Winks, *Laurance S. Rockefeller*, 154–155.

19. Winks, *Laurance S. Rockefeller*, 155–156.

20. Winks, *Laurance S. Rockefeller*, 130.

21. Robert Fitch, *The Assassination of New York* (London: Verso, 1993), 221.

22. Whyte, thank-you note to Room 5600, October 22, 1985, Rockefeller Archive Center, Tarrytown, NY.

23. Winks, *Laurance S. Rockefeller*, 50.

Chapter 9: Preserving the Last Landscape, Rural and Urban

1. Charles Abrams, *New York Times*, November 10, 1968.

2. *Last Landscape*, 79.

3. *Last Landscape*, 204.

4. *Last Landscape*, 70.

5. *Last Landscape*, 22.

6. *Last Landscape*, 70–71.

7. Doubleday contract, April 30, 1964; Pyke Johnson Jr., letter to Whyte, March 24, 1977, Rockefeller Archive Center, Tarrytown, NY.

8. J. Dryden Kuser, "The Future of Somerset County," in *Somerset County, New Jersey, 1688–1930*, edited and compiled by M. Mustin (Somerset County, NJ, 1930), 53.

9. Housing editorial, *Fortune*, September 1946.

10. E. W. Gilbert, "The Industrialization of Oxford," *Geographical Journal*, 1947, cited in Christopher Todd Green, "The Origins of Urban Sprawl" (master's thesis, University of Georgia, 2006).

11. William Lass, "The Suburbs Are Strangling the City," *New York Times*, June 18, 1950.

12. Whyte, "The Anti-city," in *Man and the Modern City: Ten Essays*, edited by Elizabeth Geen, Jeanne R. Lowe, and Kenneth Walker (Pittsburgh, PA: University of Pittsburgh Press, 1963), 46.

13. Jane Jacobs, "The City's Threat to Open Land," *Architectural Forum*, January 1958.

14. Whyte, "A Plan to Save Vanishing U.S. Countryside," *Life*, August 17, 1959.

15. Whyte, "Securing Open Space for Urban America: Conservation Easements," Technical Bulletin 36 (Washington, DC: Urban Land Institute, 1959).

16. Whyte, "Securing Open Space."

17. *Last Landscape*, 96–98.

18. *Cluster Development*, 23–24.

19. *Last Landscape*, 3.

20. Whyte, "Open Space Action: Report to the Outdoor Recreation Resources

Review Commission," ORRRC Study Report 15 (Washington, DC: Government Printing Office, 1962), 2.

21. Adam Rome (author of *The Bulldozer in the Countryside*, cited later in this chapter) traced the letter to a 1964 US Department of the Interior brochure, "The Race for Inner Space," 19.

22. *Cluster Development*, 24–25.

23. *City*, 279.

24. Louise Price Whyte, letter to the editor, *Daily Local News* (West Chester, PA), May 24, 1969, Chester County Historical Society.

25. *Last Landscape*, 148.

26. *Last Landscape*, 328–329.

27. *Last Landscape*, 227.

28. *Last Landscape*, 123–127.

29. *Last Landscape*, 256.

30. *Last Landscape*, 265.

31. *Last Landscape*, 289.

32. *Last Landscape*, 281–282.

33. *Last Landscape*, 356.

34. *Last Landscape*, 402.

35. Tony Hiss, foreword to *Last Landscape*, ix.

36. Adam Rome, *The Bulldozer in the Countryside: Suburban Sprawl and the Rise of American Environmentalism* (Cambridge, UK: Cambridge University Press, 2001), 130–136.

37. *Last Landscape*, 305–306.

38. *Last Landscape*, 295–304.

Chapter 10: Organization Man to Family Man

1. *St. Andrew's Magazine*, Spring 1999.

2. *Organization Man*, 334.

3. Class Notes, *Princeton Alumni Weekly*, December 1, 1964.

4. "Recipe: 17 Clubs, 561 Girls; Result . . . ," *Daily Princetonian*, May 17, 1946.

5. Penelope Green, "Cutting Edge before Her Time," *New York Times*, November 5, 2000.

6. Jenny Bell, *Jenny Bell's Jingle Book* (Philadelphia: Morrison, 1954).

7. Steve Cook, telephone interview, September 20, 2019.

8. "The Inventive Africans," *Time*, September 18, 1964.

9. Angela Taylor, "Maternity Styles Draw Eyes to Legs—Designer Believes That Short Skirts Are Most Flattering," *New York Times*, April 6, 1965.

10. Jenny Bell, "The Case for Marrying Later," *Mademoiselle*, January 1967.

11. Jenny Bell Whyte, "Skirts from Woven Coverlets," *Americana*, September/October 1978.

12. Bernardine Morris, "Chinese Styles for Mother and Daughter," *New York Times*, February 24, 1972.

13. Morris, "Chinese Styles."

14. Jane Geniesse, "A Simple Christmas," *New York Times*, December 21, 1978.

Chapter 11: From Men in Suits, a Radical Plan for New York City
1. *Exploding Metropolis*, 135.
2. Charles E. Little, "Holly Whyte's Journalism of Place," in *The Humane Metropolis: People and Nature in the 21st-Century City*, edited by Rutherford H. Platt (Amherst: University of Massachusetts Press, in association with the Lincoln Institute of Land Policy, 2006), 32.
3. *City*, 336.
4. Robert A. Caro, *The Power Broker: Robert Moses and the Fall of New York* (New York: Vintage Books, 1975), 776.
5. Bill Millard, "[Hillary] Ballon Reappraises Mayor Lindsay," AIA New York, April 6, 2010.
6. Richard Reeves, "New Master Plan Outlines Wide Social Changes Here," *New York Times*, February 3, 1969.
7. Whyte, letter to Elinor Guggenheimer, April 17, 1967, Rockefeller Archive Center, Tarrytown, NY.
8. Peter S. Richards, telephone interview, March 15, 2019.
9. Richard Reeves, "Final Master Plan Draft Stirs Dispute in City Hall," *New York Times*, October 5, 1969.
10. Ada Louise Huxtable, "Blueprint for City Designed for People," *New York Times*, November 23, 1969.
11. Paul Goldberger, "Why City Is Switching from Master Place to 'Miniplan,'" *New York Times*, June 27, 1974.
12. Ada Louise Huxtable, "Plan Is Regarded as Break with Tradition," *New York Times*, November 16, 1969.
13. *Critical Issues*, 6.
14. *Critical Issues*, 5.
15. *Critical Issues*, 16.
16. *Critical Issues*, 22.
17. *Critical Issues*, 5.
18. *Critical Issues*, 19.
19. *Critical Issues*, 21.
20. Robert Fitch, *The Assassination of New York* (London: Verso, 1993).
21. Jonathan Barnett, telephone interview, December 30, 2020.
22. "Master Plan's Writer," Man in the News, *New York Times*, November 17, 1969.
23. *Critical Issues*, 172.
24. *Critical Issues*, 18.
25. *Critical Issues*, 72.
26. *Critical Issues*, 67.
27. *Critical Issues*, 16.
28. *Critical Issues*, 20.
29. *Critical Issues*, 22.
30. *Critical Issues*, 33.
31. *Critical Issues*, 54.
32. *Critical Issues*, 34.
33. Center for New York City Law, video, https://www.citylandnyc.org, April 11, 2013.

34. Paul Goldberger, "Why City Is Switching from Master Plan to 'Miniplan,'" *New York Times*, June 27, 1974.

35. Katherine A. Bussard, Alison Fisher, and Greg Foster-Rice, *The City Lost and Found: Capturing New York, Chicago, and Los Angeles, 1960–1980* (Princeton, NJ: Princeton University Art Museum, 2014), 45.

36. *What Is the City but the People?*, 1969, DVD included with McLain Clutter, *Imaginary Apparatus: New York City and Its Mediated Representation* (Zürich: Park Books, 2015).

37. Bussard, Fisher, and Foster-Rice, *City Lost and Found*, 24.

38. Clutter, *Imaginary Apparatus*, 59–61.

39. *Organization Man*, 44.

40. Ada Louise Huxtable, "Thinking Man's Zoning," *New York Times*, March 7, 1971.

41. Martin Arnold, "Young Insurgents in Planning Commission Charge It Operates in Secrecy," *New York Times*, March 30, 1969.

Chapter 12: Preservation Tactics in the Urban Landscape

1. William A. Haffert Jr., Garden State Publishing Company, letter to Whyte, February 9, 1970, Rockefeller Archive Center, Tarrytown, NY.

2. Summary of Whyte's remarks to the Open Space Policy Commission, August 15, 1975, Rockefeller Archive Center, Tarrytown, NY.

3. "Carnegie Hall: Then and Now—Uncertainty and a New Beginning: 1955–1960," PDF available at "A Brief History of Carnegie Hall," https://www.carnegiehall.org/About/History/Explore-the-History-of-the-Hall.

4. *WPA Guide*, xxv.

5. *WPA Guide*, xxv.

6. *WPA Guide*, xxvi.

7. Anthony C. Wood, telephone interview, September 9, 2019.

8. *City*, 280.

9. Harmon H. Goldstone, New York Landmarks Conservancy, letter to Simon Breines, December 1, 1970.

10. *Cluster Development*, 7.

11. *WPA Guide*, xxv.

12. *City*, 279.

13. *City*, 82.

14. Oral history, New York Preservation Archive Project, October 13, 2007.

15. *City*, 279.

16. William K. Reilly, "Turning Points: Life-Altering Choices in a 50-Year Career," Harvard Law School, October 24, 2015, reprinted at https://www.williamkreilly.com.

17. Adam Rome, *The Bulldozer in the Countryside: Suburban Sprawl and the Rise of American Environmentalism* (Cambridge, UK: Cambridge University Press, 2001), 137.

Chapter 13: The Art of Small Urban Spaces

1. *City*, 233.

2. Jerold S. Kayden, telephone interview, February 25, 2021.

3. *Small Urban Spaces*, 15.

4. *Time of War*, 108.

5. *Small Urban Spaces*, 10.

6. Mark Lamster, *The Man in the Glass House: Philip Johnson, Architect of the Modern Century* (New York: Little, Brown, 2018), 247.

7. *Small Urban Spaces*, 121. Whyte credits the quotation to John W. Cook and Heinrich Klotz, *Conversations with Architects* (New York: Praeger, 1973).

8. *Small Urban Spaces*, 29.

9. *Small Urban Spaces*, 15.

10. *Time of War*, 108.

11. Ann Herendeen, e-mail, January 13, 2018.

12. *City*, xiii.

13. Bill Moody, interview, November 18, 2019.

14. *Small Urban Spaces*, 110.

15. Whyte, "Please, Just a Nice Place to Sit," *New York Times Magazine*, December 3, 1972.

16. Whyte, "Kissing Is Up on New York Streets," *New York Magazine*, July 15, 1974.

17. Margot Wellington, interview, May 21, 2019.

18. Paco Underhill, telephone interview, October 10, 2017.

19. Whyte, "Kissing."

20. Whyte, "New York and Tokyo: A Study in Crowding," in *The Essential William H. Whyte*, edited by Albert LaFarge (New York: Fordham University Press, 2000), 232.

21. Boris S. Pushkarev and Jeffrey M. Zupan, *Urban Space for Pedestrians: A Report of the Regional Plan Association* (Cambridge, MA: MIT Press, 1975); *Small Urban Spaces*, 122.

22. *Small Urban Spaces*, 112–119.

23. Miriam Fitzpatrick, "Fieldwork in Public Space Assessment: William Holly Whyte and the Street Life Project, 1970–1975," in *Architecture and Field/Work*, edited by Suzanne Ewing et al. (London: Routledge, 2011), 79.

24. *Small Urban Spaces*, 26.

25. Robert Geddes, interview, January 21, 2019.

26. Gordon Cullen and Ian Nairn, "Scale of the City," in *Exploding Metropolis*, inserted after 184.

27. Erving Goffman, *Relations in Public: Microstudies of the Public Order* (New York: Basic Books, 1971); Erving Goffman, *Behavior in Public Places: Notes on Social Organization of Gatherings* (New York: Free Press, 1963).

28. Whyte, letter to Jan Gehl, January 27, 1976, Rockefeller Archive Center, Tarrytown, NY; see also Annie Matan and Peter Newman, *People Cities: The Life and Legacy of Jan Gehl* (Washington, DC: Island Press, 2016), 30–31.

29. Madge Bemiss, telephone interview, January 18, 2021.

30. Whyte, "New York and Tokyo: A Study in Crowding," in LaFarge, *Essential William H. Whyte*, 229.

31. Whyte, "New York and Tokyo," 234.

32. Anthony Colarossi, "In Park Forest, Present Doesn't Conform to Past," *Chicago Tribune*, January 17, 1999.

33. Whyte, handwritten letter to Robert Geddes, April 19, 1973, Seeley G. Mudd Manuscript Library, Princeton University.

34. Pyke Johnson Jr., letter to Whyte, October 5, 1976, Rockefeller Archive Center, Tarrytown, NY.

35. Whyte, "Information into Intelligence," *Marine Corps Gazette*, May 1946.

36. *Small Urban Spaces*, 8.

37. *Small Urban Spaces*, 7.

38. *Small Urban Spaces*, 31, 57.

39. *Small Urban Spaces*, 37–39.

40. *Small Urban Spaces*, 101.

41. *Small Urban Spaces*, 48.

42. *Small Urban Spaces*, 43.

43. *Organization Man*, 30.

44. Whyte, "New York and Tokyo," 241.

45. Whyte, *The Social Life of Small Urban Spaces* film (New York: Municipal Art Society of New York, 1970), distributed by Direct Cinema Ltd., Santa Monica, CA.

46. Ralph Widner, interview, January 16, 2019.

47. Margot Wellington, interview, May 21, 2019.

48. Ann Herendeen, e-mail, January 13, 2018.

49. Fred Kent, interview, September 12, 2018.

50. James M. Perry, "An Amazing Eye for Detail," *St. Andrew's Magazine*, Spring 1999.

Chapter 14: From Small Spaces to the City: Rediscovering the Center

1. *WPA Guide*, 1939 preface.

2. *WPA Guide*, xxvii.

3. *WPA Guide*, 341.

4. *City Limits*, documentary film by Laurence Hyde (Montreal, Quebec: National Film Board of Canada, 1971).

5. *WPA Guide*, xxii.

6. Miriam Greenberg, *Branding New York: How a City in Crisis Was Sold to the World* (New York: Routledge, 2008), 101.

7. *City*, 287–289.

8. *City*, 295.

9. *WPA Guide*, xxxi.

10. Whyte, memo to Rockefeller Brothers Fund, November 26, 1979.

11. Dan Biederman, telephone interview, March 10, 2021.

12. Laurie Olin, telephone interview, October 16, 2020.

13. *City*, 160.

14. Andrew M. Manshel, *Learning from Bryant Park: Revitalizing Cities, Towns, and Public Spaces* (New Brunswick, NJ: Rutgers University Press, 2020), 40–42.

15. Lana Henderson, "Planners Fail to Recognize People," *Dallas Times Herald*, February 1, 1974.

16. Gail Thomas, telephone interview, January 15, 2021.

17. Bill Marvel, "A Prescription for City Hall's Plaza," *Dallas Times Herald*, May 3, 1983.

18. Whyte, "City Hall Plaza: Report to the Dallas City Council," Dallas Institute of Humanities and Culture, Dallas, TX, June 15, 1983.

19. *City*, 198–199, 315.

20. David Dillon, "Sage of the City, or How a Keen Observer Solves the Mysteries of Our Streets," *Preservation*, September/October 1996.

21. Thomas Balsley and Anya Domlesky, videoconference interview, December 9, 2020.

22. Martin Gottlieb, "Keen City Watcher Inspires Times Sq. Debate," *New York Times*, April 26, 1984.

23. Edward A. Schwartz, "Why City People Are Like Canaries," *New York Times*, February 26, 1989.

24. *City*, 204.

25. *City*, 287.

26. *City*, 301.

27. *City*, 320.

28. *City*, 328.

29. *Critical Issues*, 5.

30. *City*, 61.

31. *City*, 72.

32. *City*, 187.

33. *City*, 179–192.

34. Whyte, "What Price Sunlight?" *New York Magazine*, March 9, 1981.

35. *City*, 251.

36. *City*, 281.

37. *City*, 263–264.

38. Greenacre Foundation, e-mail, December 29, 2020.

39. *City*, 275.

Chapter 15: Revisiting the Organization Man—and Woman

1. Lena H. Sun, "And the Pipes May Return to the Streets of Old Town," *Washington Post*, November 18, 1983.

2. Whyte affidavit, *Turley v. New York Police Department*, October 7, 1994, in *The Essential William H. Whyte*, edited by Albert LaFarge (New York: Fordham University Press, 2000), appendix D, 355–359.

3. Whyte, "How to Back into a *Fortune* Story," in *Writing for* Fortune: *Nineteen Authors Remember Life on the Staff of a Remarkable Magazine*, edited by Gilbert Burck (New York: Time Inc., 1980), 187–194.

4. Whyte, "Easements: A Fair Deal for All Concerned," letter to the editor, *New York Times*, August 15, 1983.

5. Nicholas Lemann, *Transaction Man: The Rise of the Deal and the Decline of the American Dream* (New York: Farrar, Straus and Giroux, 2019), 116.

6. Kenneth T. Jackson, *Crabgrass Frontier: The Suburbanization of the United States* (New York: Oxford University Press, 1985), 296–305.

7. David Brooks, "The Nuclear Family Was a Mistake," *Atlantic*, March 2020.

8. Richard D. Heffner, interview with Whyte, *The Open Mind*, WNET–Channel 13, October 15, 1982.

9. Paul Leinberger, telephone interview, July 7, 2020.

10. Paul Leinberger and Bruce Tucker, *The New Individualists: The Generation after* The Organization Man (New York: HarperCollins, 1991), 12.

11. Paul Leinberger and William H. Whyte, "The Organization Man Revisited," *New York Times Magazine*, The Business World, December 7, 1986.

12. Leinberger and Whyte, "Organization Man Revisited."

Chapter 16: Applying Urban Principles in Suburban Places

1. Jenny Bell Whyte, *Adelaide Stories* (New York: Simon and Schuster, 1972).

2. Steve Cook, telephone interview, September 20, 2019.

3. John Cook, telephone interview, September 20, 2019.

4. Jean Hemphill, telephone interview, February 17, 2018.

5. Whyte, letter to the editor, *Daily Princetonian*, April 14, 1977.

6. Robert Venturi, letter to Whyte, February 1, 1982, Rockefeller Archive Center, Tarrytown, NY.

7. Whyte, memo to Laurance Rockefeller, March 7, 1978, Rockefeller Archive Center, Tarrytown, NY.

8. Jon D. Hlafter, letter to Whyte, May 5, 1982, Rockefeller Archive Center, Tarrytown, NY.

9. Katharine H. Bretnall, "The Head of the Environmental Design Review Committee Calls Collins Bridge over Palmer Square 'Pornography,'" *Town Topics*, March 30, 1983, Papers of Princeton, Princeton University Library.

10. James B. Harvie III, letter to Whyte, December 15, 1982, Rockefeller Archive Center, Tarrytown, NY.

11. Whyte, letter to Harvie, June 10, 1983, Rockefeller Archive Center, Tarrytown, NY.

12. Clipping from *Progressive Architecture*, February 1983, Rockefeller Archive Center, Tarrytown, NY.

13. *City*, 313–314.

14. *City*, 7.

15. *City*, 23.

16. *City*, 337.

17. *City*, 307–309.

18. Joel Garreau, *Edge City: Life on the New Frontier* (New York: Doubleday, 1991).

19. Robert Fishman, *Bourgeois Utopias: The Rise and Fall of Suburbia* (New York: Basic Books, 1987). The quotations here are from *City*, 335–336.

20. *City*, 335–336.

21. Bill King, telephone interview, October 27, 2020.

22. Whyte, memo to Carnegie Center development team, July 30, 1983, Rockefeller Archive Center, Tarrytown, NY.

23. Laurie Olin, telephone interview, October 16, 2020.

24. Princeton Packet, June 8, 1984, Rockefeller Archive Center, Tarrytown, NY.

25. Whyte, memo to development team, July 30, 1983.

26. *City*, 303.

27. Richard K. Rein, "U.S. 1's Ten Essential Truths," *U.S. 1* newspaper, November 1985, Rockefeller Archive Center, Tarrytown, NY.

28. *City*, 305.

29. Whyte, "Creating Environments . . . Not Just Buildings," *Real Estate Forum*, May 1989.

30. *City*, 305–306.

31. Lloyd W. Bookout, Michael D. Beyard, and Steven Fader, *Value by Design: Landscape, Site Planning, and Amenities* (Washington, DC: Urban Land Institute, 1994).

32. *City*, 303.

33. *Exploding Metropolis*, 19.

Chapter 17: The Final Years

1. Rutherford Platt, e-mail, December 4, 2020, and telephone interview, December 7, 2020.

2. Ann Louise Strong, "The Energizer," in *The Humane Metropolis: People and Nature in the 21st-Century City*, edited by Rutherford H. Platt (Amherst: University of Massachusetts Press, in association with the Lincoln Institute of Land Policy, 2006), 35–36.

3. Whyte, handwritten note to Laurance Rockefeller, August 27, 1984, Rockefeller Archive Center, Tarrytown, NY.

4. Stephen S. Hall, "Standing on Those Corners, Watching All the Folks Go By," *Smithsonian*, February 1989.

5. Class of 1939 notes, *Princeton Alumni Weekly*, Seeley G. Mudd Manuscript Library, Princeton University.

6. Class of 1935 notes, *St. Andrew's Magazine*, 1992.

7. Royalty report from Doubleday, December 31, 1989, Rockefeller Archive Center, Tarrytown, NY.

8. Class of 1939 fiftieth reunion yearbook, Seeley G. Mudd Manuscript Library, Princeton University.

9. Laurie Olin, oral history, Cultural Landscape Foundation, June 1–6, 2012; Laurie Olin, telephone interview, October 16, 2020.

10. Paul Goldberger, "Bryant Park, an Out-of-Town Experience," *New York Times*, May 3, 1992.

11. Congressional hearing, Community Recreation Enhancement Act, June 29, 1992.

12. Whyte affidavit, *Turley v. New York Police Department*, October 7, 1994, in *The Essential William H. Whyte*, edited by Albert LaFarge (New York: Fordham University Press, 2000), appendix D, 355–359.

13. Robert Perry, telephone interview, October 28, 2020.

14. Memo in Jackson Hole Preserve Inc. files, November 14, 1997, Rockefeller Archive Center, Tarrytown, NY.

15. Ellen Fister Oxman, telephone interview, November 9, 2020.

16. David Dillon, "Sage of the City, or How a Keen Observer Solves the Mysteries of Our Streets," *Preservation*, September/October 1996; Dan Biederman, telephone interview, March 10, 2021.

17. Penelope Green, "Mirror, Mirror, Cutting Edge before Her Time," *New York Times*, November 5, 2000.

18. Albert LaFarge, telephone interview, June 15, 2020.

19. "Herndon Werth," memorial, *St. Andrew's Magazine*, Spring 1999.

20. Paco Underhill, foreword to *City*, xiii.

21. Paco Underhill, telephone interview, October 10, 2017.

22. Lynden Miller, telephone interview, March 26, 2018.

23. LaFarge, interview, June 15, 2020.

24. Dillon, "Sage of the City."

25. Peter Katz, telephone interview, December 30, 2020.

26. *City*, 341.

27. For the full text of the Whyte tribute, see Paul Goldberger, "For William H. Whyte," http://www.paulgoldberger.com/lectures/for-william-h-whyte/, January 19, 1999.

28. Oxman, telephone interview, November 9, 2020.

Chapter 18: Whyte in the Twenty-First Century—the Urban Imperative

1. Jenny Bell Whyte died on September 1, 2002. She is buried next to Holly in West Chester.

2. The LaFarge Agency, "Rights News," http://thelafargeagency.com/2020/06/rights-news.

3. David Dillon, "Sage of the City, or How a Keen Observer Solves the Mysteries of Our Streets," *Preservation*, September/October 1996.

4. *Amanda Burden Meets Holly Whyte*, Streetfilms, Vimeo, 2012.

5. Penelope Green, "Mirror, Mirror, Cutting Edge before Her Time," *New York Times*, November 5, 2000.

6. Jerold S. Kayden, *Privately Owned Public Space: The New York City Experience* (New York: John Wiley & Sons, 2000), viii. The quotation is from the preface by Kent Barwick.

7. Jerold Kayden, telephone interview, February 25, 2021.

8. David Grider, e-mail, January 24, 2021.

9. Thomas Balsley and Anya Domlesky, videoconference interview, December 9, 2020.

10. Emily Schlickman and Anya Domlesky, "Field Guide to Life in Urban Plazas: A Study in New York City," 2019, https://live-swabalsley-2019.pantheonsite.io/wp-content/uploads/2019/08/Field-Guide-to-Life-in-Urban-Plazas_digital1.pdf.

11. *City*, 334.

12. Jeff Bornstein, "Town Fine; Office the 'Morgue,'" *Stamford Advocate*, May 18, 2017.

13. *City*, 341.

14. Robert J. Gibbs, e-mail, February 3, 2021.

15. Richard Florida, *The Rise of the Creative Class and How It's Transforming Work, Leisure, Community, and Everyday Life* (New York: Basic Books, 2002), 30.

16. *City*, 338.

17. *Cluster Development*, 8.

18. *City*, 256–283.

19. Kim Stanley Robinson, Bloomberg CitiLab, Bloombergbusiness.com, April 17, 2021.

20. Edward Glaeser, *Triumph of the City: How Our Greatest Invention Makes Us Richer, Smarter, Greener, Healthier, and Happier* (New York: Penguin Books, 2011).

21. *City*, 202.

22. Robert H. Mandle, National Landing Business Improvement District, telephone interview, May 25, 2021.

23. Glaeser, *Triumph of the City*, 42–43.

24. *Last Landscape*, 399.

25. *Last Landscape*, 356.

26. *City*, 75.

27. San Francisco Parklet Program, "San Francisco Parklet Manual," https:// groundplaysf.org.

28. Mike Lydon and Anthony Garcia, *Tactical Urbanism: Short-Term Action for Long-Term Change* (Washington, DC: Island Press, 2015), 119–127.

29. Lydon and Garcia, *Tactical Urbanism*, 155–156.

30. Paul Krugman, "The Pandemic and the Future City," *New York Times*, March 16, 2021.

31. In separate interviews three of Whyte's disciples noted that certain corners of the academic world still fail to fully appreciate Whyte.

32. Congress for the New Urbanism, "The Charter of the New Urbanism," 1996, https://www.cnu.org/who-we-are/charter-new-urbanism.

33. Robert Steuteville, "Great Idea: Architecture That Puts the City First," *Public Square*, March 9, 2017.

34. Andrés Duany, Elizabeth Plater-Zyberk, and Jeff Speck, *Suburban Nation: The Rise of Sprawl and the Decline of the American Dream* (New York: North Point Press, 2000), 264.

35. Andrés Duany, telephone interview, February 2, 2021.

36. Miriam Fitzpatrick, e-mail, March 13, 2021.

37. Kim Rollings, e-mail, March 12, 2021.

38. Ron Henderson, telephone interview, January 6, 2021.

39. Setha Low, telephone interview, December 21, 2020.

40. Leysia Palen, telephone interview, March 19, 2021.

41. Mitchell Block, telephone interview, February 16, 2021.

42. See the Project for Public Spaces' website at https://www.pps.org.

43. James Fallows, "More on Frank Gehry, Public Spaces, Etc.," *Atlantic*, July 10, 2009.

44. Project for Public Spaces, "Celebrating 75 Years of Fred Kent, and 50 Years of Placemaking," https://www.pps.org, November 2, 2017.

45. Ethan Kent, e-mail, March 9, 2018.

46. Philip Myrick, telephone interview, January 19, 2021.

47. See https://www.pps.org.

48. Samuel Zipp and Nathan Storring, eds., *Vital Little Plans: The Short Works of Jane Jacobs* (New York: Random House, 2016).

49. PlacemakingX, "About the Network," https://www.placemakingx.org/about.

50. *Is Anybody Listening?*, 235.

51. *Organization Man*, 14.

Chapter 19: Whyte in the Twenty-First Century—Battling the Status Quo

1. Deborah E. Popper and Frank J. Popper, "The Buffalo Commons: Its Antecedents and Their Implications," *Online Journal of Rural Research and Policy* 1, no. 6 (2006).

2. Deborah E. Popper and Frank J. Popper, "'The Organization Man' in the Twenty-First Century: An Urbanist View," in *The Humane Metropolis: People and Nature in the*

21st-Century City, edited by Rutherford H. Platt (Amherst: University of Massachusetts Press, in association with the Lincoln Institute of Land Policy, 2006), 206–219.

3. Whyte, "The Organization Man: A Rejoinder," *New York Times*, December 7, 1986.

4. Whyte, "Organization Man: A Rejoinder."

5. *U.S. 1* newspaper, March 14, 2018.

6. Some important insights on current employment screening practices can be found at https://www.asktheheadhunter.com.

7. *City*, 365.

8. *City*, 238.

9. James Howard Kunstler, "Jane Jacobs, Godmother of the American City," *Metropolis*, March 2001.

10. Jane Jacobs, *Systems of Survival: A Dialogue on the Moral Foundations of Commerce and Politics* (New York: Vintage Books, 1994), 83.

11. Jane Jacobs, *Dark Age Ahead* (New York: Vintage Books, 2004), 24.

12. Richard Florida, "Did Jane Jacobs Predict the Rise of Trump?" Bloomberg CityLab, December 20, 2016.

13. Eric Klinenberg, *Heat Wave: A Social Autopsy of Disaster in Chicago* (Chicago: University of Chicago Press, 2002).

14. Jacobs, *Dark Age Ahead*, 86.

15. *Organization Man*, 113.

16. Jacobs, *Dark Age Ahead*, 63.

17. *Is Anybody Listening?*, 208.

18. *Is Anybody Listening?*, 210.

19. Jacobs, *Dark Age Ahead*, 74.

20. Jacobs, *Dark Age Ahead*, 70.

21. "Group 'Orthodoxy' Held Harmful to U.S.," *New York Times*, October 19, 1953.

Afterword: Taking Cues from Whyte's Way

1. Richard K. Rein, "Sizing Up the New Lewis Center for the Arts," *U.S. 1* newspaper, May 30, 2018.

2. *City*, 191.

3. Richard K. Rein, "All Signs Point toward Progress in Trenton," *Trenton (NJ) Downtowner*, January 2019.

4. Richard K. Rein, "Letter from Barbados," *U.S. 1* newspaper, February 27, 2019.

5. *Organization Man*, 445.

6. *Organization Man*, 444.

7. Eli Pariser, interview with Brooke Gladstone, *On the Media*, WNYC, January 15, 2021.

8. See https://frontporchforum.com. The quotation is from an article by Jeff Link, "9 Projects Trying to Build Healthy Social Media Platforms," https://builtin.com/software-engineering-perspectives/new-social-media-models.

9. Diane Chaleff, "These Three Things Are Preventing Your Employees from Collaborating," Fast Company, October 10, 2019.

About the Author

After a reporting career that included stops at *Time* magazine and *People*, Richard K. Rein launched a nationally acclaimed weekly newspaper, *U.S. 1*, that helped the Princeton–Route 1 corridor become more than an "edge city." Rein now serves on Princeton Future, a nonprofit that promotes sustainable urbanism in his hometown, and edits a hyperlocal news site, TAPinto Princeton Community News.

Index

Page numbers followed by "f" indicate photos.